Science Fiction Film, Television, and Adaptation

Routledge Research in Cultural and Media Studies

1 **Video, War and the Diasporic Imagination**
  Dona Kolar-Panov

2 **Reporting the Israeli-Arab Conflict**
  How Hegemony Works
  Tamar Liebes

3 **Karaoke Around the World**
  Global Technology, Local Singing
  Edited by Toru Mitsui and Shuhei Hosokawa

4 **News of the World**
  World Cultures Look at Television News
  Edited by Klaus Bruhn Jensen

5 **From Satellite to Single Market**
  New Communication Technology and European Public Service Television
  Richard Collins

6 **The Nationwide Television Studies**
  David Morley and Charlotte Bronsdon

7 **The New Communications Landscape**
  Demystifying Media Globalization
  Edited by Georgette Wang, Jan Servaes, and Anura Goonasekera

8 **Media and Migration**
  Constructions of Mobility and Difference
  Edited by Russell King and Nancy Wood

9 **Media Reform**
  Democratizing the Media, Democratizing the State
  Edited by Monroe E. Price, Beata Rozumilowicz, and Stefaan G. Verhulst

10 **Political Communication in a New Era**
  Edited by Gadi Wolfsfeld and Philippe Maarek

11 **Writers' Houses and the Making of Memory**
  Edited by Harald Hendrix

12 **Autism and Representation**
  Edited by Mark Osteen

13 **American Icons**
  The Genesis of a National Visual Language
  Benedikt Feldges

14 **The Practice of Public Art**
  Edited by Cameron Cartiere and Shelly Willis

15 **Film and Television After DVD**
  Edited by James Bennett and Tom Brown

16 **The Places and Spaces of Fashion, 1800-2007**
  Edited by John Potvin

17 **Communicating in the Third Space**
  Edited by Karin Ikas and Gerhard Wagner

18 Deconstruction After 9/11
Martin McQuillan

19 The Contemporary Comic Book Superhero
Edited by Angela Ndalianis

20 Mobile Technologies
From Telecommunications to Media
Edited by Gerard Goggin and Larissa Hjorth

21 Dynamics and Performativity of Imagination
The Image between the Visible and the Invisible
Edited by Bernd Huppauf and Christoph Wulf

22 Cities, Citizens, and Technologies
Urban Life and Postmodernity
Paula Geyh

23 Trauma and Media
Theories, Histories, and Images
Allen Meek

24 Letters, Postcards, Email
Technologies of Presence
Esther Milne

25 International Journalism and Democracy
Civic Engagement Models from Around the World
Edited by Angela Romano

26 Aesthetic Practices and Politics in Media, Music, and Art
Performing Migration
Edited by Rocío G. Davis, Dorothea Fischer-Hornung, and Johanna C. Kardux

27 Violence, Visual Culture, and the Black Male Body
Cassandra Jackson

28 Cognitive Poetics and Cultural Memory
Russian Literary Mnemonics
Mikhail Gronas

29 Landscapes of Holocaust Postmemory
Brett Ashley Kaplan

30 Emotion, Genre, and Justice in Film and Television
E. Deidre Pribram

31 Audiobooks, Literature, and Sound Studies
Matthew Rubery

32 The Adaptation Industry
The Cultural Economy of Literary Adaptation
Simone Murray

33 Branding Post-Communist Nations
Marketizing National Identities in the New Europe
Edited by Nadia Kaneva

34 Science Fiction Film, Television, and Adaptation
Across the Screens
Edited by J. P. Telotte and Gerald Duchovnay

Science Fiction Film, Television, and Adaptation
Across the Screens

**Edited by J. P. Telotte
and Gerald Duchovnay**

NEW YORK   LONDON

First published 2012
by Routledge
711 Third Avenue, New York, NY 10017

Simultaneously published in the UK
by Routledge
2 Park Square, Milton Park, Abingdon, Oxon OX14 4RN

*Routledge is an imprint of the Taylor & Francis Group,
an informa business*

© 2012 Taylor & Francis

The right of J. P. Telotte and Gerald Duchovnay to be identified as the authors of the editorial material, and of the authors for their individual chapters, has been asserted in accordance with sections 77 and 78 of the Copyright, Designs and Patents Act 1988.

Typeset in Sabon by IBT Global.
First issued in paperback in 2013

All rights reserved. No part of this book may be reprinted or reproduced or utilised in any form or by any electronic, mechanical, or other means, now known or hereafter invented, including photocopying and recording, or in any information storage or retrieval system, without permission in writing from the publishers.

Trademark Notice: Product or corporate names may be trademarks or registered trademarks, and are used only for identification and explanation without intent to infringe.

Library of Congress Cataloging-in-Publication Data
Science fiction film, television, and adaptation : across the screens / edited by J. P. Telotte and Gerald Duchovnay.
   p. cm. — (Routledge research in cultural and media studies)
  Includes bibliographical references and index.
  Includes filmography and videography.
  1. Film adaptations—History and criticism. 2. Television adaptations—History and criticism. 3. Science fiction films—History and criticism. 4. Science fiction television programs—History and criticism. 5. Motion pictures and television. I. Telotte, J. P., 1949– II. Duchovnay, Gerald, 1944–
  PN1997.85.S38 2011
  791.43'615—dc22
  2011008276

ISBN13: 978-0-415-74383-9 (pbk)
ISBN13: 978-0-415-88719-9 (hbk)
ISBN13: 978-0-203-80572-5 (ebk)

Contents

List of Figures ... ix
Acknowledgments ... xi
Introduction: Across the Screens: Adaptation, Boundaries, and Science Fiction Film and Television ... xiii
J. P. TELOTTE

PART I
Cross-Screen Dynamics

1 Domesticating Space: Science Fiction Serials Come Home ... 3
   CYNTHIA J. MILLER

2 The Cinematic Zone of *The Twilight Zone* ... 20
   J. P. TELOTTE

3 *Voyage to the Bottom of the Sea*: Big-Screen Spectacle and Compressed Television Images ... 35
   MARY PHARR

PART II
Case Studies: Film to Television

4 Finding Sanctuary: Adapting *Logan's Run* to Television ... 53
   GERALD DUCHOVNAY

5 *Stargate SG-1* and the Visualization of the Imagination ... 67
   SHERRYL VINT

6 She's Just a Girl: A Cyborg Passes in *The Sarah Conner Chronicles* 84
LORRIE PALMER

PART III
Case Studies: Television to Film

7 *Star Trek* and the Birth of a Film Franchise 101
M. KEITH BOOKER

8 "I Want to Believe the Truth Is Out There": *The X-Files* and the Impossibility of Knowing 115
RODNEY F. HILL

9 *Serenity*, Genre, and Cinematization 127
J. P. TELOTTE

PART IV
Issues in Science Fiction Adaptation

10 *Doctor Who*: Adaptations and Flows 143
MARK BOULD

11 Déjà Vu All Over Again? *Cowboy Bebop*'s Transformation to the Big Screen 164
MICHELLE ONLEY PIRKLE

12 Fan Films, Adaptations, and Media Literacy 176
CHUCK TRYON

Notes on Contributors 191
Selective Videography/Filmography 195
Bibliography 197
Index 201

Figures

I.1	Future television recalls the "age of windows" in the film *Things to Come* (1936).	xviii
I.2	A demon comes through the rift in the British series *Torchwood*.	xxi
1.1	Youthful sidekicks, like Captain Z-Ro's cadet, Jet, mirrored a young audience's "space fever."	8
1.2	Space comes into the home, as audience members sport uniforms and even sf insignia haircuts.	13
2.1	Henry Bemis (Burgess Meredith) as part of the rubble in the post-apocalyptic world of "Time Enough at Last" on *The Twilight Zone* (1959).	25
2.2	Andy Hardy's Carvel redressed as *The Twilight Zone*'s "Maple Street" (1960).	29
3.1	The *Seaview* surfaces at an impossible angle: Spectacle in *Voyage to the Bottom of the Sea* (1961).	38
3.2	The television *Voyage* turned to guest actors (here Eddie Albert, along with series regulars David Hedison and Richard Basehart) to bolster viewership.	41
4.1	Futuristic setting: inside the domed city of the film *Logan's Run*.	56
4.2	The "hovercraft" that Logan, Jessica, and REM use for their different adventures in the *Logan's Run* television series.	59
5.1	The use of scale differentiates the film *Stargate* from its television adaptation.	70
5.2	The "event" of the stargate's opening in a first season episode of *Stargate SG-1*.	71
6.1	The cyborg Cameron (Summer Glau) and Sarah Connor (Lena Headey), absent the bodily brawn of 1980s movie heroines.	85
6.2	Cameron (Summer Glau) defeats a Terminator to protect the teenage John Connor	90
8.1	Scully (Gillian Anderson) and Mulder (David Duchovny) ponder their futures in *The X-Files: I Want to Believe* (2008).	117

x *Figures*

8.2	The mysterious conspirator "Cigarette-Smoking Man" (William B. Davis) plots his next move in *The X-Files: Fight the Future* (1998).	119
9.1	A Western-style train robbery done in space-opera fashion on *Firefly* (2002).	129
9.2	River (Summer Glau) watches a hologram viewing screens in the multiply-mediated world of *Serenity* (2005).	131
10.1	The time-and-space visualizer: television on television in "The Chase," *Doctor Who*.	151
10.2	Easter egg: the Doctor on DVD on television on television in "Blink," *Doctor Who*.	158
11.1	Opening credits of the *Cowboy Bebop* series with fragments of the "mission statement."	165
11.2	Spike investigating Rasheed in the Moroccan district on Mars in *Cowboy Bebop: The Movie*.	172
12.1	A group of (action- figure) storm troopers patrol Tatooine in Kevin Rubio's *Cops/Star Wars* crossover, *Troops*.	183
12.2	The *Star Wars Uncut* website invites users to participate in "remaking" the original film.	184

Acknowledgments

I want to express my deep thanks to J. P. Telotte, my co-editor, who originated the idea for this volume. His extensive knowledge of science fiction aided me and the other contributors in making this volume a significant contribution to science fiction studies. I would also like to thank my many undergraduates for their insights on adaptation studies and film history. I am especially grateful to the graduate students at Texas A&M University-Commerce who are pursuing a film certificate. Their continued interest in links and connections between various media have helped shape some of my perceptions about film audiences and issues of adaptation. I especially want to thank Angela Kennedy, Michelle Pirkle, and Sylwester Zabielski for their assistance on technical matters, and Erica C. Wetter at Routledge for her timely and gracious support throughout this project.

—Gerald Duchovnay

As is always the case, a great many people helped bring this book into being and deserve thanks. Foremost among them is my co-editor and good friend, Gerald Duchovnay, who started the ball rolling by organizing a conference panel on the subject, talked through the volume's concepts and organization, and then contributed his usual sharp eye for detail and good writing to the various contributions. Closely following are the various colleagues who, when asked to join this project, without hesitation agreed to contribute their time and creative efforts. Many of them I have worked with before, and I hope to have the chance to work with them all again. Erica Wetter, our editor at Routledge, was consistently enthusiastic and supportive, and she helped push this project into production with great organization and efficiency. Julie Ganz and Michael Watters saw the work through production and offered a fine eye for detail. And my students at Georgia Tech, especially those in my class on Science Fiction Film and Television, as ever proved an invaluable resource in both their interest in science fiction and their unfailing ability to ask good questions. Among this group let me specially thank Dan Fuller, Jennifer Gergely, Chris Grayson, Emily Mask, Robert Solomon, and Joshua Wilkinson. Finally, I need to thank my personal IT consultant, Gabrielle Telotte, who was always available to walk me through my various technical stumbles.

—J. P. Telotte

We also need to express our appreciation to the editors of the journal *Science Fiction Film and Television*, as well as the journal's publisher, Liverpool University Press, for permission to use expanded versions of two contributions to this volume:

> "*Serenity*, Cinematisation and the Perils of Adaptation," *Science Fiction Film and Television* 1.1 (2008): 67–80; and "In the Cinematic Zone of *The Twilight Zone*," *Science Fiction Film and Television* 3.1 (2010): 1–18.

Introduction
Across the Screens—Adaptation, Boundaries, and Science Fiction Film and Television

J. P. Telotte

I

On first consideration, many would assume that film and television naturally and rather easily feed into each other, that adapting a successful film to the television screen or a wildly popular broadcast series to motion pictures would be a simple task. And certainly, we might expect that executives in the various media industries would leap at the prospect of mining additional profits from an established, enthusiastic, and seemingly even measurable audience, just as movie moguls in the 1930s eagerly snapped up highly popular novels like *Anthony Adverse* (1933), *Gone with the Wind* (1936), and *Of Mice and Men* (1937) for glossy film treatment. Yet the histories of film and television are marked by sobering reminders of how rarely the crossover between these two screen media has been successfully navigated. Rather, it often appears that, as we have tried to move across those deceptively similar screens, to adapt from one form to another, film and television have proved to be less attuned, less mutually welcoming than we might have expected. Rather than functioning as portals of opportunity, as doors that easily swing both ways, they more often seem to demarcate rather exclusive territory. In fact, historically the two media have more commonly become, quite literally, *screens* or filters that seem to filter out something that made the program in its original medium so effective, broadly popular, or simply resonant for a specific audience.

A glance at a popular genre like science fiction (sf) quickly tells the story. Although there have been a great number of efforts to adapt successful sf films to television, it is a singular work like *Stargate* (1994), for example, that manages to generate a popular series such as *Stargate SG-1* (or its further spin-offs *Stargate Atlantis* and *Stargate Universe*) with its ten-year run, largely on cable television. Far more often, adapted films suffer the fate of an effort like *Planet of the Apes* (film, 1968; television, 1974), a series that, despite the great popularity of its various film versions and even the inclusion of several cast members from the big-screen originals, lasted for only thirteen episodes on CBS. And movement in the opposite direction has produced little more success. Although *Star Trek* (1966–69) and its many television spin-offs have inspired a number of film adventures, most efforts to adapt television sf to cinematic proportions have resulted in rather weak, unmemorable works, as in the case of the nostalgia-driven big-screen adaptations of *Lost in Space* (1998) and *My Favorite Martian* (1999). Clearly, there is a complex calculus involved in that movement across the media screens, one that this volume aims to better gauge by examining some of the key problems that have been encountered in the process of adaptation.

There are some obvious and readily understandable culprits at which we can readily point as causes for this problematic relationship. Differences in budget, running times, and cast availability; the distinct implications of televisual seriality versus the typically self-contained cinematic narrative; different audience viewing habits; even variations in screen size and shape are just a few of the factors that potentially come into play and at times seem to pose insurmountable difficulties for moving a text from one screen medium to another. As an example, we might point to the highly popular early television series *Captain Video* (1949–55) that, when adapted to film as a serial in 1951, lost much of the minimalist charm of the television original, thanks to its absorption of certain practices of the new medium, particularly the frenetic, fight-filled, action-driven conventions that propelled the movie serial but that actually had little play in the series' live-broadcast, dialogue-heavy stories about ray guns and space travel, punctuated with direct-address admonishments to the children of the audience. Meanwhile, the popularity of the television series continued unabated—despite that slight film version—into 1955. Coming from the opposite side, the widely praised film *Logan's Run* (1976)[1] would manage to last just fourteen episodes as a television series, even though it had the advantage of using recycled footage and extensive model work that had been created for the original film, and that often provided it with a far more cinematic look than was common to television narrative of the time.

One aim of this volume, consequently, is to examine a number of these issues through case studies that particularly highlight the intermedia adaptation process. By tracking a variety of these texts in the course of that adaptive journey, by following them as they struggle to move across their respective screens, we hope to begin sketching the nature of that screening process and thus to better understand both how and why that "filtering" works as it does and, as a consequence, why certain few texts have successfully managed that crossover whereas a majority have foundered in the attempt. An additional aim is that by following this admittedly rather limited adaptive path, we might also clarify some of the problems and possibilities inherent in all instances of cross-media adaptation, including instances that take us across the screens of the new digital media—the internet, video games, interactive narratives.

As the type of examples cited above should already suggest, our focus for this limited examination is not the entire field of film and television adaptation, but rather a single genre, that of science fiction. We have chosen this selective focus in part simply because it is necessary to narrow the scope of an investigation that could easily require us to consider a broad array of narrative types, each with its own range of generic and media-related conventions that pose their own problems for adaptive work. For example, tracking a domestic melodrama like *Peyton Place* (film, 1957; television series 1964–69) across the screens would immediately involve considering not only the differences between film and television melodramas (the latter, especially during the period when it aired on American television, far more bound by FCC content regulations and audience expectations) but also the relations of both to the long tradition of daytime versus prime-time soap opera, and especially to the different narrative "rhythms" of the soap opera. And given the notoriety of the Grace Metallious novel on which both were based, we would inevitably have to take into account the long-standing debate centering around source-relationships between film and literature, one that has for many decades concentrated on what ultimately seems a concern of somewhat limited significance, what is often referred to in adaptation studies as the "fidelity issue."[2]

Such questions are not of less consequence, nor do they entirely disappear when we narrow our focus to film and television science fiction. However, they do shift valence as we isolate certain common "bridges" between texts—connections afforded by such elements as the relatively constant conventions of one genre, by film and television science fiction's comparable reliance on a special effects aesthetic and an attendant emphasis on a sense of wonder, and by some of the stylistic similarities that science fiction brings to these visual media. So although the fidelity issue almost invariably haunts at some level every discussion of adaptation, bringing with it a certain implication of primary and secondary texts, or as Thomas Leitch succinctly puts it, of an all-too-common assumption that "the model is more valuable than the copy" (6), it will largely shift into the background here as we focus our main attention on a number of those various bridges between texts and media. With that focus we can also foreground some of the issues surrounding what Henry Jenkins has described as "convergence,"[3] that is, we can better understand how film and television have increasingly come to share characteristics, narrative practices, even particularly compatible subjects as their distinct identities increasingly meld into a general category of screen media and become the subject of a kind of convergence scholarship that has come to be identified as "screen studies."

Moreover, this particular genre choice, we would argue, is both an especially appropriate and potentially a most revealing one. As one support for this focus, we might note Anne Friedberg's recent effort to describe the key role the "window" has played—as architectural element, as movie screen, and as digital portal—in Western culture and its arts. To draw together a wide range of historical developments while also trying to move "across the screens" in exploring this trope, she too turns to science fiction, using the 1936 British film *Things to Come*, adapted from the work of noted author H. G. Wells, as her crucial touchstone. Late in that noted film we see a grandfather in the year 2036 showing his granddaughter filmed images of the New York City skyline of a century before, as he tells her all about "the age of windows" that had "lasted four centuries," while also lauding their own age, one that, as the film repeatedly envisions, is marked at every turn by video screens and virtual images, by the sort of electronic "windows" that are already a part of our own everyday lives. Within that science fiction text and its own forecasting of cultural and technological change, Friedberg simply locates a resonant and guiding account of how "the cinematic, television, and computer screens have become substitutes for the architectural window" (11), as well as a way of beginning to consider the various ways in which information travels across our various screens, comes in through our many windows. Although few of her other exemplary texts fall within sf, with *Things to Come* Friedberg locates in the genre's common predictive properties and image stores useful tools for contextualizing and visualizing our own experience of change.

But beyond this singular and striking example—which obviously resonates for our own trek across the screens—we would also argue that sf is especially useful here simply because it is one of the most popular genres in either film or television. Films in this genre are consistently top box-office attractions, as evidenced by such recent hits as *Iron Man* (2008) and *Iron Man 2* (2010), the latest incarnation of *Star Trek* (2009), or the box-office-leading *Avatar* (2010). Moreover, sf films have increasingly staked a claim as high art, as we see in the robust discussions that have been generated by such works as the *Matrix* trilogy, the *Alien* films, and the Steven Spielberg/Stanley Kubrick opus *A.I.: Artificial Intelligence* (2001). Meanwhile, television programming has shown a relative explosion of interest in sf, with series like *Firefly* (2002–03), *Heroes* (2006–10), and *Battlestar Galactica* (2004–09) attaining a kind of cult status; with science-fictional elements such as time travel giving a unique inflection to popular series like *Lost* (2004–09), *Life on Mars* (2006–07 UK, 2008–09 US), *Ashes to Ashes* (2008–10), and *FlashForward* (2009–10); and with cable broadcast allowing a wide variety of older series, from *The Twilight Zone* (1959–64) to all of the various *Star Trek* spin-off series, to find new and newly dedicated audiences.[4] If not yet the most popular genre in both film and television, sf has obviously attained a high level of general acceptance and is often the formula of choice for indirectly addressing a number of our most pressing cultural concerns.

In fact, that sense of the genre's *usefulness*, as a key form of cultural commentary, is another and certainly one of the more important reasons for narrowing our screen focus in this way. We only echo a number of other commentators in suggesting that sf is, very simply, the essential postmodern genre, that is, the one that most directly addresses the key issues of contemporary global culture: our inevitable interactions with technology and an increasingly technologized world; our sense of the self as a constructed and even programmed entity, marked by a precarious subjectivity; our view of the world as a fragile, even threatened ecosystem in a vast universe of diverse systems. Because of this effective cultural address, Scott Bukatman has argued that the genre provides our contemporary technology-haunted world something we sorely need, a "narrative process of technological accommodation" (28), that is, the opportunity—and the place in which—to tell stories wherein we can begin to work out the terms of life in an inevitably scientifically oriented and technologically driven culture. This science-fictional emphasis, then, allows us not only to narrow the scope of our investigation but also to bring into sharp focus some of the essential concerns that are to be found circulating in all (or across all) contemporary screen media.

Finally, we would suggest that probably the most important advantage gained from focusing specifically on sf for this sort of investigation derives from the very nature of the genre. In another effort at comparative analysis, focused on literature and film, Annette Kuhn has remarked that "the most obvious difference between science fiction as literature and science fiction as film lies in the latter's mobilization of the visible" and, consequently, its generation of a highly reflexive dimension (6) as that "visible" thrust repeatedly intersects and resonates with the film experience itself. In this same vein, Garret Stewart argues that sf has always been one of the most self-conscious of film genres, constantly "privileging the viewer" (164) by presenting him or her with tools and opportunities for reflexive study. As a result of its pervasive emphasis on viewing devices, scanners, screens, and various technologies of reproduction or replication, sf cinema, Stewart offers, "often turns out to be, turns round to be, the fictional or fictive science of the cinema itself, the future feats it may achieve scanned in line with the technical feat that conceives them right now and before our eyes" (159), as video technology "is not merely recruited ... its purposes are critically scrutinized" (161). By focusing specifically on this genre, a genre largely made possible by the very technical advances that permit its embodiment, then, we also mine that reflexive potential to better understand the "feats" that both film and television achieve in screening sf—that is, what is so peculiar about their respective screens and what is involved as we try to move across them.

At the same time, in our own reflexive turn, we hope the comparative treatment of these screen media will afford some additional insight into the nature of the genre itself. Although sf has, after a lengthy history and a long relegation to the "pulps," become a highly successful and influential *literary* form, it has—despite the recent successes noted previously—only lately achieved a similar level of critical respectability in its screen incarnations. Part of the problem is due to what Mark Bould identifies as "the special position afforded to spectacle within narrative sf cinema" (80)—a position that has never fully been shared by television,

xviii *Introduction*

although the newer form has increasingly edged closer to the older in this regard, especially as digital technology has given it more access to the "effects" and visual spectacle of the movies and as the very nature of its screen—ever larger, ever wider, with high definition and even 3-D capability—seems increasingly to model that of film. But spectacle, despite its immediate power and appeal, has almost always been critically suspect, viewed largely as an interruption in the more important business of cinematic narrative; and films that highly privilege that element, whether through images of alien invaders, scenes of apocalyptic destruction, space exploration narratives, or realized utopian cities, are approached warily by critics—and perhaps with some of the same suspicion by television producers who have had to consider how they could even make such material fit into their specific media constraints, that is, of more intimate narratives, smaller budgets, and smaller screens. Yet that element of spectacle is central to what sf has always sought to accomplish, for through its tradition of effects and extraordinary images, through its ability to let us all, as *Star Trek*'s well-known introductory injunction offers, "boldly go where no man has gone before," the genre effectively speaks to—and at least partially satisfies—what Michele Pierson describes as "a cultural demand for the aesthetic experience of wonder" (168). And its highly visible *generic* effects, those semantic elements that stand at the very surface

Figure I.1 Future television recalls the "age of windows" in the film *Things to Come* (1936).

of the sf narrative, its well-known and well-appreciated signifiers are, in fact, literally keys that serve to unlock our "wonder" and open up a new world—or universe—of experience.

In the course of being sifted out onto their respective screens, those generic elements, then, not only open onto the nature of film and television as screen media, but they also allow us to glimpse a generally unremarked character of such mediated sf. Whether it is a text that situates the audience in front of a mysterious circumstance or dazzling spectacle ("Space, the final frontier," as *Star Trek* intones), beckons viewers to step through a "Stargate" into another world, or confronts its characters with a "rift" in the space-time continuum that is disconcertingly depositing the universe's imaginary all around (as the contemporary British series *Torchwood* [2006-present], *Primeval* [2007-present], and *Doctor Who* have all recently dramatized), the sf media text also becomes a drama of screens. By that we mean to suggest a level on which this project engages—and, we hope, illuminates—the very nature of media and of media sf, as a form that continually struggles to bring its technologically based vision to the screen, while also suggesting a place for this vision beyond the limits of that same screen—as if its narratives were *always trying to reach beyond*, to escape the screen of fiction, to argue for their possible reality—that is, their very *adaptability* to other forms and, indeed, to life itself. And herein, we would offer, lies one of this book's key arguments—as scattered as it is across the various "screens" offered by our contributors' essays: that both the lure and the difficulty of across-the-screen adaptation of sf rest in that abiding effort at reaching beyond, at escaping the fictive, at, if you will, *unscreening*.

II

As we have also noted, what follows in these discussions of sf across the screens naturally plays out against the backdrop of another field of recent critical consideration, the contemporary concern with adaptation studies. As Thomas Leitch and others have noted, almost from their form's inception, "filmmakers have looked to literary works as a model for their films" (27) or sought to emulate a literary or, especially in the early cinema, a theatrical style of presentation. Particularly in the period from the late 1950s through the 1960s, adaptation research occupied a very prominent place in the burgeoning area of academic film studies, in part because it helped to claim a certain seriousness for film itself by comparing it to a more venerable literature. Film, it was thought, would make significant works more accessible to a wide audience, and film itself, after the fashion of the French "tradition of quality" of the 1940s and 1950s, would thereby gain in its own significance.

However, much of that thinking focused on texts and textual matters while giving little attention to the fact that adaptation is also and always a media event, that is, one that has to consider the impact of media properties. George Bluestone's pioneering 1957 study in this area recognized the issue. He described how, "like two intersecting lines, novel and film meet at a point, then diverge" (63), and in that divergence he would presciently observe that film represents "a different mode of experience, a different way of apprehending the universe" (20)—a point that, while resonant for our thinking about screen sf, was little appreciated in that era because it troubled what was still the more-fundamental project, that effort to legitimize film and film studies through literary comparison. The unspoken fear, after all, was that if film did see "the universe" differently, then to be properly evaluated it would have to be approached differently as well, and ultimately it might not be seen as measuring up to literature or the theater after all.

Yet the sort of comparative study that typically resulted did provide a useful model for research and analysis at a time when film studies was in need of systematic and discipline-specific methods. By linking film studies to the long critical tradition of literary theory and analysis, this early emphasis on adaptation provided not only a useful foundation for theory and criticism, but also one that easily dovetailed with that other legitimating theoretical turn that would also emerge in this era, *auteurism*. For if films could be said to have "authors," after the fashion of novels, plays, and poems, then they could also be usefully compared in terms of their authorial intentions and the way those intentions were supported, altered, or even contravened in the course of the adaptation process. Yet with the advent of a radically revisionary notion, that of the "death of the author," that advantage effectively vanished as the *authority* of authorship—if not quite authorship itself—gradually lost its traction in the academic world.

Although adaptation studies as practiced today have largely moved beyond these key early concerns with legitimacy, authorship, or as we earlier noted, fidelity, in doing so they have also bypassed or neglected two key areas of adaptation activity that also traditionally pose some challenge to the "status" of the film narrative. The first area is that of genre narratives, as most of the recent wave of adaptation study has still focused much of its energy on canonical literary adaptation, what might even be termed "high art," while giving relatively little consideration to the sort of formulaic narratives—horror, thriller, and especially the sf texts—that largely dominate the contemporary cinema. A key exception in this regard is Leitch's work, which acknowledges this problem and pointedly sets out to challenge conventional hierarchical evaluations of adaptations.

The second area of neglect is a rather different sort of adaptive activity that has tended to distract attention from the literature-film nexus on which most studies continue to focus, namely the crossover—and cross-fertilization—between film and television, as these two media have increasingly influenced each other's offerings, as we increasingly explore and

Introduction xxi

move across the screens of the two media, as both become part of that larger confluence that Henry Jenkins has evocatively labeled "convergence media." Part of the driving impulse behind this volume is the belief that we can begin to address both omissions by considering issues of adaptation from the vantage of what, as we have suggested, is arguably the most important of contemporary genres, sf, and by examining key texts on both sides of this largely unexplored media nexus, that is, by looking both at sf films that have generated television series and at series that, in their turn, have inspired popular—and in some cases, admittedly, not-so-popular—sf films. In doing so, this text hopes to offer not only a needed dimension to the current thrust of adaptation studies but also an important insight into the manner in which these two popular media interact, cross-pollinate their texts, and together participate in what the French media theorist Paul Virilio has variously termed the "mediatization" or "cinematization" of contemporary culture (6).

The contemporary concern with adaptation typically highlights two theoretical developments that we would like to mobilize, as both figure centrally to this sort of comparative study and also shed further light on the contemporary, cross-screen popularity of sf, as well as that "unscreening" impulse that I noted earlier. One is the postmodern emphasis on the pastiche text, that is, on the notion that texts are fundamentally derivative and marked by what Ingeborg Hoesterey describes as a "dual structural profile": "imitation of a masterwork" (or works) and a "pâté of components" (9). The "double-coding" that results (Hoesterey 51) insists on a level on which *most* texts should properly, and indeed inevitably, be viewed within

Figure I.2 A demon comes through the rift in the British series *Torchwood*. Copyright BBC.

a framework of adaptation, while it also underscores the significance of the pâté-like mixture or blending of different elements, which suggests both a referential quality that directly derives from those elements' prior uses and an aggregate effect, a new "flavor," if you will, that recalls yet escapes from that elemental past. Given its own blended character—already implicit in that difficult conjunction of terms, "science" and "fiction"—the sf text tends to form an inviting ground for such pastiche consideration, for *evoking* the *sense* of adaptation, as we shall see in several of the following essays. As a telling forecast, we might simply note that in order to define the pastiche and demonstrate how that concept typically functions in the arts, Hoesterey himself would in part ground his discussion in lengthy examinations of several acknowledged masterworks of sf cinema: Fritz Lang's *Metropolis* (1927) and Ridley Scott's *Blade Runner* (1982).

The second theoretical development at work here is that of liminality, or the examination of borders or boundaries—the lines that have historically and theoretically been drawn between types of texts or media and that have often worked to cut off or contain analysis and understanding, especially on a cultural level. By its very nature, of course, every adaptation asserts the hybridity of texts as it holds together works from media like film and literature, film and television, or even film and the internet to present us, inevitably, with a denser cultural picture. At the same time, it makes us mindful of borders, pointing us in a direction suggested by Michel Foucault, who observed how "the play of limits and transgression seem to be regulated by a simple obstinacy: transgression incessantly crosses and recrosses a line which closes behind it . . . and thus it is made to return once more right to the horizon of the uncrossable" (34). In that description Foucault effectively established the lure of the liminal study, for he reminded us of how illusory our historical, cultural, and textual boundaries inevitably prove to be; of how upon close examination or approach, they all too easily recede from critical scrutiny, practically seem to disappear, much as happens, we might argue, when we begin to hold examples of film and television sf in positions of opposition—and as we might increasingly expect in a period when the technological differences between screen media increasingly seem to be blurring, thanks to advances in technology as well as the introduction of yet other screens.

We would again argue for sf as affording the most fertile ground for exploring both of these key issues, and indeed for observing the sorts of "transgression" to which Foucault calls attention. It presents us not only with a field that is itself a kind of hybrid—of science and fiction, of fact and fantasy—but also one that is fundamentally concerned with going beyond normal boundaries as it creates a context that Darko Suvin has, in his influential definition of the form, termed one of "cognitive estrangement" (4) that allows for asking the basic science-fictional question, "What if?" If the genre now asks such questions from a privileged position as the primary postmodern genre, it also does so while easily crossing boundaries and frequently incorporating the conventions of other genres—as evidenced by *Blade Runner*'s re-visioning of the film noir, *Robocop*'s (1986) and *Life on Mars*' (2006–07 UK, 2008–09 US) versions of the police procedural, *Firefly*'s (2002–03) and *Serenity*'s (2005) embeddedness in the world of the media Western, or *Roswell*'s (1999–2002) and *Smallville*'s (2001–11) adaptations of the teen melodrama. Yet from the vantage of this other hybrid character, the sf text manages to voice the same sort of cultural concerns and to convey the same sort of imaginary solutions that we customarily find in all our popular screen genres.

Moreover, whereas the sf film has very quickly developed its own canon of critical commentary, science fiction television has lagged far behind, and more important, the links between the two forms have been far too little explored to this point. The recent *Essential Science Fiction Television Reader* (Telotte) does provide several essays that survey this territory, and the journal *Science Fiction Film and Television* lives at this point of juncture. However, the popularity of many of the works that have straddled the borders of film and television—including, on the one hand, series like *Voyage to the Bottom of the Sea* (1964–68), *Alien Nation* (1989–90), and *Stargate SG-1*; and on the other, films such as *Star Trek: The Motion Picture* (1979, and its many sequels), *Twilight Zone: The Movie* (1983), *The X-Files* (1998, 2008), and *Serenity*—suggests that an assessment of these cross-media adaptations is overdue and indeed essential to the developing field of adaptation studies, to the evolving genre study of sf, and to increasing academic efforts to link film and television into a common—and growing, as our inclusion here of the internet underscores—field of screen studies.

Paul Young in his recent study of cross-media influence has argued that what we commonly think of as classical cinema—and from which we derive much of our sense of what classical genre narrative is and how it works—exists only as an element within a larger industrial "system" that is constantly undergoing alteration, while also being in various ways "maintained" (7), as its institutional practices struggle against the stresses imposed by a variety of developments: in technology, in entertainment fashion, in cultural desires, and in potentially competing media. That dynamic vantage invariably speaks to the relationship between sf cinema and sf television. As has been demonstrated elsewhere (Telotte), the science fiction cinema long anticipated the advent of television and consistently sought to frame it in a less-than-positive manner: as a flawed, even dangerous method of communication and surveillance (see, for example, a most revealing title like *Death by Television* [1935]) and not as the potential competitor that the industry actually feared television would inevitably become. Yet as Young argues, there has always been more at stake in such intermedia relationships than just an industrial fear of competition or of being supplanted. There is a concern with maintaining, or at least *suggesting*, the perceived "qualities" of a medium "as compared to its newer rivals" (xxii)—"qualities" that have become linked to our

xxiv *Introduction*

enjoyment of certain types of texts (for example, the current film industry emphasis on the 3-D experience) and that have taken on a definite "value" within our culture (and here consider the importance of the "immersive" media experience). The process of intermedia or cross-media adaptation explored in this volume foregrounds the dynamics implicit in that sense of rivalry between film and television, and thus, we hope, opens a new perspective on the relative failures and successes of each medium's efforts to draw upon the successful works of the other, as each tries to establish its own "value."

III

The structure for these investigations is rather straightforward. Following this situating of the sf text as our general area of study and a description of the terrain of intermedia adaptation, we shall analyze some of the most telling efforts to adapt the science fiction film to the newer medium of television and to turn successful or significant television series into feature-length movies. Yet rather than simply focusing our case studies on variously successful and unsuccessful attempts at such cross-media adaptation, we shall concentrate on texts whose adaptation foregrounds many of the key characteristics of the media involved, thereby casting into relief that dual sense of the screen's function we noted at the start of this chapter—as both a portal and a barrier to the process of intermedia adaptation.

In order better to organize this investigation, most of the essays draw to various extents on a central touchstone, on what is not only one of the key texts in television studies but also a kind of foundational text of screen studies, John Ellis's *Visible Fictions*. In a way that has proven especially fruitful for cultivating an emergent televisual theory, Ellis isolated some of the salient characteristics of both film and television: the "radically different" weighting of the image in the two forms (127), the "segmentalisation" and "seriality" of television narratives (120, 123) versus the unitary strategy of film narratives, their differing constitution of how viewers see in the two media (137), their dissimilar emphasis on and even different visual depiction of characters (153). Ellis emphasized these and other characteristics not to produce an essentialist reading of either form, but rather to suggest ways of organizing their comparison, of framing the resulting comparisons within appropriate cultural contexts, and of better understanding the cultural voice that resides in and speaks through those traits. Thus he noted—and in a way that Young's commentary obviously recalls—that many of these characteristics have arisen from specific industrial and ideological conditions, reflecting "the typical uses to which these technologies [i.e., film and television] have been put by Western society" (13), even as he also suggested that other practices could well emerge given different technological and cultural circumstances.

Although Ellis's text may now seem somewhat dated, many of those points of comparison remain useful guides for our case studies of cross-media adaptation, particularly when they are inflected by other works that draw Ellis's analysis into the realm of fantasy and sf, such as Catherine Johnson's *Telefantasy*. Although focused mainly on television, Johnson's work, very much like this book, isolates the broad field of fantasy as its control case because, as she explains, "all texts that represent the fantastic ask questions that push the boundaries" (4) of a medium by inviting opportunities to experiment with its very nature. Thus, while ranging across different eras of television production in the US and UK, she argues that fantasy programming has consistently posed a challenge to the "dominant notions of the aesthetics of television" and, for that very reason, has become "a useful site . . . to re-examine the dominant paradigms for understanding" those aesthetics (12)—a most important step at a time when, thanks to ongoing changes in both industries, as well as the still-to-be-felt impact of the internet, those aesthetics are beginning to seem poised for change.

The resulting series of case studies, then, will range across a number of the main aesthetic issues identified by Ellis and Johnson. We shall begin by turning to several of the primary early influences on the movement of sf from film to the television screen. One is the serial narrative that provided a model, in both form and subject matter, for much early television science fiction, particularly of the popular space opera variety, typified by such series as *Captain Video* (1949–55), *Space Patrol* (1950–55), and *Tom Corbett, Space Cadet* (1950–55). As Cynthia Miller describes, the serial's B-film links made for relatively uncomplicated imitation in the low-budget, limited-ambition climate of television production in the late 1940s and early 1950s, and its narrative segmentation easily adapted to the short blocks of television presentation, resulting in a kind of "domesticated" version of the cinematic model. Another is Rod Serling's *The Twilight Zone* (1959–64), a work that, despite its links to the popular televised live-action drama of the 1950s and the frequent claims for its *literary* sources, also managed to resist the dominant televisual style Ellis has described in favor of a pointedly cinematic one. Affording some contrast to both of these approaches, in the following chapter Mary Pharr examines the troubled nature of the image in early sf adaptation from the vantage of Irwin Allen's interpretation of his own action-adventure spectacle *Voyage to the Bottom of the Sea* to television. The resulting study juxtaposes what Ellis terms the "characteristically pared down" or "impoverished" image of television (112) with the spectacular form that has typically been seen as a hallmark of cinematic sf and that has always been especially pronounced in Allen's technologically driven narratives. Through these three initial chapters, then, we hope to offer a triangulation on our subject as we suggest different—and typically unremarked—models of successful intermedia adaptation: models based on generic form, media style, and even technological capacity.

xxvi *Introduction*

The next section of the book assesses both failed and successful efforts at adapting films to the television screen. Beginning with one of the most spectacular of those failures, Gerald Duchovnay examines how the film *Logan's Run* (1976) became a short-lived series of the same title (1977–78), and in the process explores how the imperatives bound up in what Ellis terms a "dialogue/talk medium" like television have often clashed with the action dynamic of film fantasy and how context might trump either. As a balance, Sherryl Vint assesses the case of what has obviously been one of the most successful of all television adaptations, that of *Stargate SG-1* from the 1994 film *Stargate*. The series would run from 1997 to 2007, lead to two live-action spin-off series and an animated series, and would result in two direct-to-video film productions; but its success, Vint suggests, owes less to its sf elements and more to its appearance at a time when both the television and film industries were undergoing significant technological and economic changes. Examining a less-successful adaptation, that of the *Terminator* films (particularly those of 1984 and 1991) to the two-season television series *The Sarah Conner Chronicles* (2008–09), Lorrie Palmer considers how the combination of character and spectacle affects that transition from film to television. Anchoring her comparison in concerns of character, she argues that the key issue in this adaptation lies in the transformation of the *spectacle* of gender as it had been developed in the film franchise to a new, televisually developed gender vision focused on a female who could pass as a teenager. This examination situates the issue of televisual adaptation in a broad media and cultural landscape, one that has been altered in recent years by a variety of such feminine "warrior" models, but most notably by the central character in the long-running fantasy series *Buffy the Vampire Slayer* (1997–2003).

The following section focuses on a series of case studies involving the opposite movement—from television to film. As the most appropriate start for such a series of investigations, M. Keith Booker looks at what is arguably the most iconic and most influential example of television sf, Gene Roddenberry's original *Star Trek* (1966–69), as it was first translated to the big screen. In this discussion he considers how differing audience experiences and expectations inflected the cross-media adaptation and helped to shape a work like *Star Trek: The Motion Picture*—a work that, while it aimed to open up the universe originally imagined by the television series also reimagined the utopian implications that had been central to the television original and to its audience's experience. Rodney Hill then considers another popular television phenomenon, *The X-Files* (1993–2002), as it was twice translated to the screen in *The X-Files* (1998) and *The X-Files: I Want to Believe* (2008). His discussion plays against the background of the dominant serial mode of television by examining how, in the case of the series' two weak film adaptations, issues of seriality clash with the closure that is expected—and that provides a strong measure of the pleasure bound up in—the typical payoff of classical film narrative. Turning to the unusual case of a failed television series that inspired a successful film adaptation, Joss Whedon's *Firefly* (2002–03) and his film *Serenity* (2005), the next chapter examines how a cult following might empower adaptation, allowing a text to move across the screens almost in spite of its network failure. In this instance, though, the success of the film certainly also owes much to the influence of Whedon and to his particular approach to genre and its narrative possibilities.

The final section considers a number of what we would simply term "issues" that inform—and challenge—much of our thinking about cross-media adaptation. Mark Bould appropriately opens this section by looking at the longest-running of all sf series, *Doctor Who* (1963–89, 1996, 2005-present), as a way of introducing production and consumption contexts into the study of adaptation. Drawing on the view of television as an unremitting "flow," he examines how segments within that flow—serial arcs, films, and various ancillary texts and products—all contribute to a textual commodification that inevitably shapes the adaptation process. Proceeding from Dani Cavallaro's reminder that the adaptation of animation requires us to understand "a very distinctive visual language" (12), Michelle Pirkle analyzes how that special "language" worked in the case of the highly successful Japanese *anime* series *Cowboy Bebop* (1998–99) as it was adapted into *Cowboy Bebop: The Movie* (a.k.a. *Knockin' on Heaven's Door*, 2001). As Pirkle finds, the feature film tends to translate that language differently and in a way that can lose some of its resonance for the typical *anime* audience. And in what seems a particularly fitting conclusion for this sort of study, Chuck Tryon takes us across other media screens. He tracks the impact of the fan community and its life online as he discusses the transformation—through re-editing, refilming, and continual interactivity—of one of the most influential of all sf franchises, *Star Wars* (1977), into a contemporary internet phenomenon.

The aim of all of these examinations, anchored simultaneously in Ellis's pioneering screen studies and in the long tradition of adaptation studies, is to take readers on a journey across the various screens that our selected sf texts have so profitably employed and fascinatingly visualized. In the process, we hope that these essays shed a revealing light on how fundamentally linked texts can, for a variety of reasons, prove in some cases easily adaptable and in others frustratingly tied to their originary media. Moreover, we believe that sf might be the most suitable field for revealing some of the dynamics of screen adaptation, for as Catherine Johnson nicely suggests, it is in the very nature of media sf to be both "experimental and formulaic, spectacular and intimate, economically successful and aesthetically valued" (149). Of course, sf in all of its forms has always sought to pose questions of possibilities, to push at the boundaries of both subject and medium, to straddle distinctions as its very name implies. Such exploratory and combinatory possibilities thus form the core of this study, just as they also inform the best of adaptation thinking. And as the new digital regime of the internet—of video games, of interactive narratives, of forms that seem in many ways fundamentally science fictional—is already insisting, we should only expect our media, now frequently handheld and tabletlike, to expand these concerns, as we increase the possibilities for such movement across the screens.

NOTES

1. *Logan's Run* won an Academy Award for Special Visual Effects and was also nominated for Oscars in the categories of Cinematography and Art Direction. The science fiction community was also generally impressed by the film, awarding it the Saturn Award for best science fiction film and nominating it for a Nebula Award for best science fiction script.
2. For a discussion of the "fidelity issue" and a thorough explanation of what is at stake for film studies—and we would suggest, for television as well—in following the path of "fidelity as a criterion of value" (6), we would recommend Thomas Leitch's *Film Adaptation and Its Discontents*. Adaptation studies, thanks especially to Leitch's work as well as several other recent books, has entered into a dialogue with mainstream film theory and has foregrounded issues that should inform other cross-media adaptation work, including that involved in the screen studies relationships considered here.
3. Jenkins describes the operation of "convergence media" as both the intersection of different media, such as film and television, and also the "circulation of media content . . . across different media systems, competing media economies, and national borders" (3).
4. In a recent week on my local cable television system, I counted twenty-three science fiction series being broadcast. These included older series in deep syndication, such as the original *Twilight Zone*; reruns of relatively recent series like *Enterprise* (2001–05) and *Stargate SG-1*; and new efforts like *Dollhouse* (2009–10) and *Fringe* (2008-present). Of course, the very existence of a dedicated outlet like the Syfy Channel already underscores the general popularity of media science fiction to which a volume like this points.

WORKS CITED

Bluestone, George. *Novels into Film: The Metamorphosis of Fiction into Cinema.* Berkeley: U of California P, 1957.
Bould, Mark. "Film and Television." *The Cambridge Companion to Science Fiction.* Eds. Edward James and Farah Mendlesohn. Cambridge: Cambridge UP, 2003. 79–95.
Bukatman, Scott. *Matters of Gravity: Special Effects and Supermen in the 20th Century.* Durham: Duke UP, 2003.
Cavallaro, Dani. *Anime and the Art of Adaptation.* Jefferson: McFarland, 2010.
Ellis, John. *Visible Fictions.* Rev. ed. London: Routledge, 1992.
Foucault, Michel. *Language, Counter-Memory, Practice: Selected Essays and Interviews.* Ed. Donald F. Bouchard. Ithaca: Cornell UP, 1977.
Friedberg, Anne. *The Virtual Window: From Alberti to Microsoft.* Cambridge: MIT P, 2006.
Hoesterey, Ingeborg. *Pastiche: Cultural Memory in Art, Film, Literature.* Bloomington: Indiana UP, 2001.

Jenkins, Henry. *Convergence Culture: Where Old and New Media Collide.* New York: New York UP, 2006.
Johnson, Catherine. *Telefantasy.* London: BFI, 2005.
Kuhn, Annette. "Introduction." *Alien Zone: Cultural Theory and Contemporary Science Fiction Cinema.* London: Verso, 1990. 1–12.
Leitch, Thomas. *Film Adaptation and Its Discontents: From* Gone with the Wind *to* The Passion of the Christ. Baltimore: Johns Hopkins UP, 2007.
Pierson, Michele. *Special Effects: Still in Search of Wonder.* New York: Columbia UP, 2002.
Stewart, Garrett. "The 'Videology' of Science Fiction." *Shadows of the Magic Lamp.* Ed. George E. Slusser and Eric S. Rabkin. Carbondale: Southern Illinois UP, 1985. 159–207.
Suvin, Darko. *Metamorhposes of Science Fiction: On the Politics and History of a Literary Gene.* New Haven: Yale UP, 1979.
Telotte, J. P. "Lost in Space: Television as Science Fiction Icon." *The Essential Science Fiction Television Reader.* Ed. J. P. Telotte. Lexington: UP of Kentucky, 2008. 37–53.
Virilio, Paul. *The Art of the Motor.* Trans. Julie Rose. Minneapolis: U of Minnesota P, 1995.
Young, Paul. *The Cinema Dreams Its Rivals: Media Fantasy Films from Radio to the Internet.* Minneapolis: U of Minnesota P, 2006.

Part I
Cross-Screen Dynamics

1 Domesticating Space
Science Fiction Serials Come Home

Cynthia J. Miller

Before they first came to television in the late 1940s, with their spectacular tales of robots, rocket ships, and alien encounters, early science fiction serials had captured the imaginations of theater audiences one thrilling chapter at a time. Each week, futuristic heroes such as Flash Gordon, Buck Rogers, and Commando Cody championed humanity and democracy against the forces of evil, both earthly and alien, as fans watched in wonder, creating a Saturday morning tradition that would come to define youth entertainment from the 1920s through the 1950s. With their arrival on broadcast television, however, the thrills and chills of sf serials and space operas found another home—in their audience's homes—opening a new era in sf entertainment. Although only a small number of theatrical sf serials were reproduced on television, their format would provide the template for numerous televised programs that confronted producers, writers, cameramen, and actors with the challenge of adapting fantastic tales of outer space from the formalized, big-picture public screenings of cinema into the new domestic, small-screen experience of the home.

Considerations of these early televised sf series and space operas typically focus on the technical challenges of adaptation across screens, noting the inherent differences between film and television in production values, narrative structure, content, viewing styles, and the ability to create spectacle. Still in its infancy, early television production was often found lacking in comparison to its cinematic counterpart, derided for low production values resulting from the physical limitations of live studio soundstages and the creative—and budgetary—limitations of its effects technology. Whatever television was not able to duplicate (via kinescope), it also was not able to replicate (via live special effects). However, when thinking about televised sf series, a direct comparison with commercial cinema may be of limited usefulness. Early televised sf series often have less in common with seamless cinematic texts than with the comics, radio serials, and short stories from which many of them were drawn. With roots in these other "domestic" and often sequential media, televised sf series are not quite cinematic narratives out-of-place, but a different form of narrative. Indeed, their adaptation to television may be thought of as sf serials coming home.

ONE CHAPTER AT A TIME

Serials, or chapterplays as they are often called, with their high adventure, low budgets, and cliffhanger endings, played a significant role in cinematic entertainment for more than half a century.[1] Produced in episodes of fifteen to twenty minutes in length, serials such as *The Perils of Pauline* (1914), *The Master Mystery* (1919), and *The Hope Diamond Mystery* (1921) typically ran for twelve to fifteen episodes that were screened weekly in theaters. From the silent era onward, these serial dramas were popular screen attractions that netted profits for studios and theaters, advanced the careers of their stars, and contributed to a spectacle-based culture of attractions distributed in weekly installments.[2] Whereas a number of early serials contained elements of the fantastic (most notably *The Master Mystery*), sf serials, which prominently featured themes of space and superscientific technologies,[3] only became a staple of neighborhood movie houses in the mid-1930s, with serials such as *The Vanishing Shadow* (Universal, 1934), *The Lost City* (Krellberg/Regal Pictures, 1935), and *The Phantom Empire* (Mascot, 1935). Most closely identified with youthful audiences, these serials were the stuff of which childhood fantasies, and Saturday matinees, were made. As Weiss and Goodgold (1981) relate:

> The serials were a world of their own. For approximately twenty minutes you were totally involved in a series of hair-raising escapes, spectacular battles, mile-a-minute chases, hidden treasures, secret plans, and diabolical scientific devices, all held together by a plot which was at once highly tenuous and at the same time complicated almost beyond comprehension. (vi)

Avid serial fans, young viewers always watched a second time, "looking for clues [they] might have missed the first time around," becoming highly literate in the serials' narrative form and plot devices, as well as reliable consumers of serials as an entertainment genre (Weiss and Goodgold, vi). Later, as sf serials were adopted as broadcast television programming, similar young audience members, who often watched together with their parents,[4] would become the core of the genre's fan base in its new medium, as well as primary consumers of its social and commercial messages as sf series became integrated into domestic life.[5]

Because of their close identification with youthful audiences and their association with second-tier studios,[6] early sf serials were almost never shown at first-run theaters, which led both their production and content to be dismissed as inconsequential (Kinnard 5). Even so, the fantastic plots of these chapterplays breathed new life into motion picture serials and created a new era in film entertainment as they spoke not only to Americans' fascination and fear surrounding technological advancements in the machine age but to the increasing interweaving of science and popular culture.[7] The sf genre's speculative power, "its ability to speak to the wonder and curiosity that are ultimately bound up in our scientific and technological developments" (Telotte, *Replications* 3) safely cast as children's entertainment, would later become one of its most celebrated and studied qualities.

With the advent of broadcast television in the US in the 1940s, the terrain of entertainment media shifted, transporting the fantastic directly into the home. A technological marvel that, for many, seemed science fictional itself, the television had already been prefigured in numerous sf serials long before it made its way to many households, often taking the form of "remote viewing screens" for the purpose of surveillance rather than entertainment. One such example can be found in the film serial *The Phantom Empire*, a musical-Western-sf hybrid, starring soon-to-be cowboy icon Gene Autry. The film takes place in the present but showcases the futuristic world of Murania far beneath Earth's surface, where scientific marvels such as moving sidewalks, robots, video phones, a reviving chamber, and ray guns are part of everyday life, and the empire's icy Queen Tika (Dorothy Christie) uses her viewing screen to monitor both her realm and the world above—bringing all into her domain.[8] When *The Phantom Empire* was released in 1935, a good deal of experimentation had been done with television in the audience's "real" world, yet only about four hundred sets existed in the US, and it would be four more years before the beginning of commercial television broadcasting, coinciding with the technology's public debut at the 1939 New York World's Fair, would start American television's move into the domestic realm.

Between 1946 and 1948, regular network television broadcasts began on ABC, NBC, CBS, and the DuMont Television Network, and network executives anxiously grappled with the challenge of providing programming that would draw viewers to the nascent medium. First, there were the obvious postwar limitations on personnel, facilities, distribution, advertising support, raw materials needed for equipment manufacture, and programming content (Hawes 12). Beyond those overarching limitations, though, the live television format used for most programming was also constrained by small sound stages, limitations on image production, demands on actors unlike those posed by stage or film, and the rate at which audiences developed a common grammar for "reading" new televisual codes and cues. Integrating television into family life meant not only adjusting to its physical presence but also constructing an intimate, shared culture that encompassed both the world of the narrative and the world of the viewers. The industry and audiences alike were still making sense of the technologies and possibilities of the new medium. As one CBS vice president noted, "television is a challenge to creative imaginations to learn the basic characteristics of the medium and then devise suitable material for it" (Wilk xii).

And then there was the question of programming itself as major film companies, understandably wary of competition, attempted to stifle the aspirations of the fledgling medium by using threats and contractual bans to prevent actors from "crossing over" into television and claiming ownership of film rights, including the transmission of blurry sixteen-millimeter kinescope reproductions.[9] Further, motion picture studios sought to block network access to existing stage plays and scripts, which forced television studios to turn to public domain and original material for their programming (Wilk 125–26). Producers and studio executives reflected this increasing tension between older medium and new. In 1946, Twentieth Century-Fox studio chief Darryl F. Zanuck pronounced, "Television won't be able to hold onto any market it captures after the first six months. People will soon get tired of staring at a plywood box every night" (Becker 17). But only three years later, producer Samuel Goldwyn predicted that "the television age" would have "revolutionary effects" on the motion picture industry:

> The competition we feared in the past—the automobile in early movie days, the radio in the twenties and thirties, and the developing of night sports quite recently—will fade into insignificance by comparison with the fight we are going to have to keep people patronizing our theaters in preference to sitting at home and watching a program of entertainment. (200)

Goldwyn further cautioned that in direct competition with the new medium, the motion picture industry would lose: "If the movies try to lick television, it's the movies that will catch the licking." Instead, he advocated finding ways to fit movies into "the new world created by television" (200).

A DOMESTIC MEDIUM

The power Goldwyn predicted can be glimpsed in John Ellis's examination of television as an integral part of the structure and replication of domestic culture. Ellis observed that broadcast television is "a profoundly domestic phenomenon" (113)—programming that circulates in specific patterns of production, distribution, and consumption that are intricately interwoven with the culture of home and hearth. Etched into the everyday rhythms and routines of households and families, television programming becomes part of home life and the dynamic commercial culture that has been built up around it. That commercial culture makes assumptions about family composition, gender roles, and sexual orientation that, in turn, inform programming and affect not only on-screen representations, but scheduling and advertising as well. Consequently, broadcast television not only reflects but also *creates* particular kinds of viewers in service of its own social, political, and commercial agenda—and that commercialism, for many, formed the crux of the big screen-small screen divide. Films were cast as high-quality cultural products with high-quality stars, whereas television's commercialism was derided as a "corrupter of the dramatic arts" (Becker

28). Actor Dana Andrews (*Laura* [1944], *The Best Years of Our Lives* [1946]) summed up these sentiments, contending that "TV is controlled by bookkeepers who don't care about the quality of their shows as long as they reach the people and sell merchandise" (Becker 28).

Television's segmented forms of narration combined with commercialization, however, are key to both its framing of audiences and its successful integration into the domestic realm. Unlike cinema, where audiences purchase tickets for a single narrative event that is cast as spectacle and bracketed in time and space from their daily routines and relationships, early television programming had to meet the needs of a domestic setting brimming over with distractions and intrusions that were competing for the attention of the viewing audiences, from household schedules to interpersonal demands. Thus, its offerings have typically taken the form of segments—a series of sequential programs and advertisements—that accommodate natural shifts in attention. This segmentalization is television's own creation, one as innovative as the medium itself, and extends across virtually the whole of television's output (Ellis 120).

Early television's landmark forms of segmented programming were the serial and the series, two formats that contained similarities but also significant differences. Both generated multiple segments from basic thematic material, and both contained a form of continuity-with-difference that suited the medium's nature, providing recurring characters and tropes, revisiting familiar settings and locations, and supplying enough repetition to acculturate new viewers or fill in gaps from missed episodes. Serials, however, led viewers down an episodic path of accumulated knowledge to a story's conclusion, whereas series did not. Serials, with their continuing narrative progression, brought additional features to each episode's beginnings and endings, many opening with title sequences that introduced characters and relationships as well as summarized the episode's current adventure. Cliffhangers, which left characters—and sometimes, entire worlds—in peril, added suspense to each episode's closing. Their to-be-continued drama also resisted any resolution of danger or suspense, guaranteeing the weekly return of existing viewers.[10]

Successful film serials, such as *Flash Gordon* (1936), *Buck Rogers* (1939), and *Radar Men from the Moon* (1952), offered material that was adaptation-ready. Typically public domain, and thus free of motion picture studios' claims to copyright and control, the segmentation of these serials offered an ideal fit for the framework of daily television programming with its need to accommodate domestic viewing patterns and commercial interruption. It was also material for which there existed a "preconstructed and preselected audience" (Elsaesser 93), given the great popularity of cinematic serials and the more recent successes of films such as *Destination Moon* (1950). Early children's television series such as *Captain Video and his Video Rangers*; *Tom Corbett, Space Cadet*; and *Space Patrol* along with early regional offerings like *Captain Z-Ro* all helped,

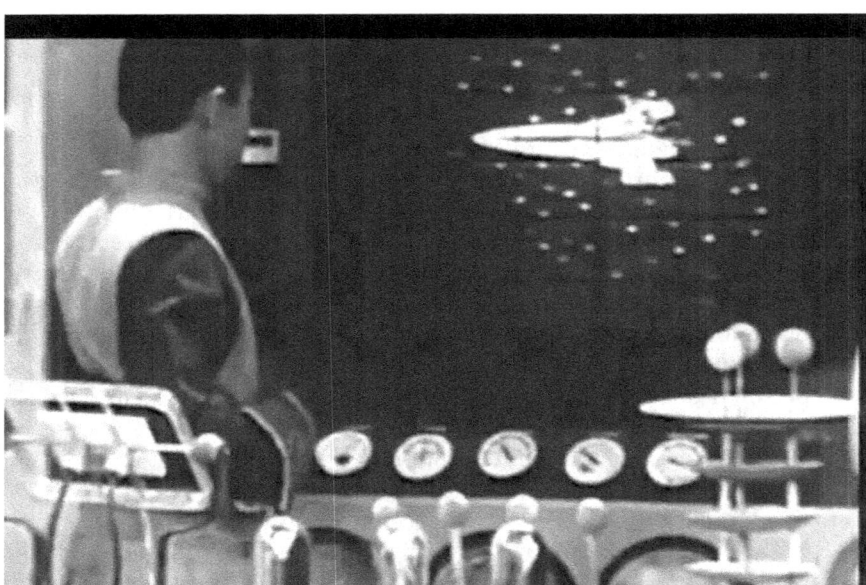

Figure 1.1 Youthful sidekicks like Captain Z-Ro's cadet, Jet, mirrored a young audience's "space fever." KRON-TV, San Francisco.

as Keith Booker notes, to "establish science fiction as a central television genre," adapting the narrative model provided by film serials to create the foundation for televised sf series and anthologies for decades to come (5). In these early years, however, bringing rockets, missiles, alien invasions, and interplanetary travel to the small screen demanded resources and creativity that other genres did not, and sf was still generally considered "a problematic genre in that its futuristic worlds and speculative storylines often challenged both the budgets and narrative constraints of the medium" (Duchovnay 69).

BIG ADVENTURES, SMALL SCREENS

When the first wave of sf series was readied for broadcast television, the new medium provided many challenges. Chief among them was how to adapt those big adventures to fit television's small screens and transport the thrills of the theater into the home. The spectacular effects that captured the imaginations and box-office dollars of youthful audiences were severely hampered by the nascent medium's lack of technological development, along with significantly smaller budgets and television's resulting inability to create special effects that rivaled those of the movies. As actor George Wallace (of *Commando Cody*) relates, the special effects and stunts used in the crafting of his serial's motion picture production already stretched the abilities of both actors and production crew, all retained by a studio that was one of the most active producers of motion picture serials:

> I started off doing [stunts] in front of the actual Republic Administrative Offices . . . [they'd] bury a spot trampoline right in front of my intended takeoff position. Then they had charges wired in the tanks, with some mattresses on the other side so I didn't break my neck. I would run, hit the dials, hit the trampoline, go sailing past the camera, and land on mattresses on the ground on the other side. (Henderson, "Commando Cody Speaks" 59)

Whereas theatergoers were able to witness the spectacular results of these stunts—Commando Cody flying through the air before their very eyes—television audiences were not so lucky.

Thanks to the resources of motion picture studios, film special-effects masters such as Republic's Howard and Theodore Lydecker crafted miniature rockets, soaring figures suspended by guide wires, and the pair's signature special effect, "melting" rocks.[11] Universal's prop man Elmer A. Johnson built countless copper-and-wood spaceships, and cinematographers like Jerry Ash and Richard Fryer shot futuristic cities and cinematic spacescapes that brought motion picture serials' fantastic worlds to life. The resources—in finances, talent, and technology—needed to support and nurture these creative efforts could only be found in established film studios, not in the small budgets and live formats of televised sf series, which often relied on paint, cardboard, and audience's imaginations to conjure effects that seldom approximated what movie studios could create.

The fledgling medium of television with its live productions, small sound stages, and smaller budgets faced an even greater challenge, and the adaptation of the sf serial model across screens was neither seamless nor unproblematic. Few motion picture serials were simply adapted or transitioned directly to broadcast television without stops, diversions, or alterations along the way, though their influences, both collectively and individually, may be readily observed in a variety of early sf series from *Captain Video* (1949–55) and *Tom Corbett: Space Cadet* (1950–55) to anthology shows such as *Tales of Tomorrow* (1951–53) and *Lights Out* (1949–52).

The exchange of material between theatrical serials and televisual sf series took an unanticipated direction when, in 1951, with cinematic serials already on the path to extinction, the adaptation process was reversed and the silver screen began to co-opt characters made familiar at home. *Captain Video*, a popular children's program featuring Richard Coogan as the titular military hero and Master of Science,[12] had begun its run on the small screen and early in its broadcast history was concurrently "cinematized" as

Captain Video: Master of the Stratosphere (1951). The televised version of *Captain Video* clearly was pared-down cinema; with a reputed prop budget of $25 per week,[13] it paled in comparison to that of film sf, although it was also widely celebrated for its down-home ingenuity: "The program is a triumph of carpentry and wiring, and the entire action takes place primarily in the headquarters of the Video Rangers—a room equipped with flashing bulbs, microphones, panels, dials, telephones which have been given names from electronic double-talk" ("Electronic Age" 6). Camera work, limited to two-shots and close-ups, failed to conceal the confined space of the program's soundstage. Apart from its iconic characters and locations, however, the theatrical serial shared neither plot nor actors with its small-screen predecessor, but it did capitalize on and expand the fan base created by the popular television program.

Few episodes of the original series survive to the present day. However, its general production values, enhanced during the program's broadcast tenure, remained relatively constant and are evident in those surviving shows. Utilizing the model established by its cinematic predecessors, each installment of *Captain Video* opened on a long shot of the Captain's (Richard Coogan) secret mountain headquarters, which more resembled a charcoal landscape sketch than a hero's power base. Orchestral fanfare accompanied Fred Scott's voice-over announcement: "Captain Video: Electronic Wizard! Master of Time and Space! Guardian of the Safety of the World!" Viewers were then oriented to the show's thematic stance, as the title credit cards appeared on screen:

> Fighting for law and order, Captain Video operates from a mountain retreat with secret agents at all points of the globe. Possessing scientific secrets and scientific weapons, Captain Video asks no quarter and gives none to the forces of evil. Stand by for Captain Video and his Video Rangers!

Recalling its serial ancestors, a brief recap of the ongoing drama typically followed and was often accompanied by a direct address to the series' young audience members: "Video Rangers, you and I know why," drawing viewers into the narrative.

Typically, only three set variations made up the interior shots for an episode: the evil scientist's laboratory—defined by the flashing lights of a huge (cardboard) energy machine; Captain Video's office—a military control room outfitted with its own collection of radios, dials, and a video screen, with a painted window view as a backdrop; and the interior of the Captain's rocket ship—a bolted cockpit door painted onto the rear wall. Across these sets, the camera's direct, unflinching gaze betrayed frequent stumbling over lines and missed cues.[14] The actors' direct address, however, filled the distance between laboratory and living room, convincing viewers that science truly was a threat to humanity. Likewise, Captain Video's futuristic technospeak, with its neologisms such as "radio scillograph" and "opticon scillometer," added to this familiarity and closeness by creating a framework of linguistic intimacy that bound together fans and fictional characters—one of the key features of the new medium, as Ellis notes—and made knowledge of the fantastic "a part of home life rather than any kind of special event" (113).

SPACE-AGE DOMESTIC CONSUMERS

Along with its educational Ranger Messages, which promoted good conduct and citizenship, the series' commercial breaks provide a clear illustration of television's adaptation of the cinematic serial format to suit its role in the domestic economy and of the ways this early programming may be understood as a "material articulation" of the era's domestic consumerism (Williams 66–68). These departures from the world of the narrative were crafted, with varying degrees of success, to give the sense of an almost seamless continuity. They utilized the series' sets, stars, and announcer (whose familiar voice already signaled "authority" to the series' young audience members) to blur the distinction between advertising and nonadvertising material, facilitating the creation (in children) and reinforcement (in adults) of the ideal domestic consumer. The interpolated commercials, typically advertisements for snack products, were similar to those found in other forms of televised children's programming. Aspiring Video Rangers were instructed, "Be sure to ask your mom to buy delicious Powerhouse bars," or advised that an ordinary lunchbox becomes "extraordinary" when it contains Johnson's Fudge squares. Series tie-in products, such as the Video Rangers ring, were frequently offered as premiums to reward young viewers for their roles as consumers.

Young audience members were already familiar with these sorts of tie-in products, which commonly accompanied their favorite cinematic serials.[15] Blended into the world of the televised narrative, however, these advertisements made it difficult for young viewers to immediately distinguish between storyline and marketing, the characters becoming that much more "real" in the space of the child's own living room.

In a particularly well-known example of *Captain Video*'s boundary blurring, the on-screen action shifts to the Video Ranger inside the familiar rocket ship cockpit as the voice-over announcer relates: "Off on another dangerous mission for Captain Video, Video Ranger dons one of his most important pieces of equipment—the secret identifying ring." Ranger, in a tight close-up, then offers the young rangers in the audience advice:

> Rangers, here's why this ring is so important to me and to all video agents: If anyone questions your identity, all you've got to do is show them this ring. . . . [Zoom in on a drawing of the ring, adorned with Captain Video's likeness] Wear it at all times to show that you're on the side of law and order!

With that message, Video Ranger gave his young fans a two-fingered salute and wink, and the screen shifted to an ad for Powerhouse candy bars, during which the youngsters were told that two nickel wrappers and ten cents in coin would earn them their own ring.

Young sf fans received similar inducements from other televised programming as well, such as an offer from the producers of *Tom Corbett, Space Cadet* (1950–55), reminding young viewers that it was not too late to use the wrappers from Kraft Caramels to obtain their space cadet membership kits:

> Now, here's what you'll get: this handsome space cadet ring, just like Tom and Astro and TJ's; your official space cadet shoulder patch; and your signed membership certificate in the Tom Corbett unit.

Such product tie-ins were not new to young audiences in the 1950s, but this networked advertising drew on the televised medium in innovative ways, creating consumer desires in the midst of the domestic environment and linking them to the world on the screen through intimate address, ties to the televised drama, and promotion by young viewers' favorite stars.

As televised sf series brought new fans to the genre, new productions emerged, such as *Space Patrol* (1950–55),[16] *Captain Z-Ro* (1951–56), *Flash Gordon* (1954–55), *Rocky Jones, Space Ranger* (1954), and *Commando Cody* (1955), and space fever swept through American homes, department stores, and supermarkets. Although, as *TV Forecast* proclaimed in an article about *Captain Video*, these series were "produced especially for the modern-minded youngsters who are seeking adventure in front of the family television set" ("Electronic Age" 6), the new wave of sf serials propelled the entire family, and domestic life itself, into the electronic age.

As televised sf series quickly caught on, *Collier's Magazine* reported, "All over the air waves, the Wide Open Spaces are being traded in for the Wide Upper Spaces. The trend may be away from horses and up in the heavens for keeps" (Robinson 31). And of course, youthful American viewers needed a "new wardrobe, new gear, and a whole new language" to keep up with the new breed of space hero (Bassior 8). The cover of *American Weekly* (10 May 1953) depicted a youthful "space man" proudly clad in his new Atomic Space Suit and helmet, handing down his outmoded cowboy boots and chaps to a dismayed younger brother, and a few months later, *Woman's Day* (August 1953) proclaimed that "A new supersonic generation is putting its cowboy suits in mothballs and encasing itself in space helmets" ("Four Flight-Tested Space Helmets" 25). As the housewife's tried-and-true advisor, the magazine offered to help mothers facing these new "space happy" demands develop new domestic skills, with the cover promising "Four Flight-Tested Space Helmets to Make," complete with full-color pictures and two pages of how-to diagrams for creating space helmets "like those seen in *Space Patrol* and *Captain Video*." One frustrated mother, perhaps less confident in her abilities, went straight to the producers of *Tom*

Corbett and pleaded with them to market a space helmet for the protection of the family pet—a turtle whose bowl became a makeshift helmet for her two-year-old each time the program aired (Bassior 9–10).

And so, as sf serials such as *Tom Corbett* and *Captain Video* propelled the American youth into the space age, their families were carried right along with them. The language of televised space series spread from the sound stage to the living room as youthful viewers traded quips with siblings such as "Plug your jets!" and "Blast me for a Martian mouse!" Adult programming was also infiltrated as comedians and talk-show performers wished viewers "Spaceman's Luck" and "Blast Your Rockets" (Thomas 50). Even everyday household objects such as appliances and automobiles took on a space-age look.[17]

The household economy was further affected by products and promotions from the series' numerous sponsors, advertised during the commercial breaks: at breakfast, families ate Kellogg's Corn Flakes, Chex cereals, and "Pep—the solar cereal" (which boasted a picture of Tom Corbett on every box) as the younger members eagerly awaited the enclosed prizes; they snacked on Nestlé's Caramels, Powerhouse bars, and Johnson's Fudge so the wrappers and labels exchanged for promotional items; they collected premiums and entered contests for larger prizes, such as *Space Patrol's*

Figure 1.2 Space comes into the home, as audience members sport uniforms and even sf insignia haircuts.

larger-than-life Rocket Club House, awarded to the winner of the "Name the Planet" contest. And for housewives who purchased these products at Market Basket supermarkets, their weekly trips also included a ride for the kids on Exhibit's *Space Patrol* rides, which were installed at many of the chain's stores.

Supermarkets and department stores alike also carried official series merchandise, such as space suits, cadet uniforms, rocket guns, and other gizmos carefully studied and coveted by their young fans, which were also interwoven into family spending and pastimes in ways that could not be ignored. A 1952 *Life* magazine photo spread illustrated a dazzling array of items—from cosmic generators to "paralyzers"—bearing the *Space Patrol* label, predicted to net $40 million in sales that year (*Life* 83). Frankie Thomas (Tom Corbett) recalled that in addition to eight hardback Tom Corbett novels and a series of comic books, there were 185 separate sale items manufactured bearing the Corbett name. Thomas, who appeared in department stores across the country, observed that "at one point it seemed like the subsidiary rights were getting bigger than the show" (Thomas 51).

So significant was sf series' impact on domestic economies and patterns of consumption, as well as on the relationships and pastimes of American families, that the programs' heroes became role models and authority figures as well. Invited each week into the intimacy of the domestic sphere, Tom Corbett, Commando Cody, Captain Video, and their cohorts reciprocated by reinforcing familial and social norms to their young audiences through modeling behaviors, enacting morality tales, and supporting parents by holding youth to the high standards of a rocketman, as can be observed in the Rocky Jones Space Ranger Code:

> As an official Space Ranger, I pledge
> To obey my parents at all times
> To be kind and courteous to all
> To be brave in the cause of freedom, to help the weak
> To obey the law at all times
> To grow up clean in mind and strong in body

Thus, through this give-and-take of multiple influences and impacts, the sf serials became adapted to and intricately interwoven not only with the domestic broadcast programming for which they were structurally so well suited but with domestic culture as well. For the resulting series' young fans and their families, the familiar heroes and villains, catchphrases, homemade space helmets, department-store ray guns, secret pictures hidden in boxes of cereal, and all the rest created a continuity between the fantastic worlds on screen and the worlds in which they lived—a world in which "real" rocket men were soon to begin their own space adventures. Serials, once one of the mainstays of neighborhood movie houses, had indeed come home.

SERIALS: AT HOME IN THE HOME

This notion of sf serials "coming home" should begin to suggest that the story of early televised sf series is not just one of producing smaller, impoverished versions of cinematic counterparts but one of a narrative form arising from, and interweaving with, domestic culture. Although television can, at particular moments, adopt a form that corresponds closely to that of cinema, overall the two have developed different forms and approaches that opened up new methods of signification. Throughout their histories, the synergy and convergence of the two has steadily increased, but as Williams offers, "the media of filmscreen and television are only superficially similar. . . . in transmission the results are radically different" (58–59). Those differences in the results of transmission are clearly at play in thinking about the media ecology of early sf series, but particularly when considered in the broader context of the archaeology of the serials themselves.

Serials featuring the fantastic did not spring into being with the birth of the moving image. As Telotte observes, serials and series routinely brought to life the iconic characters and technologies that already dominated the covers of popular fiction—pulp magazines and futuristic novels—featuring spacecraft and flying platforms, death rays and reanimators, rocket packs and robots that had already captured the imaginations of their readers (*Replications* 92–93). The serial served as one of the original and primary vehicles for these otherworldly themes and tropes for decades.[18]

But the roots of sf serials may also be found in comic strips and comic books—narratives from which the genre draws not only its amazing adventures but its essential characteristic of seriality—forms of entertainment that, not unlike eighteenth-century novels, meted out their melodramatic storylines one episode at a time. Comic strips found in the daily or Sunday newspapers served as a significant source of characters and material for serials. Universal Studios alone had used comic strips as source material for sixteen different serials, including *Flash Gordon* and *Buck Rogers*, and Columbia Pictures drew on the strips for *The Phantom* (1943) and *Brick Bradford* (1947).

One of the more complex adaptations across the screens, *Flash Gordon*, with its lavish budget and overwhelming box office success, was the second cinematic serial to be based on a comic strip (which first appeared in 1934). The serial's producer, Henry MacRae, and director Frederick Stephani exercised care to maintain the integrity of the series, from narrative structure to costuming, in order to cultivate and retain the comic strip's loyal fan base. Newspaper entertainment pages celebrated the adaptation with half- and three-quarter-page promotional features that combined scene stills with comic strip renderings. The characters—Flash Gordon (Buster Crabbe), Dale Arden (Jean Rogers), Dr. Zarkov (Frank Shannon), and the rest—were scripted as closely as possible to their print counterparts, guaranteeing recognition across media (Backer 23–25). Costumes were nearly exact reproductions of Alex Raymond's newsprint originals, even featuring the same vibrant colors, in spite of the serial's black-and-white filming. Actress Jean Rogers recalled: "Ming's costume was real fur, and that was a red velvet cloak he wore" (Kinnard, Crnkovich, and Vitone 9). To further enhance cross-media identification, the opening credits of the film serial credited "Alex Raymond's cartoon strip" just below the title and later repeated that it was "based on the newspaper feature entitled 'Flash Gordon' owned and copyrighted by King Features Syndicate."

Also preceding television, radio drama had been broadcasting its own renditions of the fantastic into American living rooms each week in a serialized format that gripped audiences and created an intimacy that television would struggle to match. Arch Oboler, a master of adaptation in radio, film, and television, explained this power:

> [W]hat comes out of that loudspeaker is not just words, or sound effects, or music, but a cohesive whole, an emotional something which plays on the stage of the listener's mind with a drive and a force that no other dramatic art medium has ever done before. (1940, n. pag.)

Radio cliffhangers, like comic strips and comic books, served as source material for some of the most successful series that would eventually make the transition to both cinema and television screens: *The Lone Ranger* (1938), *The Green Hornet* (1939), *Captain Midnight* (1942). And the tune-in-next-week formats of sf-horror-suspense hybrids like *Lights Out* served as templates for numerous others.[19] Similarly, many serial scriptwriters transitioned to television after long careers writing for radio, such as veteran writer Maurice C. Brooks, who began work on television's *Captain Video* after doing such successful radio serials as *Dick Tracy* and *Gangbusters*.

All these various media—newspaper comic strips, comic books, radio—may be seen as essentially "domestic" media. They were consumed primarily in the home or other informal settings, functioned as part of the domestic "wallpaper"—fading from visibility on coffee tables, end tables, nightstands, or under beds—and were considered casually, once drawn into the reader/listener's personal environment. Whether their narratives operated visually or sonically, they employed patterns of direct, individual address to draw their audiences into an intimate relationship with their characters, icons, and themes, and they created an atmosphere of intimate consumption as they engaged with the imaginations and inner worlds of single audience members. Moreover, one defining characteristic of this array of early media was that segmented, sequential quality that, for Ellis and Williams, defines the nature of television as a quintessential domestic medium.

As we consider the nature of sf serials' adaptation across screens, then, limiting our frame of reference to discussions of big versus small screens and shortcomings in fidelity, budgets, and technology results in an important but incomplete level of discussion. Drawing together a constellation of influences from pulp magazines, radio, comics, and sequential literature,[20] cinematic sf serials clearly are indebted to earlier forms of "domestic" media, just as they are to the seamless singular texts of feature films. Seen in this light, discussions of the adaptation of these early sf serials across screens shift from a focus on cinematic texts uncomfortably transitioning to broadcast television—where the screen size radically alters the effect of the image, light and shade are lost, and planes and perspectives flattened[21]—to a focus on the ways in which the resulting televised series more closely resemble and function as other domestic media. In their adaptation to television's small screen as popular space operas, sf serials were, in fact, coming home and taking their place as part of a complex and developing domestic media environment.

NOTES

1. For a detailed survey of silent-era serials, consult Lahue's *Continued Next Week: A History of the Moving Picture Serial*. The scope of early sf sound serials is examined in a number of texts, including Backer's *Gripping Chapters*, Barbour's *Days of Thrills and Adventure*, Cline's *In the Nick of Time*, Fletcher's *Don't Dare Miss the Next Thrilling Chapter!*, Kinnard's *Science Fiction Serials*, Parish's *The Great Movie Series*, Rainey's *Serials and Series*, Stedman's *The Serials*, Weiss and Goodgold's *To Be Continued*, and Warren's *Keep Watching the Skies!*
2. See Tom Gunning's "The Cinema of Attractions: Early Film, Its Spectator, and the Avant Garde."
3. Fletcher, for example, notes that these elements include "rocket ships, robots, death rays, lost civilizations, other planets, invisibility, and fantastic inventions, such as rocket flying suits." He further qualifies that "[m]any serials have wild inventions; the issue is whether the invention shapes the serial or is just a device in what otherwise is some other type of serial" (89).
4. In an interview with film scholar John Tibbetts, Frankie Thomas, star of *Tom Corbett, Space Cadet*, noted that an estimated 25% of the television program's viewing audience were adults.
5. Examples include *Captain Video*'s "Ranger Messages," which promoted good citizenship and social responsibility, and *Captain Z-Ro*'s world history lessons; along with commercials for products that targeted youth audiences—teaching nutrition, creating ties between television watching and snacking, and even tutoring children in party planning, as in a Nestlé's Caramel commercial accompanying one episode of *Tom Corbett, Space Cadet*, which included a recipe for "circus parade cookies."
6. The Big Five studios—MGM, Warner Brothers, Twentieth Century-Fox, RKO, and Paramount—avoided serial production, and second-tier studios such as Universal, Mascot/Republic, and Columbia dominated their release.
7. This function of early serials is explored at length in Miller's "Defending the Heartland: Technology and the Future in *The Phantom Empire* (1935)."
8. Similar remote viewing screens are used in both serials and series, such as *Commando Cody*, *Captain Video*, and *Tom Corbett, Space Cadet*. In a variation on this theme, episodes of *Captain Z-Ro* featured a viewing screen that projects real historical events that are the focus of each episode—making the series a kind of early edutainment.
9. For an in-depth discussion of the pressures and stigma attached to film actors working in television, see Becker (16–68).
10. Viewer Mike Humbert's account of the final episode of San Francisco's locally-produced *Captain Satellite* series relates that "when the show was cancelled, KTVU gave the Captain a big send-off, with many well-wishers dropping by for the final voyage of the Laser 2." <www.tvparty.com/lostsf.html>

11. Originally developed with effects engineer Jack Coyle for *The Phantom Empire*, the melting effect was created by printing a portion of film on a glass slide that was then heated. The emulsion run-off resembled molten lava—or in the case of *The Phantom Empire*, a melting world.
12. Richard Coogan performed the role of Captain Video from 1949–50, at which time Al Hodge took over until the series ended in 1955.
13. See Backer for further production details.
14. This direct gaze, along with direct voice-over address to the audience, may be seen in numerous early sf series, including *Tom Corbett, Space Cadet*, *Captain Z-Ro*, and *Rocky Jones*.
15. Typical tie-ins for Western serials were items such as Rex Allen marbles, Gene Autry Club badges, and Roy Rogers wallets.
16. The program experienced a brief hiatus in 1954, then returned until 1955.
17. See Bassior; Javna; and Gould for additional context.
18. As Telotte (*Replications* 94) and others note, various hybrid motion pictures from the 1930s through the 1950s feature themes of the monstrous and science gone awry, which are often consigned to the horror genre.
19. See Miller's "In the Blink of a Martian Eye: American Horror from Page to Airwaves to Screen" for additional discussion of radio series' adaptations to early television.
20. For more on serials' relationship with these media, see Telotte's *Science Fiction Film* (94).
21. See Williams (59) for additional discussion on the perceptual losses associated with adaptation to television.

WORKS CITED

Backer, Ron. *Gripping Chapters: The Sound Movie Serial*. Albany: Bear Manor Media, 2010.

Barbour, Alan G. *Days of Thrills and Adventure*. New York: MacMillan Publishing Company, 1970.

Bassior, Jean-Noel. *Space Patrol: Missions of Daring in the Name of Early Television*. Jefferson: McFarland, 2005.

Becker, Christine. *It's the Pictures That Got Small: Hollywood Film Stars on 1950s Television*. Middletown: Wesleyan UP, 2008.

Booker, M. Keith. *Science Fiction Television*. Westport: Praeger, 2004.

Cline, William C. *In the Nick of Time: Motion Picture Sound Serials*. Jefferson:

———. "The Space Opera and Early Science Fiction Television." *The Essential Science Fiction Television Reader*. Ed. J. P. Telotte. Lexington: UP of Kentucky, 2008. 93–110.

Duchovnay, Gerald. "From Big Screen to Small Box: Adapting Science Fiction Film for Television." *The Essential Science Fiction Television Reader*. Ed. J. P. Telotte. Lexington: UP of Kentucky, 2003. 69–89.

"The Electronic Age of Captain Video." *TV Forecast*. Chicago: Television Forecast, June 10, 1950. 6.

Ellis, John. *Visible Fictions: Cinema, Television, Video*. Rev. ed. London: Routledge, 1992.

Elsaesser, Thomas. "Introduction." *Writing for the Medium: Television in Transition*. Ed. Thomas Elsaesser, Jan Simons, and Lucette Bronk. Amsterdam: Amsterdam UP, 1994. 91–97.

Fletcher, Anthony L. *Don't Dare Miss the Next Thrilling Chapter!* Minneapolis: Mill City P, 2009.

"Four Flight-Tested Space Helmets You Can Make." *Women's Day* Aug. 1953. 21–26.
Goldwyn, Samuel. "Hollywood in the Television Age." *Hollywood Quarterly: Film Culture in Postwar America, 1945–1957*. Ed. Eric Smoodin and Ann Martin. Berkeley: U of California P, 2002. 199–204.
Gould, Jack. "Television in Review." *New York Times* 20 Nov. 1949. 63.
Gunning, Tom. "The Cinema of Attractions: Early Film, Its Spectator and the Avant-Garde." *Early Cinema: Space, Frame, Narrative*. Ed. Tomas Elsaesser. London: BFI, 2008. 56–62.
Hawes, William. *Live Television Drama, 1946–1951*. Jefferson: McFarland, 2001.
Henderson, Jay Alan. "Commando Cody Speaks: An Interview with George Wallace." *Ultra Filmfax: The Magazine of Unusual Film and Television* 69–70 (1998–99): 56–63.
———. *The Legendary Lydecker Brothers*. Lexington: Createspace, 2010.
Humbert, Mike. "Local Kids Shows: San Francisco in the 1960s and '70s." <www.tvparty.com/lostSF.html>.
Javna, John. *The Best of Science Fiction TV*. New York: Harmony, 1987.
Kinnard, Roy. *Science Fiction Serials*. Jefferson: McFarland, 1998.
Kinnard, Roy, Tony Crnkovich, and R. J. Vitone. *The Flash Gordon Serials, 1936–1940*. Jefferson: McFarland, 2008.
Lahue, Kalton, C. *Continued Next Week: A History of the Moving Picture Serial*. Norman: U of Oklahoma P, 1964.
Life. Uncredited photo of *Space Patrol* merchandise. 1 Sept. 1952. 83.
Miller, Cynthia J. "Defending the Heartland: Technology and the Future in *The Phantom Empire* (1935)." *Heroes of Film, Comics, and American Culture*. Ed. Lisa DeToro. Jefferson: McFarland, 2009. 61–80.
———. "In the Blink of a Martian Eye: American Horror from Page to Airwaves to Screen." *Adapting America/America Adapted: Cultural Adaptation in American History, Literature, and Film*. Ed. Laurence Raw. New York: Edward Mellen, 2009. 13–24.
Oboler, Arch. *Ivory Tower and other Radio Plays*. Chicago: Willam Targ. 1940.
Parish, James Robert. *The Great Movie Series*. Lancaster, UK: Gazelle Book Services, Ltd., 1972.
Rainey, Buck. *Serials and Series: A World Filmography, 1912–1956*. Jefferson: McFarland, 1999.
Robinson, Murray. "Planet Parenthood." *Collier's Magazine* 5 Jan. 1952. 31.
Stedman, Raymond William. *The Serials: Suspense and Drama by Installment*. Norman: U of Oklahoma P, 1971.
Telotte, J. P. *Replications: A Robotic History of the Science Fiction Film*. Urbana: U of Illinois P, 1995.
———. *Science Fiction Film*. Cambridge: Cambridge UP, 2001.
———. "Serenity, Cinematisation and the Perils of Adaptation." *Science Fiction Film and Television* 1.1 (2008): 67–80.
Thomas, Frankie. "Westward The Stars." *American Classic Screen* 4.2 (1980): 47–52.
Warren, Bill. *Keep Watching the Skies! American Science Fiction Movies of the Fifties*. Jefferson: McFarland, 2010.
Weiss, Ken, and Ed Goodgold. *To Be Continued*. Stratford: Star Tree, 1981.
Wilk, Max. *The Golden Age of Television: Notes from the Survivors*. New York: Delacort, 1976.
Williams, Raymond. *Television*. London: Routledge, 2003.
Williams-Rautiolla, Suzanne. "Captain Video and His Video Rangers." *Museum of Broadcast Communications*. Museum of Broadcast Communications, n.d. Accessed 18 Nov. 2010. <http://www.museum.tv/eotvsection.php?entrycode=captainvideo>.

2 The Cinematic Zone of *The Twilight Zone*

J. P. Telotte

Today we often take for granted the operation of what Henry Jenkins describes as "convergence media," that is, the ready "flow of content across multiple media platforms" (2) such as film, television, the internet, and increasingly our cell phones, with an attendant blurring of distinctions between the media forms. It is, after all, part of our daily experience, something offered—and sold—to us at every turn in what Paul Virilio describes as the "media nebula" of postmodern society (*Landscape* 69). Yet in the early days of American television, particularly as the new medium sought to establish its own identity, "convergence" was hardly considered. Rather, the film industry for quite practical reasons repeatedly trumpeted its difference from the upstart television while offering various technological enhancements that television could not match, such as widescreen formats, stereophonic sound, Technicolor and other color systems, and 3-D imagery. At the same time, television seemed rather similarly intent on distinguishing itself from its older rival. As John Ellis has shown, it very quickly "developed distinctive aesthetic forms to suit the circumstances" (111) of broadcast presentation: an emphasis on short, discrete narrative segments; a greater reliance upon dialogue than in the cinema; a kind of dislocated viewer gaze (or what, by way of contrast, he terms a "glance");[1] and an image that Ellis argues "is characteristically pared down" (112). It is this emphasis on—or rather, deemphasis of—the image, particularly in favor of a reliance on dialogue, that I want to address here in the context of one of television's golden age shows and most important science fiction entries, Rod Serling's *The Twilight Zone*. By focusing on its often-overlooked image qualities, particularly what we might for convenience simply term its *cinematic* nature, we might better appreciate the contribution this sf series made to the eventual convergence of film and television and, in the process, more accurately sketch a significant part of early film and television dynamics.

Catherine Johnson argues that such sf and fantasy television programs often challenged the "dominant notions of the aesthetics of television," and she suggests that, for this reason, they have frequently been understood not as part of a simultaneous line of development but "as exceptional in television history" (12). As a consequence, critical discussion has typically treated them in a "reductive" manner; the "issues raised" by telefantasy programs, particularly their challenges to the cultural status quo, have never been fully examined, and the series have not been properly accounted for in our television histories (12). Instead, commentary on telefantasy shows has tended to "overgeneralize" them (11), that is, to submerge them into broader generic categories that dissipate their subversive impact on both thematic and stylistic levels and result in a miswriting of television history—one that fundamentally mistakes or downplays the early contributions of sf and fantasy programming.

As a partial corrective I want to situate *The Twilight Zone* in terms of an opposition between those paradigms of convergence and difference that have, at different times, influenced our views of television history, including telefantasy. Again we might take Johnson's commentary as a lead, particularly as she, paraphrasing Ellis, describes the commonplace "opposition of television as a medium of dialogue/talk against the visual spectacle of the cinema" (11). That opposition is rooted partly in the common conception of sf as a genre fundamentally bound to spectacle—a point made in most early discussions of sf cinema, but especially in Susan Sontag's seminal essay wherein she attributes the form's popularity to its exploitation of "the imagery of destruction" depicted "on a colossally magnified scale" (216). The notion of television's "pared down" image field would obviously seem to conflict with such a characterization, and the early space operas, with their practically nonexistent effects and dialogue in place of action, only support that distinction. That sense of opposition also owes to the very power of other types of shows, other dominant genres, particularly the live-action drama that many critics view as the signal accomplishment of early television, at least in America. Powered by well-written scripts, focused on psychological revelation rather than physical action, and graced with the imprimatur of "legitimate" theater, these shows have provided a powerful "dialogue/talk" model of difference that has obscured signs of convergence, even in the area of telefantasy.

Unsurprisingly, then, most discussions of *The Twilight Zone* quickly acknowledge its indebtedness to *other television* shows, particularly to those popular dramatic anthology programs of the 1950s—shows like *Playhouse 90*, *Kraft Television Theater*, *General Electric Theater*, and others, all of which were indeed "dialogue/talk" dependent, as well as to earlier radio theater, which necessarily shared that same dependency. Yet Keith Booker offers a lead in another direction, for as he discusses standout series like *Alfred Hitchcock Presents* and *The Twilight Zone*, he notes what he terms a striking "plurality" in them, a curiously "multigeneric and multimedia" emphasis (50–51). So while acknowledging that *The Twilight Zone*, in a concerted effort to follow the general theatrical television model, "consciously strove for a literary texture" (52), he also observes how often it also foregrounded and commented on the "boundaries between different levels of reality" (62), including different media forms—a notion obviously signaled by the very in-between realm or "Zone" that its title designates. Among those explorations we might especially note the series' frequent treatment of film and television as subjects in episodes like "The Sixteen-Millimeter Shrine" (23 October 1959), "A World of Difference" (11 March 1960), and "Showdown with Rance McGrew" (2 February 1962), episodes that blur the boundaries between film and everyday life or television and reality. In fact, all these episodes similarly compare the illusionism of the movies and television with the very unreality that was coming to characterize their audience's lives in this period—lives lived within the thoroughly mediatized landscape of a postmodern society. If in such instances *The Twilight Zone* resembled, as Jeffrey Sconce describes it, a kind of "perverse 'unconscious' of television" (134), it no less began to suggest a cultural unconscious as well, pointing up the media-haunted nature of the contemporary US.[2]

Of course, the very generic character of *The Twilight Zone* is partly responsible for this reflexive dimension, for as critics have often noted, sf, at least as it developed in film and television, is among the most self-conscious of forms. Thus Annette Kuhn suggests that "the most obvious difference between science fiction as literature and science fiction as film lies in the latter's mobilization of the visible" (6). We can glimpse that mobilization at work in its pervasive emphasis on viewing devices, scanners, screens, and technologies of replication, including its enormous variety of replicated human figures[3]—elements that have led Garrett Stewart to describe cinematic sf as "the fictional or fictive science of the cinema itself, the future feats it may achieve scanned in line with the technical feat that conceives them right now and before our eyes" (159), as video technology "is not merely recruited . . . its purposes are critically scrutinized" (161). And given the genre's larger investment in satisfying—and exploring—what Michele Pierson describes as "a cultural demand for the aesthetic experience of wonder" (168), we could hardly expect television efforts like *The Twilight Zone* to be immune to this tendency.

Also contributing significantly to that interrogation were the very conditions of production for the series because, in contrast to many television shows of the late 1950s and early 1960s, *The Twilight Zone* drew on a broad variety of distinctly cinematic resources. For instance, the cinematographer for much of the show's run (117 of the total 156 episodes) was George T. Clemens, already a twenty-year veteran of the film industry, who brought a thoroughly engrained sense of traditional cinematic practice to the new medium. Among the directors signed to the series were such distinguished filmmakers as John Brahm, Richard Donner, Mitch Leisen, Norman Z. McLeod, Don Siegel, and Jacques Tourneur. A number of the series' writers, perhaps most notably Richard Matheson, already had a good deal of experience writing for the movies. Most of the series was shot on film rather than done live or on videotape.[4] And it was for the most part shot at the MGM studio, whose back lot and stages permitted a greater sense of space and more attention to mise-en-scène than are typically found in television series of the era. In fact, Richard Donner, director of six episodes, recalls how doing the series at MGM resulted in an atmosphere that was conducive to a cinematic approach: "It was extraordinary; they treated every little television show like a feature" (Stanyard 98). Moreover, although the series did not have a generous budget—despite the pilot costing an exorbitant $75,000 (Presnell and McGee 14)—shooting at MGM provided a wealth of physical resources that would show to advantage, even on the small screen; thus director Richard Bare remembers how "with access to their [MGM's] fantastic scene dock, [they] were able to provide a rich look" even on the typically restricted episode budgets (Stanyard 71). The cumulative effect is a show that, in appearance, often seems closer to film than to television of the time, that points to more of a stylistic convergence between film and television in the late 1950s than our histories have usually recognized, and that underscores the sf series' impact on—even shaping of—the new medium.

As a starting point for such an examination, I will focus on the styling of three of the better-known episodes, ones that I would argue are typical of the series as a whole and that together suggest a range of its visual possibilities. I want to begin by considering an early entry, "Time Enough at Last" (20 November 1959), a story about a literature-obsessed bank clerk, Henry Bemis. This first-season episode provides a particularly fitting start because its first half demonstrates precisely the sort of interior, dramatic sensibility for which *The Twilight Zone* has so often been praised, whereas its second half is decidedly different as it provides an unusually open, even spacious and visually rich mise-en-scène of the sort that we generally associate with feature films. We can compare that show with one of the series' later and most famous entries, "Nightmare at 20,000 Feet" (11 October 1963), an episode that, in its investigation of a troubled former mental patient, works with the claustrophobic set of an airliner whose restricted spaces clearly challenged a cinematic emphasis—a challenge that was met in part by mobilizing the filmic emphasis on the gaze. And as a final contrast, I will consider an episode that operates under a very different spatial imperative, "The Monsters Are Due on Maple Street" (4 March 1960). Shot entirely outdoors, it illustrates a different sort of visual challenge, one of openness rather than interiority. By looking at this combination of episodes, each of which involves a different visual style and a different set of spatial possibilities, even a rather different approach to what Ellis terms the "glance" emphasis of televisual narrative, we can better gauge the sort of aesthetic combination that marks the series' top episodes.

"Time Enough at Last" opens on a conventional interior, that of the lobby of the bank where Henry Bemis works, but it introduces its subject in a visually complex way. A high-angle boom shot follows seemingly random characters as they move through the lobby, and it culminates in a close-up introduction of Bemis, "a charter member in the fraternity of dreamers," as Rod Serling's voice-over terms him. Of course, we already *visually* gather as much because a cut to a reverse-angle shot, from behind Bemis, directs our gaze to reveal that he is reading a novel rather than attending to his duties, as a short-changed customer's complaint quickly underscores. It is an effective introduction for what is essentially a character study, developed through a subsequent series of rather conventional dialogue exchanges between Henry and the bank president in the president's office, then between Henry and his shrewish wife Helen in their small apartment, all done in two-shots and tightly framed interior sets. Following an atomic explosion that spares Henry (who had been reading in the bank vault) but apparently destroys everyone else, the claustrophobic interior spaces give way to "an eight-hour tour of a graveyard," as Henry characterizes his wanderings: a montage of tracking shots through a landscape of total destruction, punctuated by Henry's close-up reaction shots. The exterior images increasingly render Henry a smaller and smaller figure, an effect that is particularly vivid when he finally comes upon the monumental images of a devastated library, its pillars stretched out amid the rubble, its reading tables flung about like toys, books strewn up and down its long steps. Visually rendered almost insignificant by high-angle shots and the scale of the detritus, Henry still finds an element of hope, even pleasure in having books all around him and "time enough at last" to read all he wants. But in the sort of twist ending that would become a hallmark of the series, he bends forward to retrieve a book, drops his glasses, and breaks them, leaving him, as Serling's voice-over offers, "just a piece of a smashed landscape, just a part of the rubble"—commentary that is punctuated by a visually arresting track-back to an extreme long shot of him in this hopeless, devastated world.

In describing the complex long-take approach he took to the start of another episode, "A World of Difference," Ted Post, who directed four of the shows, recalls that *The Twilight Zone* directors were consistently encouraged to be inventive and to help "visualize the concept the story is rooted in" (Stanyard 106). It is an approach we clearly see at work in "Time Enough at Last." Although the episode relies heavily on language in its first half as Bemis's love of reading comes out in his efforts to discuss books, poetry, and even advertisements with a bank customer, the president, and his wife, the story's texture ultimately derives from its visualizations. The tracking camera of the opening suggests a freedom that Bemis, as a result of his job and his unhappy personal life, simply does not share—a circumstance emphasized when the president at one point orders him back to his "cage." Yet after the atomic explosion, the show opens up to emphasize how easily that constraining modern life—embodied in its structures and institutions—might be blasted aside, reduced to rubble. The open frames and again a freely tracking camera initially suggest Bemis's release from his "cage," only to then revert to a diminishing of the character through the long and high-angle shots I have noted. Presented as a human "part of the rubble" this world has become, Bemis is finally seen—bereft of his glasses, alone, and with a look of terror—as still little more than a prisoner, although now in an open but quite empty world.

The Cinematic Zone of The Twilight Zone 25

Figure 2.1 Henry Bemis (Burgess Meredith) as part of the rubble in the postapocalyptic world of "Time Enough at Last" on *The Twilight Zone* (1959). Copyright CBS Video.

Perhaps a more telling challenge to an effective cinematic styling shows up in those episodes that, because of their limited sets, are more spatially constrained and, consequently, seem far more like dramatic chamber plays. And here we need only think of various efforts wherein the action is confined to a small interior space, such as the stark metal room of "Five Characters in Search of an Exit" (22 December 1961), the barren apartment of "Nothing in the Dark" (5 January 1962), or especially the airliner interiors of such episodes as "The Odyssey of Flight 33" (24 February 1961) or the more famous "Nightmare at 20,000 Feet." "The Odyssey of Flight 33" particularly suggests the difficulty of opening up such confined spaces because the location for almost all the action is the airliner's cramped cockpit where the crew gradually realizes—and struggles to explain in dialogue—that they have, inexplicably, flown back in time. A primary counter strategy here is the cutaway to file footage of a contemporary jet airliner in flight in order to open up the narrative and to contrast with the dominant medium shots and choker close-ups of the crew. However, their repeated reaction shots and commentary would probably only have frustrated audiences without the payback of shots *showing* that they had indeed traveled in time—shots exploiting the possibilities and even pleasures of the cinematic gaze. That satisfaction came from inserted aerial shots of the 1939 New York World's Fair and, more importantly, from the surprising images of a prehistoric New York complete with a grazing brontosaurus. The stop-motion dinosaur scene was an unusual addition and, in fact, "the most expensive such clip ever shot" for the show (Presnell and McGee 87). It is also a scene that demonstrates the sort of creative geography on which film has always depended for much of its impact: the combination of shots and reaction shots effectively construct the dramatic space of the narrative, suture the audience into that world of changing times and spaces, as the cinematic gaze typically does, and even provide a degree of spectacle to correspond to the psychological terror this strange event has visited upon the crew.

With the more famous "Nightmare at 20,000 Feet" the combination of interior and exterior spaces takes on an added weight, particularly because the plot concerns a recently released inmate of a sanitarium, Bob Wilson, for whom the very prospect of an airline flight already represents a confrontation with his own fragile inner self, previously unable to deal with such claustrophobic situations, and even now, as he readily recognizes, leaving him "not acting much like a cured man." As the plane flies through a dark and stormy night—effects that limit our view and give further reason to the narrative's interior focus—Bob suddenly sees on the plane's wing a mysterious creature that he can only describe as a "gremlin." That strange, even illogical appearance effectively externalizes his internal conflict while it also reframes the question of his sanity. Every subsequent shot of the gremlin implicates his—and our—gaze, as either a subjective shot or one from his seat perspective, and because no one else witnesses the creature's appearance, we—as well as Wilson—are left to wonder for much of the narrative, and in a long tradition of such restricted points of view in film, if he is simply projecting that nightmarish image, giving external shape to his inner fears; or if, perhaps by virtue of his "difference," he sees more than normal people—all those others on his plane who apparently never look out, never notice, those who have perhaps been conditioned by the televisual experience to do no more than briefly *glance* at the world passing by them.

Visualizing such a psychic dilemma certainly posed a special challenge. It would be easier, after all, to fashion such a narrative around dialogue, for example, by relying on the "inner voice" of Bob Wilson and the dialogue of those who must respond to his claims of a gremlin on the plane—his sympathetic but wary wife, the harried stewardess, a humoring copilot. Yet such dialogue hardly dominates "Nightmare at 20,000 Feet," and logically so, because as both Wilson and the audience quickly realize, conversation with the others accomplishes little. They offer him pills, try to humor him, or simply stare at *him* in response to his repeated urgings to "please *look*" outside.[5] As a result, at least half of the narrative is played out purely visually, not in dialogue but in an exchange of subjective and reaction shots as Wilson looks out at the gremlin on the plane's wing and those looks are followed by cuts to his face, registering his shock and disbelief at what *he alone* sees; then, altering the process, we look into the plane from the wing, almost as if from the gremlin's point of view, and we even register the gremlin's response to Wilson's observing him. In building much of the narrative around this exchange of looks and reactions, and by mobilizing the cinematic gaze that we share with Wilson, the narrative is able—with the added sound effects of the storm raging outside the airplane—to suggest Wilson's desperate effort at confronting his fears, coming face-to-face with what he worries is simply insanity, but eventually confirming, for himself at least, that the calm, quiet, brightly lit airplane interior is itself the artificial, deluded world—just a fragile barrier against the real world outside that is dark, chaotic, and threatening, that directly abuts what Serling's voice reminds us is "the Twilight Zone." In this effect, moreover, the episode points to a kind of formula for seeing, or forcing us to see our world more clearly, that might well describe the larger reflexive thrust of the entire series, including its own questioning of television culture.

Perhaps the reason "Nightmare at 20,000 Feet" remains one of the most remembered and discussed episodes of the series is precisely because of the way it so neatly juxtaposes this confined world where dialogue rules with an outside where only a "look" will suffice. Despite a number of tracking shots as the stewardess, Wilson, and his wife move up and down the airplane aisle during the story, the narrative repeatedly reminds us with those choker close-ups, angled shots, and tight two-shots of the confining, even claustrophobic nature of this set. Only the extreme long shot of Wilson being taken off the plane on a gurney and the high-angle track-back to the plane's wing at the end afford any real relief by also providing viewers, through the privileged gaze of the camera, with a lingering image of gremlin-caused damage to the engine cowling. This final shot is, as the narrator notes, a "tangible manifestation" of the truth, a *visual* demonstration when no words have managed to convince others or to explain Bob's seeming panic. It is a scene that vividly recalls the final one of another airplane disaster tale of this period, the acclaimed feature *The High and the Mighty* (1954), in which we also see, with the plane safely landed, the extent of the engine damage that has nearly brought catastrophe; it is a scene that simply underscores a key property of the cinema that *The Twilight Zone* repeatedly acknowledges, the revelatory power of the visual image.

With "The Monsters Are Due on Maple Street," *The Twilight Zone* made full use of the legendary MGM back lot, setting its narrative about the fragile nature of modern suburban life not inside the neat and attractive houses that line the titular Maple Street—only two or three brief shots in this episode are interiors—but in the common and open spaces of the front yards and the street itself. In doing so, the episode was cannily evoking a kind of cultural cinematic consciousness, for this was the street set that had been used for more than a decade for MGM's Andy Hardy film series,[6] films that effectively visualized the safe, open, and inviting life of middle

America, epitomized by the Hardys' town of Carvel. It opens with a shot of a cloudless sky before booming down to a long shot of Maple Street as an ice cream vendor makes his way down the street, a man washes his car, another waters his lawn, yet another trims his hedges, and several children approach and then converge on the ice cream salesman. All of these people in their routine and friendly interactions are then disturbed by a strange sound and flashing light, which produce a series of reaction shots from each of them. As Rod Serling's opening voice-over announces that this is "the last calm and reflective moment before the monsters came," the narrative effectively puts all these images—and that archetypal cinematic street—at risk, suggesting that they only mask a darker reality.

When the power begins to go out throughout the street and even the cars will not start, individual reaction shots give way to a particularly cinematic approach that makes effective use of the very openness of this street scene. As one or another person notices the outage, we see through a series of surprisingly deep-focus compositions how more and more people gather in the background of each shot that indicates a rising concern, suggests a frightened tendency to group together for protection and reassurance, and produces a kind of chorus effect to various foreground characters' musings about why the power is off. Various characters ask "What does it mean?" then theorize that "Meteors can do funny things . . . just like sunspots." One young boy even concludes that it is the work of "monsters from outer space or something." And as night comes on and the power remains off, the open street scene does not simply go dark; instead, it becomes *unnaturally* lit—supposedly by random candles and flashlights but clearly by a low-key, nondiegetic lighting scheme that produces ominous facial modeling, shadows, and a generally eerie look, as if the normal world of Andy Hardy's town had suddenly become a scene from a film noir—a most appropriate setting for, as one character styles it, "some kind of madness" to take hold.

Yet given a rising mob mentality and the elaborate streetscape, with its different possibilities for emphasizing the world of the characters and presenting it as such a disturbing cognate of our own, the narrative increasingly comes to focus on small, telling details. As the various neighbors on Maple Street become more unhinged by the way their power has disappeared and then begun to reappear in unpredictable places, and as they begin to act, despite the half-hearted appeals from some of them, like a mob, and to accuse each other of being the cause, the camera picks out their fearful and gradually more frenzied faces, their hands that clench into angry fists or point accusatory fingers, and the different objects—rocks, sticks, and eventually guns—that they pick up to use on the next neighbor who might fall under suspicion. Worked into a quick-cut montage and with Dutch angles used for many of these shots—techniques seldom seen in television of the day—the neighbors, even those who have been introduced as close friends, become depersonalized, transformed into frightened types, rendered not, as the character Steve earlier and jokingly offered, in the fashion of "monsters

The Cinematic Zone of The Twilight Zone   29

from outer space . . . three-headed green men who fly over here in what look like meteors," but rather almost expressionistically, as flashing images of violence and chaos. It is a point underscored by the final boom-out shot that symmetrically returns us to the episode's opening vantage, as if it were now revealing the true nature of this idyllic community. And indeed, with the typically privileged cinematic gaze, we now look down on the whole street, no longer calm but in chaos as lights flash on and off, people begin to fight, and individuals run in different directions, giving substance to what a final track back and dissolve reveal: aliens on a hill above the street, manipulating the power and noting how these humans, under pressure, "pick the most dangerous enemy they can find, and it's themselves."

Even that final shot works to introduce a further visual complexity through the symmetry it produces. In this instance, the clear, bright sky of the opening becomes the darkness of space—emblematic of the dark side of this world and its occupants—as the alien flying saucer apparently moves on to its next target for self-destruction. It is again the sort of shot we seldom find in television—even sf television—during *The Twilight Zone*'s opening season: a complex model and matte-work combination of the sort that would have been more familiar to filmgoers of the period. And appropriately so because this shot accompanying Serling's coda to the episode was actually

Figure 2.2   Andy Hardy's Carvel redressed as *The Twilight Zone*'s "Maple Street" (1960). Copyright CBS Video.

lifted from a film, *Forbidden Planet* (1956), one of MGM's—and indeed the sf genre's—most costly and lauded productions of the period. That borrowing here—and similar borrowings from that film for several other episodes[7]—only underscores both the series' own mindfulness of the current state of cinematic sf and the efforts of its production team, and particularly Serling, to reach for or converge with the more elaborate visual styling audiences were encountering and certainly expecting in sf narratives.

Critics have often suggested that a key characteristic of the series is the use of ironic or twist endings, such as the alien vision that concludes "The Monsters Are Due on Maple Street." I have already noted another, when book lover Henry Bemis's glasses are broken at the end of "Time Enough at Last." One of the series best-known examples is the final revelation in "Eye of the Beholder" (11 November 1960), wherein a "deformed" girl whom everyone has pitied throughout the episode actually proves to be beautiful; only through a final track-out do we see that it is all the people around her who look monstrous—and whose pressure for her to conform, to become like them, visually registers as another kind of monstrousness. Such irony is, of course, popular in literature and drama, a kind of rhetorical trick that suggests two levels of knowledge at work. Most commentaries on *The Twilight Zone* have typically linked those distinctly different levels of knowledge to Serling's commentary, as they are often signaled by his nondiegetic voice-over. Yet in the best cinematic tradition, as the examples discussed here show, they are also typically given a *visual* or *spatial* representation and are tied to the sort of shifting audience point of view that could never have been achieved in the live-drama format, in fact, one that more distinctly recalls the sort of spectatorship posited for the cinema. It is, as Jeffrey Sconce explains, the special gaze of the camera that "allows the viewer to enjoy the illusion of being 'all perceiving'" (184). In keeping with this cinematic model, these revelations commonly occur through or with track-backs, boom shots moving up and out, or simply cuts to extreme long shots, all of which effectively shift the audience's vantage to provide them with a larger visual field, a cognate to that larger level of knowledge implied by Serling's rhetoric.

This seeing from a distance, from a kind of outsider's or even omniscient point of view, also typically brings the narrative back to its starting point, which often begins in traditional cinematic fashion with a long or establishing shot, a technique used to orient film viewers. As we have noted, the boom up and out at the end of "The Monsters Are Due on Maple Street" neatly matches the high-angle boom-in that opens the episode, although that final movement is inevitably more disturbing than the initial one. Whereas the opening suggests a process of familiarization, moving into a typical American middle-class community and among its people—people who look like the very audience that would be watching the show—the final movement literally embodies a recoil the audience would feel, a possibly uncomfortable estrangement effect, a shock of recognition at their own figuration as, perhaps, "monsters." Given the typically limited camera travel, or what Ellis terms the "pared down" visual style of so much early television, that embodiment of recoil seems especially noteworthy—an effect drawn from the cinematic bag of tricks, and perhaps even a recognition of the unsettling effect of the entire narrative. That pull-back here and in so many other episodes, including the endings for both "Time Enough at Last" and "Nightmare at 20,000 Feet," might also be seen as a kind of audience safety net.[8] It *permits* viewers to pull back from this discomfiting world, to regain the distance at which they began their narrative experience, to withdraw—for contemplation—to a place of greater knowledge or understanding than the characters within the narrative have usually demonstrated.

Of course, such a reading also points to a deep understanding of television's own potentially "cinematic" properties that was at work right from the start of *The Twilight Zone*, and even to a rather self-conscious use of the medium. Earlier I noted that a number of *Twilight Zone* episodes take as their very subject the nature of film or television, shows like "The Sixteen-Millimeter Shrine," "A World of Difference," and "Showdown with Rance McGrew." Rodney Hill has recently examined this reflexive dimension as it surfaces in several episodes that deal with television's increasingly pervasive eye. He notes how the show "The Obsolete Man" (2 June 1961), for example, describes how in a future totalitarian state where books are banned and television is used to beam the actions of the state into every home, one individual, the tellingly named Wordsworth, manages to turn the medium upon itself and the state, using "the revelatory role of the TV cameras" (123) to expose the contradictions in his society, and especially the intolerance of those who would oppose the written word, burn books, and control all thought. Even beyond protesting contemporary culture's attitudes toward language or attesting to Rod Serling's general "awareness of television's . . . ability to effect social change," to function as "a powerful tool for helping people to see the real shape of their culture" (124), this episode points up his implicit understanding of the impact of the visual, of what we might term the cinematic legacy that television was adapting to its own uses. Yet as I argue here, we can see that implication not only in such obviously reflexive episodes but throughout the best efforts in *The Twilight Zone* series as they repeatedly demonstrate how those cinematic possibilities might be used in concert with language, how words and images might function together to move audiences in a way that, for various reasons, was little explored by most broadcast television in the United States up until that time.

This understanding of *The Twilight Zone* has been largely obscured by the typical linking of its reputation to Serling's own skills as a writer (one for whom "words" had much "worth"), as well as his consummate ability to attract some of the other top writers of his era to produce scripts for the series. Furthermore, it is a perspective that does not quite accord with the sense of disjunction or rupture that we often find in histories of the television-film relationship during the 1950s and early 1960s. Indeed, Christopher Anderson, in his history of the emergence of a Hollywood-inflected television in this period, suggests that the primary influence on the development of a more cinematic television was the work of powerful Hollywood producers, figures like David O. Selznick and Walt Disney who sought to create television shows in the same way they did movies (69), again suggesting not so much a convergence of media as a story of competition and a collision of forms.

An alternative perspective might recognize and seek to explore the extent to which fantasy shows like *The Twilight Zone* served as pathways to convergence, as signs of how one medium might be effectively adapted into another. Of course, by its very nature the fantastic text always revisions and restructures the real, reminding us of its limits while pointing beyond. And in the process, as Catherine Johnson reminds, telefantasy shows have often opened up "the opportunity to experiment with the formal possibilities of television as a medium" (147), as well as with its similarities to film. It is a point recognized in the later Steven Spielberg and John Landis production *Twilight Zone: The Movie* (1983), which offers remakes of several key shows from the original series. In the film's third episode, an adaptation of the original series "It's a Good Life" (3 November 1961), Anthony, a child with the ability to manipulate reality at will, surrounds himself with televisions constantly playing cartoons. What he most likes about them, he says, is that "anything can happen in cartoons"—a point he then illustrates when he "wills" his sister, who has displeased him, into a horrific cartoon where she is swallowed up by a monstrous figure. In the easy way he dismisses her from the real world and into media oblivion, we glimpse the fallout from life lived not just in the realm of the imagination but in a totally mediated or cinematized realm. Through that vision the film acknowledges the television series' uncanny anticipation, its early sense of how cartoons, television, and the movies were becoming common components of contemporary culture, colonizing our consciousness and together working to control our lives.

Admittedly, Serling's only prior connection to the film industry was a single screenplay for MGM,[9] and his series had no one master director who shaped its direction. In fact, as many of its champions emphasize, *The Twilight Zone* was quite "literary," as is suggested by its repeated homages to a world of books, its similarities to the pattern of live television drama, and even the linguistic control exercised by Serling's narration. Yet as we have seen, *The Twilight Zone* adapted a wide range of pointedly cinematic effects, even the powerful cinematic gaze, and freely turned both film and television into subjects of analysis—all elements that suggest a keen awareness of just how much, as Paul Virilio offers, modern culture had already become "cinematized," held in thrall by "the vision machine" of media (*Vision* 59). Seen in this light, *The Twilight Zone* reveals not how television sought to break with cinematic tradition or, in its specific case, to embrace the conventions of literature and live drama—explanations offered by most commentators—but how this series, like the best of early television, managed to meld together a variety of media elements, opening up the possibilities for what we might term a convergence aesthetic that would, in turn, become a key part of the sort of convergence culture that Henry Jenkins describes. The result was a landmark television moment in which those various elements were, on a weekly basis, marshaled to weave their own fantasy spell, one that, in the process, also allowed audiences to better see and to some extent even resist the growing power of that "vision machine."

NOTES

1. Ellis suggests that when faced with the typical television program, "the viewer tends to delegate his or her look to the TV itself," as if the viewer "passes his or her gaze across the sights in the TV eye" (112). The result, he argues, is an experience grounded not in the *gaze* that organizes the film experience but rather in the fleeting *glance* that follows from—or as he might offer, is necessitated by—the constant flow of the televisual experience.
2. Jeffrey Sconce makes a similar point as he describes how the series "often called critical attention to the artificial, synthetic, and otherwise 'fake' world of televisual domesticity itself, standing as the most disruptive resident in . . . 'the electronic neighborhood'" (149).
3. For a detailed discussion of the science fiction film's pervasive concern with the replicated human image and the reflexive properties of that concern, see Telotte's *Replications*, especially 22–26.
4. During its second season, CBS tried to cut costs by shooting six episodes on videotape using a three- or four-camera setup after the fashion of much television of the period, particularly situation comedies. Shot at CBS's Television City studio, these episodes were done, as Don Fresnell and Marty McGee offer, in a fashion "more similar to live television than to film" using directors with a background in live television, such as Jack Smight and James Sheldon. As a result of this approach, though, the episodes suffered from a "limited range of story and locale possibilities" (18) that soon led to a reversion to the film-style approach that had previously marked the series.
5. "Nightmare at 20,000 Feet" was remade as the final episode of the 1983 *Twilight Zone: The Movie*. In that version the protagonist, renamed John Valentine, pointedly becomes the object of numerous curious and/or irritated looks from his fellow passengers, even the subject of a bothersome little girl's Polaroid picture taking. In this case, though, the various gazes serve not so much to suture the Valentine character into the space of the airliner—a far more spacious craft, in keeping with the later period—as to build an atmosphere of suspicion and alienation. The absence of a wife in the later version also contributes to this pervasive atmosphere by removing a character who readily sympathizes with the protagonist and serves as a link to normalcy.
6. The Andy Hardy series, starring Mickey Rooney, began with *A Family Affair* in 1937 and concluded, after a twelve-year hiatus, with *Andy Hardy Comes Home* in 1958. Presnell and McGee (54) describe how "The Monsters Are Due on Maple Street" uses the Andy Hardy street, as well as various other MGM sets and props, including costumes from the studio's big-budget science fiction film *Forbidden Planet* (1956).

7. We should note how often the series would employ such scenes and even props and costumes. *Forbidden Planet* footage and costumes show up in "The Invaders" (27 Jan. 1961), that film's famous Robby the Robot creation plays a key role in "Uncle Simon" (15 Nov. 1963), and Robby reappears in "The Brain Center at Whipple's" (15 May 1965).
8. I am indebted to my student Sidarth Kantemneni for suggesting this interpretation.
9. The screenplay was *Saddle the Wind* (1958).

WORKS CITED

Anderson, Christopher. *Hollywood TV: The Studio System in the Fifties*. Austin: U of Texas P, 1994.

Booker, M. Keith. *Strange TV: Innovative Television Series from* The Twilight Zone *to* The X-Files. Westport: Greenwood, 2002.

Ellis, John. *Visible Fictions: Cinema, Television, Video*. Rev. ed. London: Routledge, 1992.

Hill, Rodney. "Anthology Drama: Mapping *The Twilight Zone*'s Cultural and Mythological Terrain." *The Essential Science Fiction Television Reader*. Ed. J. P. Telotte. Lexington: UP of Kentucky, 2008. 111–26

Jenkins, Henry. *Convergence Culture: Where Old and New Media Collide*. New York: New York UP, 2006.

Johnson, Catherine. *Telefantasy*. London: BFI, 2005.

Kuhn, Annette. "Introduction: Cultural Theory and Science Fiction Cinema." *Alien Zone*. Ed. Kuhn. London: Verso, 1990. 1–12.

Pierson, Michele. *Special Effects: Still in Search of Wonder*. New York: Columbia UP, 2002.

Presnell, Don, and Marty McGee. *A Critical History of Television's* The Twilight Zone, *1959–1964*. Jefferson: McFarland, 1998.

Sconce, Jeffrey. *Haunted Media: Electronic Presence from Telegraphy to Television*. Durham: Duke UP, 2000.

Sontag, Susan. "The Imagination of Disaster." *Against Interpretation*. New York: Dell, 1966. 212–28.

Stanyard, Stewart T. *Dimensions Behind* The Twilight Zone. Toronto: ECW, 2007.

Stewart, Garrettt. "The 'Videology' of Science Fiction." *Shadows of the Magic Lamp*. Eds. George E. Slusser and Eric S. Rabkin. Carbondale: Southern Illinois UP, 1985. 159–207.

Telotte, J. P. *Replications: A Robotic History of the Science Fiction Film*. Urbana: U of Illinois P, 1995.

Virilio, Paul. *A Landscape of Events*. Trans. Julie Rose. Cambridge: MIT P, 2000.

———. *The Vision Machine*. Trans. Julie Rose. Bloomington: Indiana UP, 1994.

3 *Voyage to the Bottom of the Sea*
Big-Screen Spectacle and Compressed Television Images

Mary Pharr

In both his film *Voyage to the Bottom of the Sea* (1961) and the television series of the same name (1964–68), Irwin Allen made what many consider to be marginal science fiction, yet it was science fiction that was commercially viable and indeed proved to be highly popular entertainment. When he adapted his movie into a television show, the resulting series ran four years, a record run for prime-time television sf that would not be surpassed until the late 1980s by *Star Trek: The Next Generation*. *Voyage*'s long run also gave Allen the credibility to develop several other sf-oriented series with varying degrees of success. But the show's most crucial significance may be its simultaneous demonstration of two conflicting sides of the adaptation issue, for it both offered a viable formula for adaptation and underscored the difficulty of replicating a cinematic feel, especially for spectacle, on the television screen.

A much earlier and more gifted voyager actually mapped out much of the route Allen's work would follow. In his cinematic adaptation of Jules Verne's *Le Voyage dans la lune* (1902), Georges Méliès had demonstrated film's capacity to turn narrative description into eye-opening visions of a universe that, although scientifically suspect, still had the power to bombard an audience's senses and engage its imagination. With every turn of technology, film increased that capacity, eventually to a point that neither print nor radio could match. After the mid-century establishment of television as its major rival, Hollywood accelerated not only the size of the screen and the intensity of image color but also a correlative reliance on spectacle in any genre that could remotely bear it. Allen understood this reliance; indeed, Richard Scheib argues that "to Allen everything was spectacle" (n. pag.). When Allen turned his cinematic *Voyage* into a television series, his ownership of the property must have given him confidence that he could make the adaptation he wanted, and as Gerald Duchovnay notes, "[a] key difference between *Voyage to the Bottom of the Sea* and most other adaptation efforts is that this series had continuity and a controlling creative presence in Irwin Allen" (70). Knowing what he wanted, Allen produced a series focused on the expectations of an audience fascinated by a view of exploration and the unknown. But television in the mid-1960s was still viewed within a smallish square box, the medium itself compressing and impoverishing the impact of even the most spectacular images. Reduced by its medium, drained of some of its original visceral impact, the television *Voyage* could never quite visually compete with its source film. And the more its creator tried to make his series an endless replication of his film, the more he diminished its quality as television. Given this paradox, we might judge it a notable achievement that he succeeded as well as he did.

When the *New York Times* ran a major story on Irwin Allen in 1974, it headlined the article "He's the Master of Disaster," a sobriquet he never objected to as it accurately depicted his raison d'être. Born in 1916, Allen dropped out of college and moved to Hollywood during the Great Depression. Defying the odds, he quickly became a magazine editor, then the creator of a radio program, a syndicated gossip column, and an early television celebrity show. Crucial to his development, Allen also became a literary agent. As Dennis Fischer notes, "[a] born wheeler-dealer, he represented many famous figures and started a new career as a packager, putting together directors, actors, and a script and selling the production package to a studio" (31). After producing a couple minor narrative films, Allen won an Oscar for the *The Sea Around Us* (1953), a documentary that brought Rachel Carson's book on oceanic life to the screen, demonstrating in the process two components in Allen's cinematic bag of tricks: a reliance on stock footage and an interest in striking underwater photography. Over the next several years, Allen used 3-D, more animal stock footage, special effects, familiar narrative bases, and recycled spectacle to make movies that were profitable but garnered little critical attention. As he moved into the most important decades of his career, he was able to turn his concentration on spectacle and technology into A-level sf projects—which would further bear out his remark to the *Times* that "people are observers of the macabre. . . . It doesn't speak too well of us . . . but it's good for the box office" (qtd. in Klemesrud D13).

By 1960, Allen had moved his production unit to Twentieth Century-Fox, a sure sign that he had clout in the film industry. Initially, the middle-aged producer did not seem well suited for the culture of the radical sixties. Unlike Roger Corman, Allen demonstrated little awareness that America was on the edge of a major youth movement, about to undergo tremendous shifts in society's perception of race, disability, class, and gender. Generally, his films and TV shows ignore minorities, except as stereotypical representatives of something inimical or (in the case of the disabled) something distasteful. More and more fantasy-based, Allen's works generally focus on prosperous white males, which makes economics a nonissue, and women are usually absent when the action starts. The few females who do enter center screen tend to be figures of corruption or temptation. Nor was Allen prescient regarding the military precipice upon which America stood as the 1960s moved on. Both the cinematic and televised versions of *Voyage to the Bottom of the Sea* rely on an image of the American military that seems at once reckless (with much destruction of and by military equipment that is consistently un- or underguarded) and jingoistic (American know-how and might, represented by the submarine *Seaview*, always triumphs).

Yet in one vital respect, Allen did understand the era: he saw it as a time of technological advances, and his work gloried in the idea of exploration made possible by technological progress. Most of the nation's attention focused on space exploration, an emblem of hope, as Gene Roddenberry would grasp in the first *Star Trek* series. Allen himself produced a space exploration series a year before *Star Trek*, but his tendency to repeat well-tried narrative ideas made his *Lost in Space* (1965–68) a re-visioning of *Swiss Family Robinson*—a family show that lacked the resonance of Roddenberry's landmark program. Earlier in the decade, Allen was more comfortable with ocean exploration. His best received work had been *The Sea Around Us*, and he had further reasons to use the ocean as the setting for his largest film yet: "a national interest in the nuclear-powered submarine *Nautilus* and its top-secret crossing of the North Pole in 1958, and his childhood love of Jules Verne's *20,000 Leagues Under the Sea*" (Duchovnay 71). Named after Captain Nemo's submarine, the American *Nautilus* "could do things that an earlier generation would have scorned as fantasy" (Lawless 4). In 1960, as *Voyage to the Bottom of the Sea* was in production, the first Polaris missiles were successfully test-fired off Cape Canaveral, adding the ultimate weapon to the post-*Nautilus* nuclear submarine fleet—unimaginable power, unseen but always available anywhere around the globe. For Allen, this nexus between fantasy and reality was an opportunity to use his well-honed production techniques and make an sf movie topical enough to interest whatever audience members cared about nuclear potential and visually spectacular enough to sell tickets to those—the majority, in his opinion—who just wanted to see big danger on-screen. He had a precedent, moreover, in Disney's 1954 adaptation of Verne's novel, a movie whose success had proved there was a market for underwater sf—and Allen liked the comfort of precedent.

As *Voyage*'s auteur, Allen produced and directed the movie from his own story and a script cowritten with veteran screenwriter Charles Bennett. The film certainly demonstrates the tight strictures Allen later put upon his TV writers: hasty exposition and casual denouement, minimal characterization and no consciously Aristotelian catharsis—nothing to slow the emphasis on effects and action. Nor was Allen especially concerned with the particulars of science or scientific method. He did want technology, as well as catastrophe; these were all elements of the "wonder" typically associated with sf narratives. What he emphatically did not want was explanation *or* extrapolation, both of which he seems to have regarded as something that might bore or frighten an audience, or distract from his spectacular images. When the noted sf author Theodore Sturgeon wrote the film's novelization, based on an early draft of the screenplay, he added detail to both the story's science and its characters' motivations. Although Sturgeon's psychological and emotion-driven detail is effective at fleshing out (or more aptly, ensouling) characters like troubled hero Lee Crane and secret villain Susan Hiller, no writer could make Allen's pseudoscience plausible. Nonetheless, the producer's ability to get a major genre writer to do the novelization is another indication that the film was meant to be noticed, especially by sf fans.

In spite of its creator's "no message" attitude, the film does reflect an amalgamation of cold-war anxieties and arrogance, but their presence is hidden amid post-Vernean wonders created by cost-contained but impressive effects. The care with which Allen selected and directed his craftsmen is a sure sign of his strength as an impresario. The title song, played over a Cinemascopic, DeLuxe color display of bubbling water and credits, is a sappy ballad, but Paul Sawtell and Bert Shefter's orchestral score effectively underscores Winton Hoch's and John Lamb's arresting underwater cinematography. Allen spent approximately $400,000 on his submarine models and interior sets ("Trivia"), and he chose his first shot proper to highlight the results and underscore his narrative's chief focus. Presenting L. B. Abbott's model cinematography at its finest, the shot shows the *Seaview* leaping, nose up, out of the Arctic water. Done with a miniature in a tank, the shot is, if not quite realistic looking, still memorable in its homage to the glory of technology. Presented as roughly six hundred feet in length with tail-lit Cadillac fins that would be of no practical value undersea, the *Seaview* etches itself into movie history at a sixty-degree angle that, if physically possible, would endanger everyone aboard. But that signature visual spectacle, the look of the submarine practically soaring, is all that matters. It shows what cinema can do better than any other medium: the screen, with its magnitude and clarity, can open up a penetrating but protected view of something well beyond the scope of reality. Whenever *Voyage to the Bottom of the Sea* is remembered, this first shot, not of a journey down but of a triumphant leap into a hitherto inaccessible zone, serves as a spot of time for the film's place in its exploratory culture.

Figure 3.1 The *Seaview* surfaces at an impossible angle: Spectacle in *Voyage to the Bottom of the Sea* (1961). Copyright Twentieth Century-Fox.

The uniqueness of that exploration is hammered home from the film's use of TV newscasts viewed through the *Telstar*-like technology (this before the real *Telstar 1* was launched) incorporated into the *Seaview* by the maverick genius of its creator, Admiral Harriman Nelson. Retired from the regular navy, Nelson and his Captain, Lee Crane, work under the loose auspices of the Bureau of Marine Exploration. Their nuclear-powered research ship (it is big enough to be a ship rather than a boat, even in submarine parlance) is decidedly idiosyncratic: it includes missiles, a minisub, satellite television, a transparent observation nose, and an open shark aquarium outside the reactor room. The first three innovations are explained by the navy's reserve use of the *Seaview* and the sub's subsequent need for the newest communication technology. The transparent nose, nonsense science, is unexplained in the film but rationalized in Sturgeon's novelization as "X-tempered herculite," invented by Nelson to form "oversized hull plates which just happen to be transparent" (10). The pool-sized shark aquarium, which seems to lack a cover and so should be spilling sharks out into mayhem right from the film's first shot, is beyond anyone's rationalization. Yet the set as a whole, like the quirky figure of Nelson (happily played by Walter Pidgeon as an Americanized Nemo), is eye grabbing and audience friendly, designed to hold viewers by appearance rather than application.

The *Seaview* is, as already suggested, the real star of the film, its literally glowing interiors and remarkably high ceilings far more spacious than those of any reality-based submarine. With no irony apparent, the admiral describes the most complex machine on Earth by referring to its control room as the "brain" and the reactor room as the "heart" (*Voyage* film)— perhaps with an eye to a similar duality set out in that most famous of sf films, Fritz Lang's *Metropolis* (1927). The colorful, winking equipment (some of it borrowed from earlier Twentieth Century-Fox films like *Desk Set* and *The Fly*) looks so dazzling in its big-screen setting that it is easy to ignore the triviality of the dialogue and the inattention to purpose. The green lights of the dive control do reference reality, but the large ballast control red-lit numbers are never shown functioning as the hatch closure indicators they must be. They just look good—like the steady blue lights and twinkling white lights present in the background equipment. Nelson says it's always Christmas in control, and the imposing yellow, blue, and red buttons attached to the missile launcher certainly make the device look more benign than its function suggests. The wonder of the whole setting is augmented by the audible blips of the protective sonar. Confirmation that this sub sails beneath the seas of Planet Hollywood comes from the presence of Dr. Susan Hiller (Joan Fontaine), aboard in high heels and white gloves, ostensibly to study the crew's response to confinement. As for the aquarium outside the reactor room, it's uniquely Allenesque. Outside the laws of either physics or common sense, it may exist only because Irwin Allen knew that an open shark tank situated near nuclear rods would be a hazard an audience would inevitably find intriguing.

The film's plot is a cascade of disasters. After being struck by glacier ice irrationally sinking underwater, the *Seaview* learns that the Van Allen Belt (its existence confirmed in reality just three years before the film) has ignited after being hit by meteors, setting the sky on fire. Once again, the physical impossibility of this event is irrelevant; it is topical, and the wide, flaming sky is an effective visual effect, created by a flame thrower whose twenty-foot jets were photographed repeatedly and then combined in an optical printer (Fischer 34). In short order, Nelson comes into conflict with the United Nations through his plan to save the world by shooting a nuclear missile into the Van Allen Belt. Ignoring the UN's rebuff, Nelson and crew crash dive the *Seaview* into its vital mission. As spotty TV reports show catastrophe across the globe, the *Seaview* endures sabotage, suicide, a death threat, fire, a mutiny, and attacks by a giant squid, a UN sub, and a giant octopus. Hiller proves to be the unlikely cause of the ship's internal chaos, a revelation disclosed just before she falls into the—finally useful—open shark tank. Nelson then prepares to fire the healing missile when another researcher temporarily onboard pulls out a small bomb and threatens the ship. His irrational reason is that "[n]o man has a right to challenge God's will" (*Voyage* film). Fortunately, Crane manually fires the missile, its destructive technology turned into our salvation. In a surprisingly underrealized scene, although one that again inscribes the film's concern with visual spectacle, the *Seaview* surfaces to let the principals watch the good nuke do its work, after which the admiral cheerfully orders the captain to head for home. Nobody speculates on the impact of the Van Allen Belt disaster on whatever is left of humanity. Tellingly, the last shot simply shows the submarine underway in perfect weather.

Despite its gaping script flaws, the film *is* visually impressive. The depths through which the *Seaview* travels are as alien and alluring as space, though the film's true draws are the submarine itself and the literal firestorm of catastrophes it must navigate. Still, the absence of hard science and meaningful speculation in the script are among the factors diminishing the film's place within the history of sf cinema. What commentary on the film has accrued over the years tends to the acerbic. Bill Warren calls it "amazingly stupid," despite fast pacing and good effects (2:596), and Dennis Fischer says that to call this movie "misconceived is putting it mildly" (34). More forgiving in a time when sf film was less scrutinized than it is now, contemporary reviews were not as harsh. *Variety* settled for mild wit: "*Voyage* is a crescendo of mounting jeopardy, an effervescent adventure in an anything-but-Pacific Ocean" (*Variety* staff). Howard Thompson of the *Times* began his review with faint praise: "Good color, handsome photographic effects and a submarine to end them all make 'Voyage to the Bottom of the Sea' a mildly diverting but far from memorable screen plunge." Eight paragraphs later, Thompson fell back on his own dismissive wit with a concluding reference to the absurdity of Joan Fontaine's character: "She will never make it back to Manderley now. Not on Mr. Allen's submarine" (n. pag.).

The mix of movie metaphors is appropriate. Allen's sf is a platform from which his audience can safely enjoy the chance to see the sweet Mrs. de Winter of *Rebecca* become a mad saboteur, turned inside out by an impossibly awful occurrence. Actually, the film has plenty of subtext: the jingoism evident in Nelson's dictatorial actions vis-à-vis the UN, the chauvinism that reduces a female scientist to a senseless villain, and the impiety of technology's triumph over faith. It's just that none of this dares speak its name, and virtually no one then or now has bothered to look for subtext in Allen's action-oriented films. Yet however feeble its status as serious sf, *Voyage* did please moviegoers, especially those whose imagination was fired by a big-screen vision of catastrophe first unleashed, then allayed by American technological expertise. A hit, *Voyage* grossed $6-$8 million off a budget of $1.5-$2 million (Colliver).

In the wake of this success, Allen decided to adapt this act to another arena. In 1961, Gladwyn Hill had noted the signs of a "science-fiction stampede" making its way across the silver screen (X9). Hill pointed out that television had robbed the cinema of patrons by co-opting the Western, once a cost-controlled film staple but now the province of long-term weekly series. According to Hill, sf had become the answer to this dilemma, especially the kind that could use public domain writers like Verne for source

Figure 3.2 The television *Voyage* turned to guest actors (here Eddie Albert, along with series regulars David Hedison and Richard Basehart) to bolster viewership. Copyright Twentieth Century-Fox Television.

material, eschew stars in favor of story, and contain costs through a studio's resources (X9). Inevitably, in another turn of the seasonal cycle, television networks noticed the success of sf film just as series like *Wagon Train* and *Rawhide* were winding down long runs—and the cunning showman Allen saw an opportunity to become a mogul in two media. Ever practical, Allen knew that his own hit sf film's name recognition would stir up interest in any TV adaptation he might make and that the expensive submarine sets he already owned would lend instant credibility and perhaps an unusual level of spectacle to the television version. Using his Fox connections, a library of stock footage, a stable of gifted craftsmen, and a warehouse of models left over from the film, Allen premiered the *Voyage to the Bottom of the Sea* series in the fall of 1964.

Even more than film, television is a producer's medium, and Allen stamped his name directly onto each of *Voyage*'s 110 episodes. As with the film, he set the series in the near future (never more than fifteen years ahead of each episode's air date), thus protecting its fantasy science and topical references. With the fundamentals of time, location, and crew set, Allen hired Richard Basehart to play a more vigorous Admiral Nelson than the one portrayed by the arresting but elderly Walter Pidgeon, then used Basehart's reputation to convince David Hedison to come aboard as a physically dynamic Captain Crane, a part he had earlier refused for the movie. Both lead actors made the commanding officers of the *Seaview* stalwart heroes, whose military prowess was modified by a combination of curiosity and humanity—a fitting description of the New Frontiersman of Kennedy's just-lost Camelot era. Without doubt, the casting was fundamental to the adaptation's success—and Allen's good judgment in actors went well beyond the leads. Well connected throughout show business, he persuaded well-known mid-level performers (e.g., Eddie Albert, Nick Adams, and Richard Carlson) to accept guest roles on the series. He also hired actors who would soon find fame, like Carroll O'Connor and Robert Duval, actors who could handle thin characterizations that might have defeated weaker performers. Allen got lucky (or perhaps negotiated the slot with the network) in ABC's first-season placement of the show on Monday night at 7:30 p.m., in competition with the game shows *To Tell the Truth* and *I've Got a Secret* on CBS and a weak comedy called *90 Bristol Court* on NBC (Castleman and Podrazik 172). The absence of powerful competition allowed the series to reach a wide demographic and make a strong start. As Mark Phillips notes, *Voyage* occasionally reached the top ten its first season and finished thirty-third out of one hundred shows that year ("Memories"). Its renewal was never in doubt.

John Ellis has observed how often TV series rely "on repeating a basic problematic which is worked through on each occasion without a final resolution" (125). Viewed as a virtual friend whose serial trials and triumphs continually grab the attention of viewers no show will ever willingly abandon, television tends to build a loyalty factor into its dramatic structure—something that almost certainly kept *Voyage* on air for its third and fourth seasons. But that foundation cloaks another troublesome paradox, for the lack of resolution always threatens serial television's creativity, as narrative patterns are repeated rather than expanded and climax is inevitably postponed. Character and situation development in particular may suffer, with neither growth nor change allowed in viewer favorites. Allen, it seems, had no interest in such development, encouraging his writers to use the same plot with the same character responses as often as possible. Thus in episode 50, "The Sky's on Fire" (23 January 1966), the series actually replicates the Van Allen Belt disaster scenario from the movie, as though the film itself did not exist. The problem with this selective amnesia was obvious: most home viewers knew about the original and could not help but notice the relative slightness of the fifty-minute TV version.

More generally, as part of that formulaic foundation on which Allen built the series, the episodes' plots typically involve a potential catastrophe (often created by someone recognizably evil or mad or both) narrowly averted by the technological know-how of Admiral Nelson and the macho heroism of Captain Crane and the crew of the *Seaview*. Script structure is usually network classical: something goes wrong just before the opening credits; a worsening crisis develops during two acts separated by commercials; Nelson et al. turn the table during the third act, followed by another commercial; then a brief fourth act provides an "all's well that ends well" denouement leading to the closing credits. Despite the efforts of multiple writers and the lead actors to circumvent this formula, the most devoted viewers still knew almost nothing about Nelson's and Crane's personal "lives" or their philosophical stances at the end of the series. But those viewers did know a lot about the *Seaview* and its fantastic—if temporary— triumphs. The terrible knowledge unleashed by all those mad enemies, knowledge that lay just beneath each triumph, was simply ignored. When the show was new, this lack of reflection may not have mattered in the enjoyment of the triumph; later, the increasingly obvious deficiency became more apparent as the series grew older but not wiser.

The technical know-how that had worked well on film also seemed less appealing on television. For Allen, this conundrum may have been the greatest challenge in adapting his film to television. The show's pilot was shot in color but televised with the rest of the first-year episodes in black and white as a practical matter while the series was, effectively, in its sea trials with the public. The lack of color photography immediately diminished the spectacle that is the core of Allen's work, deleting as it did the vivid oceanic palate surrounding the *Seaview*, still a reserve naval vessel but now based at the Nelson Institute of Marine Research (NIMR). The loss of color affected not just a sea change but a land loss as well. In the pilot, "Eleven Days to Zero (14 September 1964), the Arctic landscape is central to the plot, but with the exception of stock footage shots, the polar ice and snow look washed out and artificial. With the subtle contrasts within ice lost to the black-and-white broadcast, everything is a dirty white or dull grey—and obviously fake. All this is made much worse by the loss of scale. The tremendous size of both the polar setting and Nelson's submarine is marginalized by their placement inside a bit of furniture in the viewer's living room. However good Abbott's models are, once reduced to the size of miniatures on a twenty-one-inch screen, they look like toys. Too, those who had seen the movie recognized many of the models as just what they had previously experienced on a more impressive scale. This impoverishment of image was exacerbated by Allen's cost-cutting determination to reuse as much of his earlier footage—not just stock but narrative-specific footage—as he could. Old shots of the *Seaview* leaping and an enemy sub imploding found their way not only into the first episode but into multiple others. With Allen himself both writing and directing the pilot, its inability to replicate the wonder of the film presaged a major problem for the series.

Voyage's creator did not write most of the series' episodes, but his imprimatur was always required. Allen's craftsmen were loyal to his vision, but he was often in conflict with his writers. Ironically, that conflict produced some of the series' most intriguing episodes in its first season, when the show tended to view sf through a cold-war lens that reflected both the valor and distrust prevalent in the New Frontier America. But even these shows reveal the difficulty of replicating spectacle inside a TV set. In "The Price of Doom" (12 October 1964), for example, a heat-seeking Antarctic plankton devours the young scientists who discover it, leading to a search that brings the man-eating plankton aboard the *Seaview*. Nelson must deal with both the killer plankton on the loose and the presence of a spy amid the team sent to uncover the truth. Team members hurl allegations at the one foreigner in the group, allegations intensified by the confined environment under attack. As both movie and series, *Voyage* reflects an awareness of what claustrophobia can do to judgment—one reason viewers may have found Nelson and Crane's grace under pressure comforting. Ultimately, the spy turns out not to be the foreigner but the team's lone female, who falls prey to the plankton just before Crane destroys it with freezing water. Harlan Ellison wrote the initial version of this episode but disliked its development under Allen and insisted that it be aired under a pen name. Nonetheless, Ellison's concept was good, and director James Goldstone did an effective job of weaving together the human and unnatural threats within the confines of a submarine. However, the episode's key element, the spectacle of nature distorted by science, threatens to deteriorate into parody. Neither actors nor director could make the plankton look frightening. Shrunken by the small screen and its TV budget, the monster looks like the rubbery mock-up it is—leaving the episode sucked dry of spectacle and visually underwhelming.

In contrast, when the visuals worked harmoniously with the story, the show could be gripping. Allen's fascination with sea lore provided the impetus for one of the first season's best episodes, "The Ghost of Moby Dick" (14 December 1964), wherein Dr. Walter Bryce uses the *Seaview* to track the world's largest whale, ostensibly for scientific study but actually for revenge because the creature had killed his son. Intrigued by the unknown, Nelson first assists in the hunt, then tries to help Bryce's abused wife stop his increasingly mad quest. Gifted with a rich voice, Richard Basehart often used a slight stutter and a nervous laugh to indicate Nelson's wonder at the marvels his ship uncovered and the misuse of those marvels by men like Bryce. Not even Nelson's genius can stop Bryce from becoming a second Ahab, dragged down by the great whale in a scene inspired equally by Melville's novel and John Huston's film. Both aboard ship and in the water, the story emphasizes the emotional and physical perils of the sea, but this time the death scene is shot through modern binoculars that compress it into a harrowing glimpse of nature's revenge against human obsession. The adaptation here is both visually and emotionally successful.

Mark Phillips and Frank Garcia believe that despite its first-year ratings success, Allen's show "lacked the complete audience that ABC was seeking" (536). ABC switched *Voyage* to Sunday nights at 7:00 p.m. for its last three seasons, setting it up against *Lassie* and *My Favorite Martian* on CBS and *Walt Disney's Wonderful World of Color* on NBC (Castleman and Podrazik 182). The primary focus of the 7:00 hour was family entertainment, and both ABC and Allen may have wanted more family-oriented fare than the show had presented its first season. In season two, Allen added a high-tech flying sub to give more range to a slickly refitted *Seaview*. With "entertainment" the operative word, the series was also now broadcast in color—rich hues that enhanced the oceanic terrain and the technological appeal of the submarine. Everything looked great: the ocean (even at depths when it should have been nothing but blackness) outside the sub and the mise-en-scène inside (Christmas lights again in the control room and actors with tinted hair in color-coordinated uniforms). The additional hardware and color photography did move the series closer to its parent movie in visual spectacle, but the eye-candy appeal did not draw a larger audience. It could not solve the series' essential dilemma: a general inability to replicate the large scope or "first sight" quality of the film.

Yet the new effects did contribute to several memorable episodes. Abandoning all but the facade of science, Allen sent the show into the belly of a giant sea creature in "Jonah and the Whale" (19 September 1965). And as in the "Moby Dick" episode, the scale of the catastrophe works in "Jonah," with models of the *Seaview* and its diving bell convincingly set against stock footage and an animatronic model of a whale created at Fox. After the bell (with Nelson and a female Soviet researcher in it) has been swallowed by the whale, Crane leads a dive team through the creature's mouth and into its stomach, attaching a rescue cable to the bell that saves everyone in the nick of time. A striking combination of underwater and model effects is revealed in medium shots of the whale and the bell it swallows, alternating with close-ups of the two people trapped inside. Although the mechanical effects that reveal the inside of the whale are not as impressive, the claustrophobic setting of the bell within the belly is ideal for TV. Working within this constricted set, the camerawork accentuates not only the sweat and stress on the faces of the trapped, but also the human sympathy that develops between an American and a Soviet as they wait for almost certain death. Ellis has observed that, due to its smaller size, "the TV close-up generates an equality and even intimacy" diametrically opposed to the hyperbole of the cinematic close-up (131), and the visuals within this episode capitalize on such intimacy in the most extreme of situations. In fact, in what could have been an important lesson in adaptation strategy, here the spectacle of near disaster is not reduced but enhanced by confinement and limitation.

"Jonah" was an expensive-looking episode with some definite tension added by the woman-in-peril angle. Nonetheless, Phillips and Garcia note that despite a campaign by the lead actors and the writers to get a female regular on the show, "[r]esearch showed that viewers wanted more monsters and action, not women" (536). Allen readily complied, reducing the show's casting budget while still doing what he wanted to do. He revisited dinosaur islands of stock footage and imperiled his magnificent submarine with a further variety of giant monsters—including spiders, jellyfish, more whales, and even an alien amoeba—but the more they appeared, the less impressive they were. What may have been the best episode of the second year was something different, a retelling of the Flying Dutchman myth. In "The Phantom Strikes" (16 January 1966), a dead U-boat captain from World War I overwhelms the *Seaview*, abandoning it only after Crane launches a missile at him, which leads the phantom to realize that by being outside time he is also out of date. Much of the tale takes place on foggy nights, damping down but not destroying the color. Director Sutton Roley uses tracking and low-angle shots to emphasize the dominance of the lost U-boat and its phantom over the nuclear *Seaview* and its admiral. Such shots, along with a memorable but futile attempt to bury the dead captain at sea, are authentically eerie.

Yet ratings declined in the second season, perhaps because shows like "Jonah" and "The Phantom Strikes" were the series' exceptions rather than its weekly rule. This uncertainty of expectation may have been part of a larger ambiguity regarding the series' demographics. Phillips and Garcia say that *Voyage*'s Sunday night audience consisted "mainly of children and women" (538); in 1966, however, Richard Basehart told an interviewer that a survey had revealed that 80% of the show's audience was adult (*Voyage* TV). As a pioneer of sf film to television adaptation, Allen was testing not just the process of adaptation but also the placement of sf series in the broadcast schedule. Something may have backfired as Allen tinkered with his adaptation and the network moved the show to Sunday. By adding color and new technology, by following the source movie, in effect, Allen did what he could to attract the family audience considered most suitable for early Sunday evening programming in the 1960s—but *Voyage* had too much military focus to be a major competitor to Disney's *Wonderful World of Color*. Yet some of its audience—the adults—must have remained interested in the exploration element of the show and its attractive imagery, allowing it to survive even in the new time slot.

By season three, Allen had expanded his sf horizon, producing *Lost in Space* and *The Time Tunnel*. But with its auteur distracted across a variety of small screens, Jon Abbott notes that *Voyage* drifted downwards: "location shooting had ground to a halt, the writing started to get lazy, stock footage and other short cuts were rampant, and the actors were getting tired and frustrated" (13). The craft work remained good, but what had been at least borderline sf now too often became middling horror. In "The Wax Men" (5 March 1967), a small, mad clown almost effortlessly gets aboard the *Seaview* and tries to replace its crew with wax dummies. The effect of faux Nelson's waxen visage is oddly unsettling (again thanks to television's affinity for close-ups), but the choice of villain is both physically and morally offensive. In its later years, *Voyage* had a habit of using cartoonish creatures or even animated toys as alternatives to the more obvious human, alien, and beast monsters, but the effect was more often ludicrous than hazardous. In this case, dwarf actor Michael Dunn, playing the villainous clown, manages to be disturbing but in the wrong way—a reminder that Allen's work uses disability as a sideshow. At this point, according to Phillips and Garcia, "*Voyage* had metamorphosed into true camp" (539). Of course, the camp element was probably influenced by the meteoric success of another near-sf series, the deliberately outrageous *Batman* (1966–68), but if so, it was a bad bet as *Batman* fell from ratings grace almost as fast as it rose.

Voyage, too, had relatively low ratings through the fourth and final season, when a crustacean from space appeared in episode 100 and became a camp icon—but not an audience draw. Allen had unleashed a plethora of natural and unnatural threats on the small screen; most did not seem very threatening due to the medium's diminutive scale and their creator's propensity to repeat any intriguing visuals long past their maximum impact. By the time "The Lobster Man" (21 January 1968) aired, *Voyage* seemed intent on caricaturing spectacle instead of enhancing it or properly fitting it within the small screen. As so often in this last year, the plot is bizarre: a smallish spaceship picked up by the *Seaview* releases a man-sized golden crustacean with a very human face, more Halloween than Hollywood. Suspicious of this alien's announced peaceful intentions, Crane recalls the Trojan horse trick—and sure enough, the lobster-man proves to be the vanguard of an invasion that wants to destroy all life on Earth. As proof of his malevolence, this Trojan lobster tries to shoot Nelson into space, but the admiral uses his watch to short circuit the alien spacecraft while Crane uses one of Nelson's ultrasonic weapons to destroy the would-be invader. The episode has a certain mad panache to it, but the audience had already seen too many half-realized monsters and quickly concocted weapons to watch more of the same en masse.

Allen dropped the now-underwatched underwater show for a guaranteed slot for his *Land of the Giants* in the 1968–69 season. In the 1970s, he returned to the silver screen, where his spectacle-indulgent productions of *The Poseidon Adventure* (1972) and *The Towering Inferno* (1974) became the greatest commercial hits of his career. Like the cinematic *Voyage to the Bottom of the Sea*, Allen's disaster movies gave their audience technofantasy, at once visually pleasing and safely detached from reality. They were too big for TV—and maybe, in its day, the picture of a colossal submarine leaping out of the ocean was too big as well. Certainly, Allen's attempts to replicate the largest images of the *Voyage* film had only a limited success within the television technology of the time. On the other hand, when the series emphasized the dangerously claustrophobic nature of a submarine of any size within the vast oceanic unknown, it reached emotional depths well beyond its source movie. And it endured.

Image production remains a major issue in the exchange between screen and television sf narrative. Even if unable to match cinema's imagery—particularly its delivery of spectacle—television can still invest characters and situations with an intimacy that no single film has the time to match. The case of *Voyage to the Bottom of the Sea*, however, demonstrates just how difficult it is to balance essential continuity and creative flexibility in the transition from source film to serial rendering. It also demonstrates that a level of success is possible. But the paucity of long-run television adaptations of sf film over the decades since *Voyage* suggests that the fiscal realities of TV, its "endless" chronology, and its in-home technology are but rarely successfully negotiated by producers in either medium. Twenty-first-century adaptation would seem to have the advantage of advanced technology, obvious in the increasing attempts of home screens to emulate the look and sound of the theatrical experience. Yet the most popular technology of the postmodern, thoroughly mediated world is now playing out on the micro screens of iPads and smartphones, implying a shift in audience perception regarding the importance of spectacle versus intimacy of image. Consequently, the voyages set in motion by such new technology may one day go places not even the *Seaview* could reach.

WORKS CITED

Abbott, Jon. *Irwin Allen Television Productions, 1964–1970*. Jefferson: McFarland, 2006.

Basehart, Richard. Audio Interview. 1966. *Voyage to the Bottom of the Sea*. Season 3. Twentieth Century–Fox Home Entertainment, 2007. DVD.

Castleman, Harry, and Walter J. Podrazik. *Watching TV: Four Decades of American Television*. New York: McGraw-Hill, 1982.

Colliver, Tim. Voice-over commentary. *Voyage to the Bottom of the Sea*. Twentieth Century–Fox, 1961. Fox Home Entertainment, 2007: Global Warming edition. DVD.

Duchovnay, Gerald. "From Big Screen to Small Box: Adapting Science Fiction Film for Television." *The Essential Science Fiction Television Reader*. Ed. J. P. Telotte. Lexington: UP Kentucky, 2008. 69–88.
Ellis, John. *Visible Fictions: Cinema, Television, Video*. Rev. ed. London: Routledge, 1992.
Fischer, Dennis. *Science Fiction Film Directors, 1895–1998*. Jefferson: McFarland, 2000.
Hill, Gladwin. "Hollywood Cycle." *New York Times* 26 Mar. 1961: X9.
Klemesrud, Judy. "He's the Master of Disaster." *New York Times* 29 Dec. 1974: D1+.
Lawless, Chuck. *The Submarine Book*. Rev. ed. Short Hills: Burford, 2000.
Phillips, Mark. "Memories of Watching *Voyage to the Bottom of the Sea*." Part 2. *Mike's Voyage to the Bottom of the Sea Zone*. Michael Bailey. 2 July 2010. Accessed 22 July 2010. Web.
Phillips, Mark, and Frank Garcia. *Science Fiction Television Series*. Jefferson: McFarland, 1996.
Scheib, Richard. Rev. of *Voyage to the Bottom of the Sea*. *Moria: The Science Fiction, Horror and Fantasy Movie Review Site*, 19 Feb. 2010. Accessed 12 July 2010. Web.
Sturgeon, Theodore. *Voyage to the Bottom of the Sea*. From the screenplay by Irwin Allen and Charles Bennett, based on an original story by Irwin Allen. New York: Pyramid, 1961.
Thompson, Howard. Rev. of *Voyage to the Bottom of the Sea*. *New York Times* 20 July 1961: n. pag. *Nytimes.com*. Accessed 12 July 2010. Web.
"Trivia." *Voyage to the Bottom of the Sea*. *Internet Movie Database*, 2010. Accessed 25 Aug. 2010. Web.
Variety Staff. Rev. of *Voyage to the Bottom of the Sea*. 1 Jan. 1961: n. pag. Rpt. in *Variety Movie Guide*. New York: Prentice Hall, 1992. 654.
Voyage to the Bottom of the Sea (TV). Twentieth Century-Fox Tele./ABC. Prod. Irwin Allen. Sept. 1964–Mar. 1968.
Voyage to the Bottom of the Sea (film). Dir. and prod. Irwin Allen. Perf. Walter Pidgeon and Joan Fontaine. Twentieth Century-Fox, 1961.
Warren, Bill. *Keep Watching the Skies!* Vol. 2. Jefferson: McFarland, 1986.

Part II
Case Studies
Film to Television

4 Finding Sanctuary
Adapting *Logan's Run* to Television
Gerald Duchovnay

Although film and television are similar in many ways, adapting a work from the big to the small screen is especially complicated in the case of science fiction, thanks in part, as Michele Pierson argues, to its emphasis on an "aesthetic experience of wonder" (168) that always entails additional, usually highly technological concerns. Much critical discussion of filmed adaptations has focused on the fidelity to the source or the importance of the director's input. For television broadcasters, however, the aim was to adapt a film to meet the medium's demands regarding technology, narrative, audience, and financing. Of the nearly twenty sf television shows that have been adapted from films, 70% ran for only one or two seasons. Why has there been such a high failure rate for sf television? One often overlooked factor, sometimes beyond the control of television or studio executives, is the timeliness of television productions in relation to cultural and historical events. Quite simply, sometimes a series appears too early or too late for a broadcast viewer who is also a cinema spectator. Such is the case with *Logan's Run*. What follows is a consideration of what happened to a fairly successful sf movie from 1976 when it was adapted into a television series just a year after its big-screen debut and how various elements of the production, such as narrative patterns, visual effects, financing, and especially timing impacted its demise.

Prior to recent developments in Blu-ray, 3-D, digital technology, and screen size, as John Ellis and others (Noël Carroll, Vivian Sobchack, and Patricia Mellencamp) have noted, the resolution of image, sound, and size on television have had "profound effects on the kind of representation and spectator attitudes that broadcast television creates for itself" (Ellis 127). To Ellis, television images are "stripped-down, lacking in detail," in part because producers and directors have been unwilling to fund any details that are "inessential," given broadcast television's historically low definition and small image (130). For the film version of *Logan's Run*, those details, because of the emphasis on technology and the need for special effects that would support the "experience of wonder" Pierson notes, often involved more time and planning than the conventional considerations of script and acting. Unlike the television image, which tends to be simple and straightforward, the film conveys dramatic events with grandeur and in a more detailed format. Saul David, the producer who spent two and a half years bringing the film to the big screen, recalls:

> There is, in the end, very little room for inspiration. It's the kind of film that depends very heavily on planning, because so much of it dealt with magic. That is to say, so much of it is involved with effects. The director has little of the liberty that a director usually has, and likes to have, because he is confined to those things which will match what the special effects are going to produce later on. A picture of this type has almost endless effects—mechanical, photographic and every other kind. (674)

The film *Logan's Run* was directed by Michael Anderson and adapted from a novel by William F. Nolan and George Clayton Johnson (1967), which had itself gone through several iterations. It started as an idea for a short story about a rebel cop living in an overpopulated world who, when faced with compulsory death at age forty (Nolan was playing with the idea that "life begins at 40"), decides to run from other cops who are hunting him down. Johnson and Nolan subsequently changed the story to a novel, the age from forty to twenty-one, and created an "unstable world of youth where runners (those who refused to die on schedule) would be pursued by an elite futuristic police corps [they] called Sandmen" (Nolan 8–9).

The backstory for moving the adaptation of the novel to the big screen included several years and many twists and turns before MGM, which purchased the screenplay also written by Nolan and Johnson, first hired George Pal to produce the film and asked for a script by Richard Maibaum, who had written several James Bond films. With a change in studio executives, the project was shelved for a time, only to have Irwin Allen, the producer and director of such sf and overproduced television fantasies as *Voyage to the Bottom of the Sea* (1964–68) and *Lost in Space* (1965–68), try to revive the project after completing *The Poseidon Adventure* (1972). Allen wanted to go back to the novel for his screenplay and was willing to spend $15 million to produce the film, but that proposal fell through. Then, in November 1973, *Daily Variety* announced that Frank Rosenfelt, the new president at MGM, had chosen *Logan's Run* to be his first "quality" project. Saul David, who had produced *Von Ryan's Express* (1965), *Our Man Flint* (1966), and *Fantastic Voyage* (1966), was brought in to produce, with an initial budget of $3 million. David worked with two screenwriters and "compressed" elements of the novel by having the events take place under a "single domed city, with the undersea section below the city-surface and the ice cave on top" in order to save money on set construction and location shooting (Nolan 11–13).

The film's story takes place in a postapocalyptic age (the year 2274) where everyone lives in a domed city and enjoys free recreational drugs and sex until age thirty (Lastday). At thirty a flashing crystal in one's palm indicates it is time to enter the coliseum-like Carrousel to seek Renewal, although each only finds death. Those who refuse become Runners and attempt to escape to Sanctuary, a mythic place outside the domed city. Logan 5 (Michael York), a Sandman and killer of Runners, questions the process and befriends Jessica 6 (Jenny Agutter); together they escape the domed city, with Francis (Richard Jordan), Logan's fellow Sandman, in pursuit. Once outside Logan and Jessica discover a desolate and vine-infested Washington D.C., and encounter an old man (Peter Ustinov) living in that postapocalyptic world. When Francis catches up with them in the US Capitol building, Logan kills Francis. Logan, Jessica, and the old man then journey to the domed city to prove to the inhabitants that life beyond thirty is possible outside their sterile existence. When Logan is interrogated by the main computer, the unsettling information that there is no Sanctuary causes the computer to crash, resulting in the destruction of the domed city. After fleeing the city, the inhabitants encounter the wrinkled old man and see that further life is possible, even in such difficult circumstances.

Thanks to popular books like Paul Ehrlich's *The Population Bomb* (1968) and D. H. Meadows's *The Limits of Growth* (1972), the concern with overpopulation had especially worked its way into our culture as what Brian Stableford calls "a consequence of an already-widespread dystopian pessimism, which it then helped to maintain and amplify" (901). Although Logan's story is "life-affirming, love-affirming [and] speak[s] out, through a glass darkly, for the joy of living," William F. Nolan rightly notes that "[n]o amount of publicity or promotional hype can create a popular phenomenon if the audience is not responsive" (7–8). The novel received high critical praise, and the film received the 1976 award for best sf film of the year from the Academy of Science Fiction, Fantasy, and Horror Films (Logan 6), but the story and its topicality were not the only reasons for its big-screen success and domestic gross of $25 million. In fact, in this decade a number of films such as *Silent Running* (1971), *The Omega Man* (1971), *Soylent Green* (1973), and *The Noah* (1975) developed rather similar apocalyptic or postapocalyptic scenarios that emphasized overpopulation.

The Academy Award for Special Achievement in Visual Effects awarded to *Logan's Run* (shared with *King Kong*) and its nomination for Oscars for Art/Set Direction and Cinematography also suggest why the film won acclaim for elements that might be seen as fundamental to its sf gestation: visual design and special effects that, as one commentator asserted, provided a "visual dazzle rarely affordable in past science fiction films" ("*Logan's Run*" 45)—a claim that within a year would be passé. To Ellis, the cinema spectator "is already specified on entering the cinema as someone who is curious or expectant about a particular enigma" and who identifies with "the images and figures," either human or mechanical, on the screen (79, 41). For *Logan's Run* those cinema spectators consisted primarily of a youth culture that had an affinity for individual liberty, had ideas about the population crisis and options for euthanasia, and took to heart slogans such as "live, love, and renew" and "don't trust anyone over thirty." But it was also an audience interested in sf films and their technological creations, in works that could entertain and startle in a way that small screen television sf had not—and some would argue, still has not—managed.

Producer Saul David, who was well into his fifties when he began work on *Logan's Run*, believed that sf was replacing the Western, the primary film genre of his generation. This idea was not new. Gene Roddenberry had sold *Star Trek* as the "*Wagon Train* to the stars" in the early 1960s, but within the decade, as David's comments suggest, it had seeped into the ethos of "old guard" Hollywood: "You only have to look at what interests the kids to see that that's where it's going. They may not have discarded the Western [and its mythologized reality], but they certainly are fascinated by the ideas involved in science. In fact, many of them are much more at home with it than many of us who are actually making the pictures" (702).

David knew that spectacle and futuristic settings were essential if his film was to be successful. He had been executive story editor at MGM when George Pal and Irwin Allen wanted to make the film, so he knew the project well (David 637). When given the green light to produce the film, he put together a carefully designed team of photography and effects experts, including L. B. ("Bill") Abbott for visual effects, Dale Hennesy for production design, Glen Robinson for mechanical special effects, Ernest Laszlo for cinematography, and Strawberry Gatts for new hologram technology. Because Hennesy, Abbott, Robinson, and Laszlo had worked with David on *Fantastic Voyage*, the ensemble hit the ground running on this project.

In articles for *American Cinematographer*, L. B. Abbott and Glen Robinson detail the various unique processes that went into matching individuals with matte shots in the domed city and in Washington, D.C.; the devices used for the flying stickmen and the effects created to "clean up"

Figure 4.1 Futuristic setting: inside the domed city of the film *Logan's Run*. Copyright MGM.

incinerated Runners; the need to create a "futuristic hand-gun that would shoot green fire"; and their most demanding challenge—designing and devising Carrousel, a "mechanical masterpiece" that "required that a huge crystal on the floor and another high up on the ceiling be able to revolve synchronously, while [15–18] condemned citizens . . . levitated [on unseen wires] in a 'force field' to desperately bid for life renewal" (Robinson 647). We need only consider the current "wire" complications of the $60 million Broadway production of *Spider Man* to put in perspective the challenge of this latter effect.

A producer, screenwriter, or director might describe what is wanted for an effect in a sentence or two in a script. For example, in the scene when Michael York is being interrogated by the computer that controls the population, one writer's suggestion was to use "something like six glass figures," but when one member of the team realized holograms would be more effective and because "visualization is everything" in this type of film, David pushed for the use of new hologram technology. As a result, when the computer asks Logan questions in a "surrogation" process, his brain is separated into multiple images created by holograms (Gatts 650). Having created this effect, David felt it was important to transfer "the wonders of this three-dimensional imagery to a two-dimensional theatre screen with out [sic] losing the mystery and thrills." Prior to the film's release he claimed that he could have had the images projected "out among the audience. . . . But we decided that would stop the picture cold. Once it was done, we could never get the audience's attention back to the screen" ("3-D Pix" 93). Those who worked on the effects for the film championed not only the holograms and the creation of Carrousel but also several other unique aspects: Box the Robot, the computer control room, shots with specially created filters borrowed from Robert Wise, and the use of an extreme wide-angle lens not yet commercially available ("Photographing" 664, 698).

Two other elements designed to keep audiences looking at the screen were the costumes and the sets. For a film set in 2274, the futuristic design of the sets was important, especially because David had a limited budget. He saved nearly $3 million on back-lot sets when he and members of his design team found "the most advanced architecture in America" in several buildings in Dallas, the Water Gardens in Fort Worth, and a hotel in Houston, and supplemented those locations with sound stage constructions for interiors ("*Logan's Run* and How It Was Filmed" 631, 697). The costumes and sets were aimed at an under-thirty audience, with the women wearing brightly colored, flesh-revealing and braless outfits or no clothes at all at the Love Shop, where nudity (shot in a low light, with an occasional bright light for effect) and "free love" without emotional commitments were there for all to enjoy. The flashing crystals, mirrors, and twinkling lights associated with Carrousel appealed to an audience enamored of psychedelic imagery and decorations found in disco clubs and their appeal to a unfettered lifestyle.

Logan's Run, grossing over $2.5 million in its first five days of release in 1976 (sizeable for that era), "proved that, unlike the fifties, there was . . . a large audience eager for sf movies" (Brosnan 174). But what troubled Michael Crichton and others about the film is that it "is really a statement about contemporary America's preoccupation with youth" (Peary 250). And to the novel's coauthor William Nolan, it moved away from what he saw as the "deep theme" of the novel—that "a youth-dominated culture would be shallow and fad-like, that it takes experience, wisdom, and age to sustain a genuine culture—the young can't impart the essence of the culture to those younger still" (Wilcox). While lamenting the film's pandering to "mass public tastes" and "ecology conscious sloganeering," one commentator for *Cinefantastique* viewed the film as "the acid test in Hollywood for determining whether it's now the time of science fiction boom or bust" ("*Logan's Run*" 45).

Very much at odds with those who worked on the film and the Academy members who awarded the film an Oscar for special effects, C. J. Henderson claims "the effects really weren't even all that special by contemporary standards," especially when compared to more recent sf (252). Certainly true of films produced in the last several decades, Henderson no doubt was thinking about two visually stunning films released the very next year—*Star Wars* and *Close Encounters of the Third Kind*. Nonetheless, as John Brosnan and Peter Nichols note, *Logan's Run* was generally perceived to be "[o]ne of the largest, most 'prestigious' sf films of the decade" (728). The financial success of the film and its young audience reflected a time when Hollywood and the networks realized demographics and new fare mattered. Again, timing was of the essence. All three networks, knowing that their primary audiences were under twenty-five and that they were competing with more and more cable channels, were looking for fare that would appeal to them and engaged in massive marketing campaigns.

Critics may have described *Logan's Run*'s blatant appeal to the young, but network executives, hungry for acquisitions to fill evening time slots and aware of the film's box-office success, saw the film as a strong possibility for a television series. Louis Giannetti and Scott Eyman contend that the mindset of film industry executives in the early and mid-1970s was such that, because money was being made from films "on relatively small budgets and even without important stars, . . . studio executives were willing to gamble on new talent and fresh story ideas. Anyone capable of relating to the 'youth market'—or anyone claiming to—was now a viable commercial possibility" (277). Such was also the case with executives at CBS and MGM Television, who thought a series based on *Logan's Run* would be a sure thing, if there is ever such a thing in television. That MGM released the film aided its offshoot, MGM Television, in saving money on some production costs and allowed them to use the opening sequences from the film in the series. But the project still proved costly. According to John K. Muir, Nolan was paid $9 million by the network for the franchise to *Logan's Run*

Finding Sanctuary   59

Figure 4.2   The "hovercraft" that Logan, Jessica, and REM use for their different adventures in the *Logan's Run* television series. Copyright CBS Video.

and to secure his commitment to the series. By early September 1977, one national publication cited *Logan's Run* as being one of the new series having a good chance for a successful run ("Most Likely Hits"). Why, then, did such a seemingly promising show fail to last even one full season?

In describing the importance of putting together the right team for a successful television production, I have argued elsewhere that collaboration through leadership often determines a show's success. The producer Irwin Allen, for example, was the key creative presence and driving force behind *Voyage to the Bottom of the Sea*, both the film and television series. For the film version of *Logan's Run*, Saul David was the engine that drove the production, as evidenced by his more than two years in preparation and production and desire for even more time to make it "better" (Domeier 30). David was scheduled to be the producer for the television series and would have lent the project continuity had he not been replaced by Ben Roberts and Ivan Goff. Both had limited production experience (a few *Mannix* episodes and one *Charlie's Angels* show), were primarily writers, and had no experience with sf as authors or producers. In fact, none of the key creative people involved with the original film worked on the series, although Nolan's "Dark Universe" website indicates he wrote a treatment for an episode (*Thunder Gods*, a.k.a. *Thunder Sentinels*) that was never produced and Nolan and David received credits on the pilot. Because of the formulaic frame used for the series (Logan, Jessica, and android REM travel in a hovercraft and solve the problems of a new community each week, something akin to *Star Trek* plots), Nolan considered the series "doomed" (Wilcox) and walked away. Without Nolan, the show employed a series of writers, but only one, Al Hayes, worked on more than a single script—and he only worked on two.

The arc of the television pilot tries to appeal to the film's audience by following aspects of the movie's plot but without the figure of the wise old man or the spectacular destruction of the domed city. In addition, a Council of Elders replaces the computer, and they tell Francis that if he captures Logan and Jessica and brings them back, he can join the Council and live to old age. Also added is REM, the android who helps them escape a mountain city in a solar-powered hovercraft, which becomes the primary means of transportation in the series. REM serves as a replacement for the old man in the film and joins the pair in their quest to find Sanctuary. As Jessica explains in several episodes, Sanctuary is a place "where they can be free, grow old, raise families, and be happy," social bromides that connected to an audience still weary from recent conflicts such as Vietnam, Watergate, and the intrusion of government in all aspects of their lives.

As Eric Greene notes, the basic plot line of *Logan's Run* is a staple of a number of other sf shows of the seventies, including *Planet of the Apes, Starlost, Space: 1999, Fantastic Journey, The Incredible Hulk,* and *Battlestar Galactica.* They all focused on "a group of fugitives or wanderers moving from place to place, often after some kind of cataclysm, encountering and aiding various cultures and subcultures. . . . In most of these shows, . . . the characters are in a situation not of their own choosing . . . and are running or wandering with little or no direction. The format . . . appears to express a feeling of lack of control over one's life," which Greene attributes to "a cultural response to the feeling of disorientation inspired by the political conflicts of the era." Except for *Space: 1999* and *The Incredible Hulk,* each show was canceled after or within its first year (157n7). One series not mentioned by Greene, but certainly an influence on *Logan's Run,* was *The Fugitive* (1963-67, with David Jansen), which also uses the journey/quest motif for each episode.

One of the challenges for a sf series' survival is for the writers to work on a tight schedule, within the formula, while coming up with enough new ideas to fill out a season of shows that will appeal to the broadcast viewer and, hopefully, mesh with the special effects. Unfortunately for *Logan's Run,* whose initial appeal was to a young audience interested in sf, the effects were still limited by budget and technology, so the writers fell back on an old studio trick of retooling previously used narratives but dressing them differently. One representative example is the episode "Capture" (30 September 1977), in which Logan, Jessica, and REM are captured by a hunter and his wife, who set them loose to be hunted as prey. This is a direct theft of "The Most Dangerous Game" (the story and movie). A similar re-treading is "Fear Factor" (14 November 1977), in which the trio come upon a California-style mansion in the middle of nowhere—an asylum where the director is trying to produce a master race by eliminating the inmates' emotions and feelings, a situation that echoes the sf classic *Invasion of the Body Snatchers* (1956).

Perhaps the best episode in the series, "Man out of Time" (17 October 1977) has Logan, Jessica, and REM encounter a time traveler who leads them to Sanctuary. David Eakins, the time traveler, has come forward in time to find out what caused the great holocaust. By doing so, in twenty-two hours, he hopes to return to December 2118 and prevent Armageddon. Eakins leads them to Sanctuary, which is a village of Seekers living in tents or sets reminiscent of those from some episodes of the failed *Planet of the Apes*. The villagers pray for everything in their holy search for light and guidance. Although the named characters have computer-related names—the leader is Analog, a boy is called Binary—all of the inhabitants lack rudimentary knowledge: they are unable to read and have no knowledge of science. Eakins finds the Sanctuary Project under a cloth covering the altar in the temple and, with REM's help, reenergizes the computers and gets data that he hopes will change history by saving seven billion lives from the holocaust. With minimal special effects, no tension related to the twenty-two hour deadline, and low-tech computer panels, the episode manages to touch on time travel, religion versus science, using and worshipping computers, and where the quest for knowledge can take us. With much concluding commentary about how important it is to help people, Eakins returns to 2118, unable to save the world. However, he transports a computer and disk forward in time to the trio to tell them that he could not prevent the holocaust because he caused it. When the world learned that time travel was possible, each nation saw it as a weapon—the ultimate weapon—and all nations went to war in an attempt to secure the secret to time travel. This was a didactic episode that tried to use special effects, but they came across as rudimentary, if not feeble, to a mass audience familiar with *Star Wars*.

One episode near the end of the series, "Carousel" (16 January 1978), offered the producers and special-effects personnel the opportunity to revisit the most significant special effects object of the film. The episode centers on Logan being "tranquilized" while in the "polluted" world and then being sent in "transit" back to the domed city where, due to the drug-induced "memory warp," he is interrogated and "scanned" to see if he can regain his status as a Sandman. To do so, he must testify at an assembly before Carousel (spelled with one *r* in the television series) and renounce his life as a Runner. The Higher Authority (the elders who run the city) plan to kill Logan after he testifies, but the effects of the drug wear off and he remembers Jessica and REM. We never see the full Carousel set. The only echo of the original film's effects is one large red flashing crystal shown in long shot. Most of the episode is spent running through mazelike tunnels under the domed city or walking its corridors (so obviously walkways in a mall), and eyeing the scantily dressed women and the uniformed men. There is one prolonged kiss between Logan and Jessica (while he is still under the influence), but again the special effects are limited to some teleporting scenes, a blinking computer backdrop where the elders congregate, and some shots from their ray weapons.

If a sf television broadcast's production values of the special effects do not draw in the audience, and if the scripts are weak, sometimes the production can rely on its stars to sustain the show. In the 1960s and 1970s, when film theorists and journalists began to champion the importance of the director (the auteur), the star remained the drawing power for a project. Ask directors then or now about casting, and chances are they will say that although they are always interested in the selection of cinematographers, soundmen, and special-effects personnel, casting frequently determines the success of a project. Robert Altman has said it is 90% of the process (Braudy and Kolker 5), and Clint Eastwood, famous for his love of jazz, considers casting to be the equivalent of putting together a jazz ensemble (Gentry 7). In 1976 CBS "promoted its array of prime-timer performers with 'catch the brightest stars'" (Edgerton 290) as an ad campaign. Competing networks did just that with *The Six Million Dollar Man* (Lee Majors, 1973-78) and *The Bionic Woman* (Lindsay Wagner, 1976-78). For *Logan's Run*, the producers chose actors with experience, but not in lead roles. Gregory Harrison, later known for his role as "Gonzo" on *Trapper John, MD* (1979) would play Logan 5. Heather Menzies, who had her film debut as Louisa von Trapp in *The Sound of Music* (1965), played Jessica 6; and Donald Moffatt, a well-established character actor, added humor and a Spock-like flavor to the show as the android REM. But the combination of a sexually attractive Heather Menzies (who had previously posed nude in *Playboy* and willingly wore revealing outfits to bring in an audience), a handsome and somewhat rugged Gregory Harrison, and a humorous Donald Moffat did not equate to star power. Harrison, grateful for a chance to star and learn about weekly television production, candidly remarks that with the main characters "either being captured, chased, threatened, or forced to rescue others . . . [it became] a 'road show' in a science fiction arena," and instead of portraying characters with human frailties and limitations trying to survive in challenging circumstances, the writers repeatedly turned to REM to make sure they survived (Phillips and Garcia 178, 181).

Logan's Run demonstrates that when a series has little room for character development, not much conflict, one-note plots, conventional genre situations, limited budgets (which could always be reduced if the ratings declined), and short (two-week) deadlines in which to complete an episode, what we generally think of as production values will predictably suffer, and audiences can quickly disappear. But as suggested earlier, factors outside of the production also impact a show's success. We often hear that "timing is everything," and that, too, becomes a significant factor. Depending upon where you lived in the country, CBS aired eleven to fourteen episodes from 16 September 1977 to 7 January 1978, originally from 8:00 p.m. to 9:00 p.m. on Fridays, which was competing against the ABC *Friday Night Movie* and NBC's *The Rockford Files*, but later changed to different days and times. Broadcast spectators like the comfort of regularity, so the schedule changes only compounded the various problems the show faced. The series' audience and ratings, which even with a much-advertised pilot drew less than 30% of the available audience (Brown), quickly declined. But beyond all these factors, there was a game changer that few foresaw. The film version of *Logan's Run* came out a year before *Star Wars*, but that film would influence the look and appeal of sf in a way that had not been seen since Stanley Kubrick's *2001: A Space Odyssey* (1968). That film's influence on the series can clearly be seen in the introduction of REM (android version of R2D2 and C-3PO) and characters in "The Collectors" (23 September 1977) episode that seem to have come straight from the Mos Eisely Cantina. With the quality production of *Star Wars* (story, action, sound, and special effects) playing over and over again in the minds of sf fans, *Logan's Run* must have seemed like child's play, a *Captain Video* version of what was then possible—and of what sf at its best was capable of. Once Gregory Harrison saw the movie, he recognized that "it made everything we had done look like the old black-and-white Buck Rogers serials. It sort of made us obsolete immediately (Phillips 1780). When the ratings for *Logan's Run* steadily declined, CBS cut its losses and canceled the show after less than one full season.

Historically, sf has been less successful than many other genres on the small screen because of budgets, casting, visual design, sound, and a host of other technical and economic issues. Such was certainly the case with *Logan's Run*, where the initial success of the theatrical version was not able to sustain the television series. Although the series has its devotees, as is evidenced by the many comments on websites, with very little science and limited effects it could not match the visual pleasures offered by theatrical fare such as *Star Wars* and *Close Encounters of the Third Kind*. In 1977 television producers and networks simply could not present the kind of spectacle sf television audiences suddenly craved.

The 1970s was a decade of great change in the historical and cultural fabric of the United States. Coming out of the "love" decade of the 1960s, the assassinations of two Kennedys and Martin Luther King, the riots in Chicago, and the war in Vietnam, the United States was wracked by Watergate and the painful and humiliating withdrawal from Vietnam. In film the old Hollywood was disappearing and being replaced by the "film school" generation of Lucas, Spielberg, Coppola, and others. Films and television programs were two primary sources of information and entertainment, and sf was a genre that was increasingly being used in both media to indirectly address our pressing cultural and social issues. *Logan's Run* the film, adapted and altered from a novel with a somewhat satirical attack on youth, became a cinematic commentary on free love, drugs, an all-controlling government, and the impact of technology in a world in which everyone was promised renewal at age thirty but the promise proved to be a lie. The television adaptation, meant to appeal to a youth market, tried to build on the film by reprising many of its elements in a few episodes, but then followed a formulaic pattern in which the lead characters either ran for their lives or, while searching for Sanctuary, helped a particular isolated community. While the characters experienced new and surprising situations each week, the viewer had seen them before. The scripts, acting, and especially the special effects simply did not meet the expectations of the targeted audience—the young and those interested in sf, especially its generic promise of an "experience of wonder."

Compounding the show's many weaknesses, its reception was impacted by the appearance four months earlier of George Lucas's *Star Wars*. Lucas's creation of a special company, ILM, to develop a new generation of special effects, along with his use of THX and other improvements in sound quality in the theatres, influenced the entertainment culture and the audience's expectations for films in a way few movies have before or since. The cultural phenomenon of *Star Wars*, followed six months later by *Close Encounters of the Third Kind*, helped suggest the important place of sf in the culture and on television; it also sounded the death knell for inadequately funded and impoverished special effects and created a new, more demanding audience for sf programs and movies. Subsequent adaptations of sf films to television, shows such as *Stargate SG-1* (1997–2007), would have to invest far more substantially in effects and have stories that appealed to audiences if they were to survive more than a season or two. Although looked at with nostalgia by some in today's audience familiar with the original film and television production, the television adaptation of *Logan's Run* was a victim of both poor production values and bad timing. It proved once again that an idea for a television show can only be as good as its execution, and that for television shows the zeitgeist is everything.

WORKS CITED

Abbott, L. B. "Magic for the 23rd Century." *American Cinematographer* (June 1976): 642–63, 676–77, 700–01.

Braudy, Leo, and Robert Kolker. "Robert Altman: An Interview, Part I." *Post Script* 1.1 (Fall 1981): 2–7.

Brosnan, John. *The Primal Screen: A History of Science Fiction Film*. Boston: Little Brown, 1991.

Brosnan, John, and Peter Nicholls. "*Logan's Run*." *The Encyclopedia of Science Fiction*. Ed. John Clute and Peter Nicholls. London: Orbit, 1999. 728–29.

Brown, Les. "ABC Dominates Ratings." *New York Times* 21 Sept. 1977: n. pag.

Carroll, Noël. "TV and Film: A Philosophical Perspective." *Journal of Aesthetic Education* 35.1 (Spring 2001): 15–29.

David, Saul. "Behind the Scenes of 'Logan's Run.'" *American Cinematographer* (June 1976): 636–37, 674–75, 702–05.

Domeier, Doug. "Dallas' Architecture Meets Metro's 23rd Century Sci-Fi Needs." *Variety* (23 July 1975): 30.
Duchovnay, Gerald. "From Big Screen to Small Box: Adapting Science Fiction Film for Television." *The Essential Science Fiction Television Reader*. Ed. J. P. Telotte. Lexington: U Kentucky P, 2008. 69–90.
Edgerton, Gary R. *The Columbia History of American Television*. New York: Columbia UP, 2007.
Ellis, John. *Visible Fictions: Cinema, Television, Video*. Rev. ed. London: Routledge, 1992.
Gatts, Strawberry. "The Use of Holograms in '*Logan's Run*.'" *American Cinematographer* (June 1976): 650–51, 669, 706.
Gentry, Ric. "Clint Eastwood: An Interview." *Post Script* 17.3 (Summer 1998): 3–24.
Giannetti, Louis, and Scott Eyman. *Flashback: A Brief History of Film*. 6th ed. Boston: Allyn and Bacon, 2010.
Greene, Eric. Planet of the Apes *as American Myth: Race, Politics, and Popular Culture*. Hanover: Wesleyan UP, 1998.
Henderson, C. J. *The Encyclopedia of Science Fiction Movies from 1897 to the Present*. New York: Facts on File, 2001.
"'Logan,' 'Burnt,' 'Holes' win Sci-Fi Laurels." *Variety* (22 Dec. 1976): 6.
"*Logan's Run*." *Cinefantastique* 5.1 (1976): 44–45.
Logan's Run. Dir. Michael Anderson. Perf. Michael York and Jennie Agutter. MGM, 1976.
Logan's Run. MGM Television. Exec. producers Ivan Goff and Ben Roberts. Sept. 1977-Jan. 1978.
"*Logan's Run* and How It Was Filmed." *American Cinematographer* (June 1976): 630–31, 697.
Mellencamp, Patricia. "Prologue." *Logics of Television: Essays in Cultural Criticism*. London: BFI; Bloomington: Indiana UP, 1990. 1–13.
"Most Likely Hits Among New Fall TV Shows." <http://www.snowcrest.net/fox/logan/articles/enquirer/enquirer.JPG>
Muir, John Kenneth. "*Logan's Run*: The Series [1977]: A Retrospective." Accessed 30 Nov. 2010. <http://www.johnkennethmuir.com/JohnKennethMuirsRetroTVFile_LogansRun.html>
Nolan, William F. "Introduction, Logan: A Media History." *Logan: A Trilogy* [*Logan's Run, Logan's World, Logan's Search*]. Baltimore: Maclay, 1986.
Nolan, William F., and George Clayton Johnson. *Logan's Run*. New York: Dial, 1967.
Peary, Danny. "When Men and Machines Go Wrong: An Interview with Michael Crichton." *Omni's Screen Flights/Screen Fantasies: The Future According to Science Fiction Cinema*. Ed. Danny Peary. New York: Doubleday, 1984. 250–59.
Phillips, Mark, and Frank Garcia. *Science Fiction Television Series: Episode Guides, Histories, and Casts and Credits for 62 Prime Time Shows, 1959 through 1989*. Jefferson: McFarland, 1996.
"Photographing '*Logan's Run*." *American Cinematographer* (June 1976): 632–35, 664, 698–99.
Pierson, Michele. *Special Effects: Still in Search of Wonder*. New York: Columbia UP, 2002.
Robinson, Glen. "Mechanical Special Effects for 'Logan's Run.'" *American Cinematographer* (June 1976): 646–47, 649, 685.
Sobchack, Vivian. *Screening Space: The American Science Fiction Film*. New York: Ungar, 1987.
Stableford, Brian. "Overpopulation." *The Encylcopedia of Science Fiction*. Ed. John Clute and Peter Nicholls. London: Orbit, 1999. 901.

"3-D Pix Making a Comeback Via Laser Technology in 'Logan's Run.'" *Variety* (7 May 1975): 93.

Wilcox, Roger M. "The Highly Unofficial *Logan's Run* FAQ." Accessed 30 Nov. 2010. <http://www.stellar-database.com/non-ISDB/LogansRun.html>.

"William F. Nolan's Dark Universe." Accessed 30 Nov. 2010. <http://www.snowcrest.net/fox/loganbook/index.htm>.

5 *Stargate SG-1* and the Visualization of the Imagination

Sherryl Vint

Stargate SG-1 is arguably the most successful sf adaptation measured in terms of sheer magnitude: whereas Roland Emmerich's 1994 feature film had a marginal opening and was only moderately successful in gross sales, Brad Wright and Jonathan Glassner's television series ran successfully for ten years from 1997 to 2007 and has generated two further series, *Stargate: Atlantis* (2004–09) and *Stargate Universe* (2009–11), as well as two television films, *Stargate: The Ark of the Truth* (2008) and *Stargate Continuum* (2008), with talk of more to come. The success of *Stargate SG-1* is perhaps more surprising when one factors in its relative lack of critical acclaim. The film was disparaged by reviewers who saw in it only a sampling of earlier films, ranging from *2001* (1968) to the original *Star Wars* trilogy (1977–83), intercut with massive special effects sequences. Leonard Klady, writing for *Variety*, sums up this reaction when he acerbically concludes, "despite the ever-present, state-of-the-art technology, there's hardly a single indelible image in the course of two hours. One walks away uncertain whether there is a film called 'Stargate,' or if it was merely a dream composed of badly remembered movie clichés." The series too has won few awards, although it has generated a substantial fan base, and academic writing on the genre has generally neglected it, which is in marked contrast to the commentary on other roughly contemporary series such as the rebooted *Battlestar Galactica* (2003–09).[1]

To explain the "mystery" of *Stargate SG-1*'s success, then, we might ask why the combination of sf cliché with a preference for special effects over narrative proved such a successful formula for adaptation. The answer largely lies in the timing of *Stargate SG-1*'s release, coinciding as it did with a moment in which both television and film industries were undergoing significant changes. *Stargate SG-1* was well poised to capitalize on these shifts, and it thus became one of the most successful sf adaptations by virtue of being the right show for its time.

The franchise emerged when Hollywood cinema was moving toward the production of what Alison McMahan has termed the pataphysical film, a type more dependent on special effects than narrative, that in postmodern fashion privileges style over meaning and is interested in

68   Sherryl Vint

intertextuality or, more specifically, the promotion of ancillary products that increase a film's profit. "Few contemporary films are meant to be standalone texts," she argues, "but rather [are] intermediate texts, drawing meaning from and feeding meaning into other media forms such as commercials, print ads, television shows, previous and later films, comic books, games (both board and computer), novels and other books, magazines, newspapers, the web, paintings, music videos" (16). The *Stargate* franchise has mastered this market-driven context with its ever-expanding canon of texts.[2] More important, perhaps, the debut of *Stargate SG-1* coincided with a parallel shift in the television industry toward what John Ellis has called "the era of plenty" (*Seeing* 39)—that is, a context in which viewers can select programming tailored to their specific interests from many broadcast and cable stations. *Stargate SG-1* is one of the first sf series produced by a cable network (first Showtime and SciFi, later SciFi/Syfy only). Matt Hills and Glen Creeber refer to this context as TV III, stressing in addition to plenitude the expectation that television and other texts will be consumed across a variety of platforms (cellular phones, laptops, DVDs, broadcasts).[3] Competition for viewers in this context produces the phenomenon of "fiction-as-brand," which privileges the ready-made audiences for shows premised on characters "whose roles have been established elsewhere" (*Seeing* 167).

These changed regimes of production and consumption have served to reduce the gap between television and film texts that had previously been a major hurdle for adaptations. We might see the success of the *Stargate SG-1* adaptation, then, as a result of a production context in which the visual capacities of film and television began to converge, and the advent of a consumption context in which spectacle and intertextuality became privileged features.

BIG AND SMALL SCREENS: "CHILDREN OF THE GODS"

The feature-length series pilot "Children of the Gods" (27 July 1997) effectively moves the series from big-screen to small-screen aesthetics. Adaptation theory, largely focused on the long history of adaptation from print to screen, is often concerned with fidelity to the source and thus is anxious to understand the new text as a version of, commentary on, or analogue to the original.[4] More recent theory has questioned this privileging of the original, rejecting fidelity as a criterion of worth and the inherent privileging of print over visual texts that has often been the corollary.[5] Instead of comparing a work to its source text, the emphasis in postfidelity adaptation theory has fallen on noting medium specificities and analyzing each text as its own kind of original, drawing on the features of its medium. Before turning to a more detailed discussion of "Children of the Gods," it is necessary to distinguish film and television to note how this episode successfully mediates the transition between them and establishes the series as one well positioned to succeed in the context of TV III.

Ellis argues that film and television are differentiated by a number of factors related to both production and consumption. Cinema is an event in which viewers are compelled to give their full attention to a screen bigger than they are, which has a high degree of resolution, and on which a narrative is generally completed or closed within the run time. In contrast, television is consumed in the home, often interrupted by commercials and quotidian activities, is viewed on a smaller screen, and compels viewers to return regularly to watch an ongoing narrative. Thus, Ellis argues, whereas cinematic spectatorship is characterized by the gaze, television viewing is that of the glance. From these essential differences, he deduces a number of others in how each medium constructs its image and addresses its audience. Changes in both industries since Ellis formulated his ideas have significantly eroded this gap. For example, television viewers are no longer limited to viewing during the broadcast time but may instead use DVRs and watch at their leisure in conditions of concentrated spectatorship that strongly resemble those of cinematic viewing—all the more so given advances in consumer home electronics that encourage the approximation of big-screen sight and sound.[6] Similarly, the sale of DVDs of both film and television means that they are often watched in identical ways, including repeated viewing. The emergence in Hollywood of the blockbuster franchise, designed to produce sequels, also means that the formally closed nature of filmic texts (in contrast to television's open narratives) is no longer as dominant.

Conditions for consuming television and film have become more similar, and new technologies have also reduced the gap between their formal elements. New and less expensive CGI special effects have simultaneously engendered a return in film to what Tom Gunning has called the "cinema of attractions," with its emphasis on spectacle over narrative, and the introduction to television of a new regime of texts characterized by what John Caldwell has termed "televisuality." Indeed, televisuality and advances in home electronics are dialectically related as breakthroughs in one provoke interest in greater capacities in the other and vice versa. Jan Johnson-Smith argues that complex narrative dramas such as *Babylon 5* (1994–98), a series imagined as a novel for television and unfolding over a multiseason arc, were made possible by the new regimes of televisuality and the era of plenty, and that "watching television today is not inherently about distraction: it is about the choice to pay painstaking attention" (71). The success of *Stargate SG-1* can also be explained by this new context, but here the emphasis falls differently: instead of requiring a loyal audience that is compelled to view each episode faithfully so as not to become lost in the complex narrative, *Stargate SG-1* emphasizes the filmic quality of spectacle, focuses on bigger and better explosions, more and longer fire fights, and of course the spectacle of the stargate itself to capture the viewer's gaze and promote return viewing. Some additional differences between television and film spectatorship shape the discussion of adaptation, and "Children of the Gods" foregrounds them as it moves from a mostly filmic mode of visualization in the episode's first part (as the stargate is opened and a team returns to Abydos, the name given to the planet in the film) toward a more televisual mode in the latter part when the team visits Chulak, a planet invented for the show's new mythology. Evidence of visual echoes is apparent from the series' opening credits, which repeat the slow pan over details of an Egyptian mask that serves as a backdrop to the film's credits, but here the camera moves more quickly, not only because fewer names need to be shown, but also because the object itself has less intricate visual detail in the series. Director Emmerich's opening film sequence shifts from silver to red and blue hues as lighting captures the mask from many angles, while the series stays within tones of bronze and gold that are the colors of the mask itself. This palette reduction also recurs in the costuming of the guards, named Jaffa in the series. Ra's guards in the film have panels of vibrant reds, blues, and purples in their costumes, and some have earrings of brightly colored feathers. Their intricate helmets, modeled on the Egyptian gods Horus and Anubis, feature brightly glowing blue eyes and retract in a complicated pattern through a CGI effect. The series' Jaffa are clad in silver and gold uniforms that more closely suggest armor, and their snake-head helmets are mechanical and open clumsily.

The difference in scale that continues to differentiate film and television is evident in a number of ways. The film frequently evokes vast size, and many of the shots are either low angle to emphasize the grandeur of pyramids and alien spacecraft looming over the protagonists or high shots that show human figures dwarfed in a vast landscape. The series cannot reproduce this scale, but it works to reduce the gap between big and small screens in the way it films early scenes in the pilot. Many shots, especially in the gate room, repeat

Figure 5.1 The use of scale differentiates the film *Stargate* from its television adaptation. Copyright MGM.

the film's tendency to use high and low angles to convey a greater sense of scale, but long shots looking out across the landscape are avoided because the smaller scale would become too evident were the series to try to repeat such shots, many of which show lines of human figures back to the vanishing point. Selective CGI shots recall scenes from the film, such as the view out the door from the pyramid on Abydos of two obelisks or an extremely high shot of armed figures walking down its ramp. In others, lighting techniques convey a sense of the earlier scale, such as the group meal held in the center of the stargate chamber, which is lit as if by candlelight to explain why the chamber falls into darkness beyond the central pillars, suggesting that the room itself is much larger, as it is in the film.

The filming of the stargate is one of the most telling differences. This technology—both the diegetic stargate and the nondiegetic technology used to create the effect—is the real star of both film and series. In the film, the first opening of the stargate is an event: it is preceded by seismic activity (preserved in the pilot but then dropped in the series), and the fountain of water that spews from the front to mark the connection is matched by a funnel of water filmed as if emanating behind the gate (only the former was kept for the series). The gate emits a strong bright light from its center that connotes spiritual and otherworldly qualities and lights up the faces of the soldiers as they walk up the ramp. At the event horizon, the reflective surface produces an image of those who approach it, and its fluid properties are made spectacular as people cautiously dip their hands into the surface. Archaeologist Daniel Jackson (James Spader) pauses and gazes about in wonder, an emotion surely meant to be shared by the audience. His moment

Figure 5.2 The "event" of the stargate's opening in a first season episode of *Stargate SG-1*. Copyright Showtime.

of passing through the gate is a prolonged pause in which a close up shows his face hesitantly entering the surface and hovering half in and half out the other side, before the camera shifts quickly forward and cuts to a long tunnel sequence of rushing and twisting light, reminiscent of *2001*.[7]

In the "Children of the Gods" episode, this marvel associated with the image of the gate is preserved, particularly in a scene in which the camera moves slowly from the front of the open gate over its height, to track down to a position looking *through* the event horizon, level with Jack O'Neill's (Richard Dean Anderson) eyes as he tosses a Kleenex box through the wormhole as a message to Daniel Jackson (Michael Shanks). Quickly, however, the series establishes the shot of the gate opening as a normal part of each episode. When Carter (Amanda Tapping) pauses in wonder at the event horizon, O'Neill impatiently shoves her through. We might recall Ellis's argument that television uses rapid cuts much like film uses image detail, for *Stargate SG-1* represents the stargate in just this way. Whereas we see the stargate open twice in the film, it opens four times in the series' pilot alone, making up in one kind of excess (number) for what it cannot reproduce in another (detail). The stargate image also changes. The surface is far less reflective, we never see approaching figures in its surface, and the brightness of the light at its center is diminished from that presented by the film and more evenly distributed across the image surface. When the team arrives on Chulak, they exit the gate not to a room of great scope, as in the film and as implied by the pilot's representation of Abydos, but rather to a forest clearing surrounded by hills—the familiar landscape of British Columbia that will be featured in most of the rest of the series.

From its opening credits to the final shot, then, "Children of the Gods" moves from an aesthetic adapted from film toward one that demonstrates the series' distinctly televisual identity. High and low shots give way to dominant level shots, medium distances become the norm, and the emphasis is increasingly on the quick cuts of action sequences in the numerous firefights rather than on close-ups of exotic technology as in the film. The pilot also more fully establishes the series regulars and thus puts an emphasis on the audience's desire to regularly see these individuals, establishing a world rich enough to sustain multiple encounters rather than the single climax of the film. *Stargate SG-1* also broadens the cast to add new characters, like Samantha Carter, presumably to appeal to female viewers who had been established as genre fans via the *Star Trek* franchise; and Teal'c (Christopher Judge), an alien outsider figure who provides an estranged perspective, another well-established sf stereotype. Yet *Stargate SG-1* is most emphatically not *Star Trek*. It is interested in military adventure, not diplomacy, and its mythology is important only as a site of these adventures. The series revises and rewrites not only the film *Stargate* but also many other sf texts as needed to make the next adventure, and the next technology, ever more spectacular.

Lincoln Geraghty argues that in the era of technological plenty, television series must "adapt quickly to changing and diverse audience tastes" (96), and in this framework the formulaic qualities of *Stargate SG-1* have become an adaptive strength rather than a weakness. Thus M. Keith Booker describes the series as being "highly flexible, if sometimes unfocused" (178), an apt description of its process of adaptation that quickly departs from the mythology established by the film and allows maximum latitude to the series' writers. The movie's antagonist is an alien parasite who—in human-host form—was identified as the ancient Egyptian god Ra. He was ousted by a rebellion, but not before moving a population through the stargate to another planet where they continued to serve as his slaves who mined the mysterious metal from which the stargate is made. The series keeps this premise of hostile aliens, the Goa'ould, purporting to be gods, but quickly moves on from Egyptian to other pantheons, eventually establishing the premise of a group of System Lords at war with both one another and Earth, thus allowing for the dramatic defeat of archvillains at key series moments while not exhausting the store of antagonists. In later seasons, the premise expands to include other mythologies, including Roswell-like "grey" aliens as friendly aliens who have appeared as Norse gods; threatening mechanical replicators; and a two-season story arc drawing on Arthurian mythology; and a new religion of the Ori that is vaguely Christian in its stylization but resists directly collapsing Christianity with other myths. In later seasons, the enslaved Jaffa race become independent and shift from allies to a militant threat, allowing the reuse of the many sets of Goa'ould ships as well as furthering the military adventure thrust.[8]

Thanks to its long form, the series builds a more complex background world in which its stories take place, but unlike many other sf series, it does not depend on this vision of another or future world for viewer loyalty. *Stargate SG-1* is set in the present and implies its action is something that might be contemporary with viewers' lives, although the fact that it is an alternative present is made increasingly clear in post 9/11 episodes that begin to feature political characters. For example, "Smoke and Mirrors" (28 December 2002) involves the attempted assassination of presidential candidate Senator Kinsey, one of the key players in a series of episodes about the NID, a black-ops alternative to Stargate Command, in an ongoing narrative about appropriate military use of the technologies they find and appropriate relations with the civilizations they encounter. Yet the series does not offer a utopian or even coherent vision of this other world. Instead, the mythology is largely a premise to find new and more amazing weapons through the stargate, along with new and more threatening villains to defeat. The risk that *Stargate SG-1* runs in propelling its series through the logic of a film franchise is that each season, like each new sequel film, needs somehow to provide "more" than the last. The complexity of the series' world is located almost entirely in its visualization of technology, with hastily compiled explanations of new alien races used mainly as a pretext for the technology's existence.

REFLECTING ON SPECTACLE: "WORMHOLE X-TREME!" AND "HEROES"

As the series continued, it increasingly became clear that the stargate could no longer provide the same visual thrill it did in early episodes, so plots began to rely more on travel in ships. Huge, effects-driven space battles take the place of the frequent ground firefights that had previously served as episode beats. And in season 10 these two sites of spectacle were brought together with the introduction of the supergate, a huge stargate formed in space through which entire ships can travel. This drive to expand perhaps reaches its apex in "The Pegasus Project" (28 July 2006), a crossover episode with *Stargate Atlantis* that culminates in using the same explosion to destroy an Ori ship in our galaxy and a Wraith ship (the new enemy introduced in the spin-off) in the Pegasus galaxy via a supergate connecting the explosion.

Two episodes in which *Stargate SG-1* reflexively comments on its production of such spectacular images offer some insight into what is enabled and limited by this mode of televisuality that follows in the footsteps of the blockbuster sf film.[9] In "Wormhole X-Treme!" (8 September 2001), the show's hundredth episode, the team learns that a show is about to air on cable that uncannily echoes their exploits, and they go to investigate a possible security breach. The episode's plot centers on the show's creator, Martin Lloyd (Willie Garson), an alien who has lost his memory except in faint traces, and its resolution is that the US military decides the show presents an opportunity for plausible deniability rather than a security breach should information about the "real" stargate leak out. However, the function of this episode has little to do with plot, but rather, like the series as a whole, with the production of spectacle and in an ironic way. Throughout the episode, the SG-1 team and others comment frequently on the inadequacies of *Wormhole X-Treme!*, a tactic that functions dually to display their sense of humor about the limitations of the "real" show *Stargate SG-1* but also to highlight its strengths through contrast. For example, the show's version of O'Neill, Colonel Danning (Michael DeLuise), ends the episode in loving embrace with the beautiful alien-woman-of-the-week, presumably a comment on the amorous adventures of television's Captain Kirk. We watch the director, Peter Deluise, who is also the "real" director of this and many other *Stargate SG-1* episodes, staging this final scene, in which the bodies of dead aliens clutter the small stage and prevent Danning from easily sweeping the woman into his arms. When he complains, the director quickly decides upon a convention by which three shots from the ray gun will disintegrate bodies, thereby allowing those actors to exit the stage—exactly the convention used for *Stargate SG-1*'s zat guns.

Many other jokes about the limitations of producing a sf show with limited resources propel the episode. In the midst of a fight, Colonel Danning dramatically exclaims, "Actually, it does say colonel on my uniform," and then the actor, Nick Marlowe (Michael Deluise), breaks character to point out, "It doesn't say colonel anywhere on my uniform. Did anyone think of that?" Actor Yolanda Reece (Jill Teed)[10] queries the episode's premise about her character being "out of phase" with other matter—a recurring motif in *Stargate SG-1* episodes—wondering why her character does not then fall through the floor, an issue similarly unresolved in the "real" series. A production assistant going toward the set with a bowl of fruit is chastized for the fruit not looking "alien" enough and challenged, "Do you think aliens eat apples?" to which he replies, "Why not? They speak English." He is told to get some kiwis and paint them red, a low budget solution to the problem of making things look alien. In *Wormhole X-Treme!* Teal'c's character is replaced by a robot, Grell (Herbert Duncanson), thereby revealing the degree to which *Stargate SG-1*'s creators were thinking formulaically when they devised this character.

In these and other ways, this episode mocks both the typical plots and the typical visual elements of sf series, particularly the original *Star Trek* (1966-69). This episode is also willing to mock its own series as regards its implausible plots and scientific premises. Yet at the same time it works to differentiate *Stargate SG-1* from earlier sf shows precisely on the basis of its own more powerful visual qualities. In the episode's conclusion, Martin's alien companions (who have not suppressed their memories) arrive in their spaceship to take him away, interrupting the filming of a scene in *Wormhole X-Treme!* to which a spaceship effect will be added. As the "real" spaceship—that is, the special effects version that can be achieved by *Stargate SG-1* but which is beyond the reach of the production of *Wormhole X-Treme!*—arrives, the cast and crew stand and look up in awe, modeling in their response the kind of wonder that was modeled for the audience of the *Stargate* film by James Spader's Daniel Jackson. "We're going to win an Emmy for this," Martin whispers reverently, "Visual Effects category." Thus, *Wormhole X-Treme!* concludes by reinforcing the real strength of *Stargate SG-1*, its own ability to provide visual spectacle that rivals the big screen's.

This episode also underscores a confused diegesis that puts into suspension the category of the "real" when talking about the show (*Stargate SG-1*), the show-within-the-show (*Wormhole X-Treme!*), and notions of what is the "real" outside. Parts of the episode involve actors from the show-within-the-show breaking character, by asking for clarification of their characters' motivation, for example, or by complaining about casting and other production choices. Yet there is another level upon which they are acting as the actor characters; that is, the "real" actors hired by *Stargate SG-1* continue to play the actors of *Wormhole X-Treme!* portrayed in this episode, thus not breaking the illusion of the world of *Stargate SG-1* as real. There are moments, however, when the scene disrupts this notion of the "real" as well, when it is unclear whether the individual is speaking to us in character as a *Wormhole X-Treme!* actor or has fully broken the illusion of the diegesis and is speaking as a "real" actor. In one, Christian Bocher, playing (or perhaps not playing at this moment) actor Raymond Gunne explains to interviewers that he is playing Dr. Levant, and adds that this character was originally portrayed by James Spader. In another, production crew members explain to actor Nick Marlowe that what they are filming is not a "real show"—a point that begs the question of whether they explaining this to "real" actor Michael Deluise. "How can it not be a real show," he asks, "when we are filming it right now?" And although this scene and the entire episode are clearly played for humor, this moment raises the issue that, in some ways, *Wormhole X-Treme!* is just as "real" as *Stargate SG-1*.

This confusion of the diegetic with the nondiegetic is not of significant import when it comes to an episode like "Wormhole X-Treme!" but it does prove more problematic when *Stargate SG-1* takes a more serious turn, as in the two-part episode "Heroes" (3 and 10 February 2004). The premise for this episode is that a documentary film crew is going to "provide insight into what has really been going on" in the military installation, the quotidian life of Stargate Command (SGC) that is not captured by mission reports. Unlike "Wormhole X-Treme!" which pushes the show's diegesis in the direction of admitting that it is all a construction, "Heroes" attempts to push in the direction of collapsing the distance between a fictional representation of military service and the "reality" of such service as it has been captured by embedded journalists (keeping in mind that the documentary form is a representation of reality rather than the thing itself). The episode begins with its usual humorous tone, mocking the pretensions of director Emmett Bregman (Saul Rubinek) who insists on this endeavor's importance to future generations who will learn of the Stargate Program once it is declassified. Whereas Bregman refers to cinema verité, the show's regular characters behave more like they have been conscripted into a reality television program, either avoiding any appearance on camera or else creating false drama, as when Daniel runs to an office to get a fax "just to see if you would chase me." The episode switches between the style that has become typical of *Stargate SG-1* episodes (this one directed by one of the series' regular directors, Andy Mikita) and footage shot with a handheld camera that is shaky at times, badly framed, and grainy in resolution. The former footage remains within the show's diegesis, while the latter is the SGC as seen through the evident scripting and staging of Bregman's documentary.

This episode also comments on the ubiquity of action over substance that is typical of *Stargate SG-1*, although in this case characters insist that their "real" work is not sensationalist and consistently resent Bregman's attempts to add drama to his documentary using precisely the techniques regularly employed by the series. For example, while interviewing Carter, Bregman presses her to reveal that her feelings for O'Neill go beyond the professional, a recurrent series motif; but she resists this line of questioning, commenting instead on his professionalism, service to his team, and willingness to sacrifice himself for others. Similarly, Bregman tries to convince Daniel that his hours of footage of ancient ruins make for boring viewing and that, instead, while off world he should point his camera at the action and capture something of its drama for future generations. Daniel also resists, insisting that the greater purpose of the Stargate Program is the valuable knowledge about ancient and other cultures his work offers; however, regular viewers know the series rarely devotes much time to Daniel's work of translation and cultural exchange, and indeed the actor Michael Shanks was absent from the previous season because he felt his character was being underutilized as a nonsoldier who had nothing to do during the frequent firefights.[11]

The characters also comment on notions of truth and representation in a number of other ways in the episode, culminating in a question about the moral status of footage of someone's death that Daniel inadvertently catches on camera. A group of soldiers was under attack, and series regular Dr. Janet Fraiser (Teryl Rothery) assisted a wounded soldier who, it appears, will die before being transported back through the gate. Fearing the worst, the soldier begs Daniel to record a goodbye message to his pregnant wife, and Daniel complies; but while recording they come under fire again, and Dr. Fraiser is killed but the soldier is saved. Back at the SGC, Bregman intuits from everyone's charged emotions that something significant happened off world and demands that he be given the camera, a request that succeeds because the president, we are told, wants to ensure positive documentation of the Stargate Program exists to preserve his political reputation at some future date when the program goes public. Yet, when Bregman sees the footage, he chooses not to use it, feeling that it would be too exploitative to turn the personal moment of death into simply a recorded fact. Instead, he makes a film that heroically charts the honor and self-sacrifice that he suggests is the "truth" of the soldier's experience more than is the blood, pain, and fear of death the camera captured. The television audience sees the concluding scenes of this film, along with the series regulars who watch it in their briefing room; the film concludes with a montage, some of it historical, of footage that connects the activities of the SGC with those of American soldiers in a number of other wars (although notably not the Iraqi war) and a voice-over praising "all those willing to die for the preservation of our way of life" over a background of a proudly waving American flag. The episode concludes with a funeral for Fraiser in which, in lieu of a eulogy, Carter reads the list of names of all those who would not have been alive were it not for the service of Dr. Fraiser, thereby implying that the military is more about life than death.

This two-part episode was highly regarded by the fan community, garnering one of only two Hugo nominations the series received in the category of Best Dramatic Presentation.[12] Yet it is also a very anomalous episode for the series, condemning the very techniques of representation that are the grounds for the show's success and introducing an overly sentimental and earnest tone that is out of tune with the rest of the series. Indeed, in pushing toward collapsing the diegesis with reality instead of pushing it further toward artifice, "Heroes" at times threatens to give away the game, described by Jean Baudrillard in his essay "The Gulf War Did Not Take Place," that real service to the military is in many ways a performance, that wars are fought for reasons of representation and for motives other than those given as their cause. Indeed, the suddenly serious tone of "Heroes," combined with its unreflective praise of military service, in many ways makes this episode less truthful and less plausible than its most imaginative fancies. As Baudrillard reminds us, wars fought through representations and the construction of consent have a sinister aspect, which is an "assault on the reality principle" that belies the real damage of war through its "transformation of corpses into extras" (309) in a media performance. *Stargate SG-1*, with its interest in innocuous spectacle and its ever-changing cast of archvillains, is simply not equipped to comment visually or narratively on the reality of warfare. The series can tell us stories about the stories we tell ourselves, but it falters when it tries to tell us stories about our material world.

POSTMODERN SCIENCE FICTION: "200" AND "UNENDING"

In its blurring of reality and representation and its embrace of surface spectacle over cognitive substance, *Stargate SG-1* might best be understood in the context of postmodern sf. Baudrillard framed the Gulf War in another sort of adaptive context as "the decoy of the event" that replaced the real war, one readily embraced by the public because "we have neither the need of nor the taste for real drama or real war" (309). In their own ways both *Stargate* and *Stargate SG-1* share this postmodern sensibility of lacking "real drama," and herein we perhaps find the clue to the success of this adaptation. Robert Stam, rejecting the standard of fidelity to evaluate adaptation, understands texts as permanently open structures rather than fixed entities, ones that "fee[d] on and [are] fed into an infinitely permutating intertext, which is seen through ever-shifting grids of interpretation" (57). Thus, he argues, it is ultimately impossible to distinguish original from adaptation, as both are formed by multiple antecedents: all texts are "tissues of anonymous formulae, variations of those formulae, conscious and unconscious quotations, and conflations and inversions of other texts" (64). Similarly, Fredric Jameson argues that postmodernism is characterized by, among other things, heterogeneity without a center, a dead imitation of styles of the past rather than a reactivation of their emergent qualities as expressions of living, collective human endeavor. One of the aesthetic impulses of postmodernism is a shift away from parody, with its inherent notion of critique, and toward pastiche, an imitation "amputated of the satiric impulse, devoid of laughter and of any conviction that alongside the abnormal tongue you have momentarily borrowed, some healthy linguistic normality still exists" (17). Understanding *Stargate SG-1* as a postmodern, postfidelity adaptation can help explain why episodes such as "Heroes," with its sentimental angst about military service, can comfortably exist side-by-side with episodes such as "Wormhole X-Treme!" without any sense of contradiction troubling the audience.

The series' treatment of cliché is perhaps one of the best ways to grasp its qualities as postmodern pastiche. *Stargate SG-1* is, finally, an unashamedly derivative series. Even its most emotionally intense moments, such as Daniel's ascension at the end of season 6, cannot claim any originality: Sheridan (Bruce Boxleitner) similarly ascended at the end of *Babylon 5* and Sisko (Avery Brooks) joined the Prophets in an otherworldly realm at the end of *Star Trek: Deep Space Nine* (1993-99). Over the course of *Stargate SG-1*, the characters themselves comment on the often clichéd and implausible nature of their own lives/stories: in "The Other Guys" (2 August 2002), for example, O'Neill informs the scientists captured with SG-1 what to expect next, namely, "some over-dressed, over-the-top bad guy glides in gloating about what evil fate awaits us"; in "Fragile Balance" (20 June 2003) the team quickly accepts that a teenage boy purporting to be an age-regressed O'Neill is telling the truth, noting "stranger things have happened," before recalling examples from previous episodes; in "Inauguration" (24 February 2004) the president is almost convinced to disband the team based on evidence of the risk they pose, documented by recounting the plots of previous episodes[13] and noting the frequency with which team members have been taken over by aliens; in "Citizen Joe" (18 January 2005) a man experiencing O'Neill's life as dreams tries to turn these adventures into short stories and is rejected 326 times by various magazines, prompting a friend to comment "we are all just regurgitating the same ideas over and over, boiling them down to a great pot of mediocrity"; in "Arthur's Mantle" (24 February 2006) Mitchell (Ben Browder) becomes confused and needs the difference between alternative realities and alternate dimensions explained to him, and then concludes, "Hell, all I need is a good time-travelling adventure and I'll have hit the SG-1 trifecta"; in "The Shroud" (30 January 2007), Daniel argues to O'Neill that it is necessary they follow through on a plan because "the fate of the galaxy hangs in the balance," to which O'Neill replies, "that old chestnut"; and so on.

Thus, knowing they are repeating sf clichés becomes a part of the fun in *Stargate SG-1*, a quality that is nowhere more apparent than in the two-hundredth episode titled simply "200" (18 August 2006). Here Martin Lloyd returns to announce plans for a film adaptation of *Wormhole X-Treme!* and to seek input from the SG-1 team on the script. What follows is a series of scenes that switch from his discussion of the script to the regular cast performing the imagined film footage and back to their discussion, which dismisses the implausibility of most of these scenarios. Mitchell, for example, imagines the need to fight zombies produced by an alien device in the SGC, and it seems not that far a stretch to imagine this as a possible script rejected for the series itself: zombies are among the few clichés not visited. Martin proposes a scenario in which the team flees an overwhelming number of replicators, only to be cornered on a cliff overlooking a valley filled with Jaffa warriors, which quickly cuts to them walking safely out of the gate. Criticized by others for this too-convenient rescue, he insists just-in-time rescues are standard writing techniques, made palatable to the audience by "hang[ing] a lantern on it," that is, by having a character comment on how convenient it was, thus demonstrating the show's self-awareness. Various other in-jokes and parodies of similar sf shows ensue, including both *Star Trek* and *Farscape* (1999–2003), the previous show of series regulars Ben Browder and Claudia Black. All of this activity culminates in the wrap party for the two-hundredth episode of *Wormhole X-Treme*.

A number of *Wormhole X-Treme!* cast members are interviewed in the episode's final moments, most of these interviews making light of both shows. For example, Raymond Gunne/Dr. Levant comments on "not really leaving the show" but just gaining some distance to get back to the "craft" of acting, rather than always working with "people throwing paper-maché boulders at you," quickly adding that "both are good." Yet the episode ends on an oddly serious note, similar to the tone of "Heroes": Douglas Anders (Herbert Duncanson), the actor/character who plays Grell, looks solemnly into the camera and says, "Science fiction is an existential metaphor that allows us to tell stories about the human condition. Isaac Asimov once said that individual science fiction stories may seem as trivial as ever to the blinder critics and philosophers of today but the core of science fiction, its essence, has become critical to our salvation, if we are to be saved at all." Such a claim seems curious appended to a series that is perhaps better described by Booker's comment on contemporary series *Andromeda* (2000–05) that it "touches on topical issues, but these tend to be treated in rather banal and uncontroversial ways" (190). And indeed it is telling that this episode, although a fan favorite, was not the final episode of *Stargate SG-1*.

Like Martin's envisioned *Wormhole X-Treme!* movie, *Stargate SG-1* was premised more strongly on the axiom that "big explosions make good trailers, simple fact," than it was on any cognitive estrangement from our world or existential metaphors for the human condition. Jameson claims that in postmodernity we have lost the material world, which has been replaced by sheer images, and that we have lost history as a dimension of human collective action vital to a better future; instead, we have merely "a vast collection of images, a multitudinous photographic simulacrum" (18). *Stargate SG-1* finally might be seen as just such a collection of images. Its final episode, "Unending" (13 March 2007), takes place predominantly in a "time dilation field" in which the slower passage of time allows the crew to live approximately fifty years. During this time, Daniel supposedly studies and learns all the vast knowledge of the Asgard race, but when

Stargate SG-1 *and the Visualization of the Imagination* 81

time is reset in the episode's conclusion, he loses it again. Yet this loss does not matter because *Stargate SG-1* was never about these things in the first place: as the crew stand for one final walk up the ramp and into the stargate, they joke about all the things he has learned and forgotten, which they encapsulate in a series of clichés they exchange: "it's always darkest before the dawn," "life is too short," and the like. Such last lines are matchlessly suitable for this series, the sf of spectacle, a show that might be understood not merely as an adaptation of the film *Stargate* but, indeed, as an adaptation of the genre of sf itself, "an infinitely permutating intertext" (Stam 57) that transforms the genre's most well-worn conceits into the visual realm of spectacle.

NOTES

1. In contrast to this lack of critical acclaim, the series has been well regarded by the US military. The *SG-1* team purportedly works for the US Air Force, and real Air Force Chiefs of Staff have made cameo appearances, General Michel E. Ryan in "Prodigy" (2 Feb. 2001) and General John P. Jumper in "Lost City: Part 2" (19 Mar. 2004). As well, Richard Dean Anderson received the Special Air Force Salute, an award given to civilians.
2. Stargate has been less successful with other ancillary products. Hasbro produced action figures, and board games, trading cards, and comic books have all been successfully marketed. Two series of novelizations, one based on the film and another on the series, have met with less success. A number of digital games have been in development, but various financial problems have prevented their release. According to the DVD commentary on this episode and the Stargate Wiki (http://stargate.wikia.com/wiki/Avatar), CGI from one game was incorporated into the diegesis in the episode "Avatar" (13 Aug. 2004).
3. They link TV I to Ellis's era of "scarcity" when few stations broadcast programs and only during specific parts of the day and TV II to Ellis's era of "availability" in which a greater variety of programming times meant niche programming began to emerge.
4. See Wagner.
5. See Stam.
6. See Nelson.
7. It is almost impossible to chart the degree to which *Stargate*, both film and series, are derivative of other sf. The light from the stargate reminds one of *Close Encounters of the Third Kind* (1997); the shots of hands playing with the gate surface recall *The Abyss* (1989). The series draws frequently and overtly on other texts, reaching a kind of self-reflective point of absurdity in the episode "Citizen Joe" in which a man attempting to recount an SG-1 adventure to his friends about an asteroid about to strike Earth is interrupted and told, "I've seen the movie. It hit Paris." My reference to Kubrick's film is thus meant to convey the visual quality of these effects, not to contribute to a list of the many texts used to quilt together both film and series.
8. This reinvention of villains is perhaps at its most foolish when the Lucian Alliance of humans takes the form of drug dealers selling addictive corn, but the *Stargate Universe* series, with its darker and more "adult" tone, striving for something closer to the new *Battlestar Galactica*, has recently reinvented these antagonists with more menace.

9. It is a frequent complaint among sf fans that the genre is best defined as a "literature of ideas," and thus sf film is an inferior or inadequate form. One of the many ways that *Stargate SG-1* differs from other sf shows is in its impatience with technological rationales for its inventions and indeed its mocking of those interested in science as geeks in episodes like "The Other Guys." It is worth note that Roland Emmerich would direct many of the films that are staples of spectacle-with-sf-premise, such as *Independence Day* (1996), *Godzilla* (1998), *The Day After Tomorrow* (2004), and *2012* (2009).
10. In the later episode featuring these characters, "200," she comments that the show didn't seem to know what to do with her character, female scientist and soldier Stacy Monroe, a statement equally true of *Stargate SG-1*'s clumsy attempts to deal with Carter's gender. When Carter is introduced, she is characterized as a defensive "feminist," telling O'Neill, "Just because my reproductive organs are on the inside instead of the outside doesn't mean that I can't handle anything you can handle" ("Children of the Gods"). An alternative-world version of this character later considers this line and rejects it as ridiculous in the episode "Moebius Part II" (22 Feb. 2005). Various alien love interests are introduced for Carter, but none of these relationships ever progresses, and an ongoing thread about her and O'Neill's mutual attraction (upon which they cannot act, given their military relationship) persists throughout the series but is left ambiguously resolved. The series is praiseworthy for its refusal to sexualize Carter in costuming as happens with many women in sf series.
11. When Shanks returned in season 7, his character was given a more active role as a military presence based on his experience in the field, although he remained a civilian. In the final three seasons, he spends more time holding a gun than holding a reference book and in many ways becomes interchangeable with the military characters.
12. The film also received a nomination in this category. *Stargate SG-1* has never won a Hugo, although it did receive Saturn Awards for Best Syndicated/Cable Series in 1997, 2003, and 2004. The other episode to receive a Hugo nomination ("200") won a Constellation Award for best script.
13. This episode is one of many that cobble together footage from previous episodes under the rubric of a review or other premise. The series includes at least one such episode each season after season 3. This technique saves on the budget for new episodes, allows maximum use of battle-sequence footage, and demonstrates the degree to which imitation, even of itself, is embedded in the show's aesthetic.

WORKS CITED

Baudrillard, Jean. "The Gulf War Did Not Take Place." *Jean Baudrillard: Selected Writings*. 2nd ed. Ed. Mark Poster. Stanford: Stanford UP, 2001. 231–53.
Booker, M. Keith. *Science Fiction Television*. Westport: Praeger, 2004.
Caldwell, John Thorton. *Televisuality: Style, Crisis, and Authority in American Television*. New Brunswick: Rutgers UP, 1995.
Ellis, John. *Visible Fictions: Cinema, Television, Video*. Rev. ed. London: Routledge, 1992.
———. *Seeing Things: Television in the Age of Uncertainty*. London: I. B. Tauris, 2000.
Geraghty, Lincoln. *American Science Fiction Film and Television*. Oxford: Berg, 2009.

Gunning, Tom. "The Cinema of Attraction: Early Film, Its Spectator, and the Avant-Garde." *Film and Theory: An Anthology.* Ed. Robert Stam and Toby Miller. Blackwell, 2000. 229–35.

Hills, Matt, and Glen Creeber. "Editorial: TV III." *New Review of Film and Television Studies* 5.1 (Apr. 2007): 1–4

Jameson, Fredric. *Postmodernism, or the Cultural Logic of Late Capitalism.* Durham: Duke UP, 1990.

Johnson-Smith, Jan. *American Science Fiction TV: Star Trek, Stargate and Beyond.* Middletown: Wesleyan UP, 2005.

Klady, Leonard. "Stargate." *Variety* 24 Oct. 1994. Accessed 12 Dec. 2010. <http://www.variety.com/review/VE1117909323?refcatid=31>.

McMahan, Alison. *Films of Tim Burton: Animating Live Action in Contemporary Hollywood.* London: Continuum, 2005.

Nelson, Robin. "HBO Premium: Channelling Distinction through TV III." *New Review of Film and Television Studies* 5.1 (Apr. 2007): 25–40.

Stam, Robert. "Beyond Fidelity: The Dialogics of Adaptation." *Film Adaptation.* Ed. James Naremore. New Brunswick: Rutgers UP, 2000. 54–76.

Wagner, Geoffrey. *The Novel and the Cinema.* Rutherford: Fairleigh Dickinson UP, 1975.

6 She's Just a Girl
A Cyborg Passes in *The Sarah Conner Chronicles*

Lorrie Palmer

There is a moment in the feature film *Terminator 3: Rise of the Machines* (2003) in which a deadly female cyborg from the future is pulled over for speeding. She avoids a ticket when she glances at a Victoria's Secret billboard and quickly inflates her breasts just before the male police officer reaches the side of her stolen car. Not only does the television series *Terminator: The Sarah Connor Chronicles* (2008–09) revise the narrative timeline of the film series by eliding the events depicted in *T3*,[1] it also—and this is perhaps more significant—revises the traditional, gendered (and largely negative) depiction of female cyborgs in science fiction cinema. In its crossover from film to television and in the years since the first two *Terminator* films, *The Sarah Connor Chronicles* emerged onto a television landscape that had been altered by a new feminine warrior model in *Buffy the Vampire Slayer*—an alteration that inflects the new Sarah Connor (Lena Headey) character as well. Part of this revision can be seen in the shift from a male cyborg protector in *Terminator 2: Judgment Day* (1991) to a female (played by Summer Glau)[2] in the Fox series that foregrounds the heroism of women and teens (*without* Arnold Schwarzenegger) in its apocalyptic narrative. During the twenty-four-year time period between the first chapter of the *Terminator* film series (1984) and this twenty-first-century television adaptation, the (pop) cultural representation of female heroism has changed dramatically, inevitably influencing characterization as it moves across screen formats.

These intertextual references play across a media-literate audience that is now accustomed to slightly built, unapologetically feminine women taking over the job of butt kicking from the hypermuscular and excessively gendered stars of 1980s and 1990s cinema. The website *Rankopedia*, which assembles the votes of cinema and television fans for their twenty-five favorite science fiction/fantasy screen heroines, lists Buffy in the number one slot, followed by Ripley (#2) from the *Alien* series and Sarah Connor (#3) from *both* film and TV versions of that narrative.

The other characters in this ranking account for both movie and television representations, gathering together Xena, Princess Leia, Wonder Woman, Trinity, Dana Scully, Nyota Uhura, Jaime Summers, Caprica Six,

Figure 6.1 The cyborg Cameron (Summer Glau) and Sarah Connor (Lena Headey), absent the bodily brawn of 1980s movie heroines. Copyright Warner Bros. Television.

Captain Kathryn Janeway, Seven of Nine, Neytiri, Leeloo, and at #13, Summer Glau's cyborg from the *Sarah Connor Chronicles*.[3] These characters also literally visualize, over time, the ways in which a gendered and newly embodied female heroism has traveled across screens. The accretion of such evolving archetypes allows films and series, even as they develop, flourish, and disappear, to become part of the cultural imaginary. And this continuous development has enabled an ongoing sf franchise like *The Terminator* to redraw its own borders (and accommodate a changing audience) as it shifts media formats. The viewing practices of a fan culture that does not delineate between film and television characterizations further reveals the symbiotic link between the multiple screens across which it reads so fluidly. It is that increasingly conjoined relationship that *The Sarah Connor Chronicles* effectively taps in its adaptation of gender imagery.

In *Visible Fictions*, John Ellis resists previous assumptions about the interchangeability of film and television by suggesting that their cultural, aesthetic, and industrial aspects instead highlight a mutual "interdependence" (1). My analysis of the relationship between the cinematic and televisual versions of the *Terminator* saga starts from the position that these *interdependent* media have further evolved, stretching Ellis's description. His view of film as part of a network with "a mass of references" (31), for instance, similarly applies to television. His differentiation (50) of spectatorial *looking* between cinema (a gaze) and TV (a glance) is one that demarcates active versus passive viewing and that has been significantly revised by the newer technological delivery systems and intertextual narrative relays embedded in the contemporary television experience (for example, by TV on DVD and extended, character-driven story arcs on network television). In fact, I would argue that it is no longer the case that the "broadcast TV viewer is not engaged by TV representations to any great degree," any more than it is now true that the medium does not attract "telephiles to match the cinephiles who have seen everything and know the least inconsequential detail" of their onscreen favorites (Ellis 162). Certainly, the core viewer of *The Sarah Connor Chronicles* enters into a networked relationship with an *interdependent* mythology, characters, and performers, actively accumulated across narratives (both cinematic and serialized), as well as across myriad screen experiences. This interdependence between film and television marks the evolution of both on-screen characters and off-screen spectatorship, visibly adjusting the fictional images that bring them together. The current TV viewer is one who is plugged into a narrative and media multiverse and to a particular mode of looking (the intensified gaze, rather than the diverted glance), in all of which we can trace out the reformulated models of gendered heroism that have traveled from cinema to television.

"Come with me if you want to live." This line of dialogue first appeared in James Cameron's *The Terminator* (1984) and recurred in his sequel, *T2*. It is also spoken in *The Sarah Connor Chronicles* by the female cyborg Cameron to fifteen-year-old John Connor (Thomas Dekker), the future resistance leader in the war against the machines. As in *T2*, it signifies the moment when humans join forces with technological others. This trope of assimilation and resistance between humanity and technology forms the backbone of many sf narratives. But the male-to-female transition of the cyborg character heralds something more. I propose that we see it as a site of cultural interrogation that addresses what Susan George refers to as "our problematic attitude toward both gender and technology" (160). In her discussion of the sf series *Battlestar Galactica*, George notes that the show's multiple Number Six Cylons (Tricia Helfer), depicted both visually and behaviorally as "hypersexualized," function to "inhabit traditional feminine roles—as objects of man's desire and his helpmate in distress" (163). Drawing the line between the evil robot Maria in Fritz Lang's canonical sf film *Metropolis* (1927) and these television incarnations of AI femmes fatales, George describes another tendency in the genre: sf's "misogynistic tradition . . . of associating technology with women's bodies to represent the threat of unleashed female sexuality" (164). Similarly, Christine Cornea situates *Star Trek*'s Borg queen as a "femme fatale" (157) who deploys her "sexualized, female body" (158) in an effort to "seduce and tempt" the android Data (Brent Spiner) during her first appearance in the film *Star Trek: First Contact* (1997). But whereas the depiction of the Sixes in *Battlestar Galactica* and the female cyborg in *Star Trek* align largely with traditional cultural fears, *The Sarah Connor Chronicles* departs from that pattern. This sf convention of presenting female sexuality as analogous to threatening, embodied technology has increasingly been interrogated—and reconsidered—as it has passed from cinema to television. For example, the deadly, seductive Borg queen in *First Contact* was followed by the *Star Trek: Voyager* TV incarnation of Seven of Nine (Jeri Ryan) who, although presented in skin-tight costuming (frequently attributed to the network's pitch to *Trek*'s male demographic) was neither written nor performed as a character whose sexuality was deliberately mobilized for power. The televisual female cyborg lineage subsequently passes, in *The Sarah Connor Chronicles*, to Cameron who is younger, more physically kinetic, and more realistically (and modestly) attired than her antecedents. From the original male Terminator to these evolving female incarnations, gendered imagery has obviously moved across sf screens in a transformative guise.

In *Terminator 2*, Arnold Schwarzenegger's muscular cyborg (in a 1991 London screening I attended) roused audience cheers at the moment he emerged from the roadhouse, clad head-to-toe in fetishistic black leather and, accompanied by the aggressive sneer of George Thorogood and the Destroyer's bad-boy rock anthem "Bad to the Bone," swung his leg over a gleaming black Harley-Davidson "Fat Boy" motorcycle. His character was built on the performer's extratextual identity as a hypermasculine conflation of Conan the Barbarian and Mr. Universe. The extreme musculature of Schwarzenegger's body was highlighted through costuming (or the absence thereof), its hard contours visible through the leather trousers, tight T-shirts and, most overtly, the nudity of his cyborg character when it first materialized out of an electric blue sphere (in both *T1* and *T2*). Visually foregrounded in full-figure shots, his naked physique bulged with excessive and spectacular muscles; this image linked power to a specifically sexed body.

In *The Sarah Connor Chronicles*, on the other hand, Cameron, like Sarah, dresses without excess or spectacle, both of them usually wearing jeans or fatigue-style pants, T-shirts, jackets, and sturdy boots. Occasionally, and in keeping with current fashion trends, a few inches of midriff will show on the younger woman. Her femininity is never far from the surface—she wears light yet flattering makeup and lacy undergarments—but unlike the cyborg dominatrix in red leather with the inflatable breasts of *T3*, Cameron is not positioned as sexually threatening.[4] She frequently observes other girls her apparent "age" and copies their grooming, their poses, and their vernacular. Blending in provides her cover in her pose as John Connor's sister. In her discussion of *Buffy*, Sara Buttsworth similarly notes that the vampire slayer, "although 'sexy,' does not use her sexuality as an artifice or a weapon, nor does it detract from her ability as a warrior" (190). This characterization is certainly true for Cameron. The slayer and the cyborg, then, challenge these essentialist notions by *not* abandoning their femininity and, instead, by incorporating it into their full identities. Such deft incorporation of female complexity into active heroic characters is not simply a generic marker of recent sf (or localized in *Buffy* alone) but has become evident in a wide range of television narratives. Women with both understated and quite visible femininity operate throughout such series as *NCIS: Naval Criminal Investigative Service* (2003) in the figure of former Mossad Army and special-ops officer Ziva David (Cote de Pablo); or as NYPD homicide detective Kate Beckett (Stana Katic) in *Castle* (2009); as well as the multilingual spy Sydney Bristow (Jennifer Garner) in *Alias* (2001); the übercompetent fugitive Kate Austen (Evangeline Lilly) in *Lost* (2004); the former IRA bounty hunter and explosives expert Fiona Glenanne (Gabrielle Anwar) from *Burn Notice* (2007); and the latest incarnation of the fierce operative (Maggie Q) in *Nikita* (2010) who, like Sarah Connor, has moved from cinema to the small screen. As these characters have accumulated in such widely varied TV texts in the last decade, so have diverse alternatives to the highly masculinized movie heroines that preceded them.

When the *Chronicles* series begins, Cameron is presented as an outwardly typical high-school girl integrated into ordinary daily life, much like Linda Hamilton's Sarah Connor as we first see her in *The Terminator* (1984). The mainstream femininity of these characters—one a student, the other a waitress—allows them to travel from a culturally stable starting point to the divergent paths opened up in the move from cinema to television. The respective narrative arcs as well as the physical depiction of these female figures mirror that split. Whereas Hamilton's Sarah morphs into a steely, masculinized mental patient/guerilla fighter, the television heroines—Cameron and Headey's Sarah—are able to be formidable warriors without the visible gender coding of previous decades in which power was equated with bodily brawn. This shift is further emphasized by the *Chronicle*'s male-to-female substitution. Summer Glau is a trained ballet dancer, fine-boned and graceful. She is the physical, visual, and iconographic opposite of Arnold Schwarzenegger's weighty and slow-moving Terminator. And like Buffy, her gender is her camouflage because "nothing visibly distinguishes" her from other girls (Buttsworth 189). Buttsworth claims that although "this camouflage releases Buffy from some of the constraints which conventionally operate for the gendered warrior, it also reflects part of a broader Western tradition of the exclusion, and invisibility, of female heroism" (191). I would invert the "invisibility" Buttsworth describes here to instead underscore the characteristic of *lack* it implies about those who are doing the looking, and to further note that, for all its supposed negativity this perceptual disconnect has practical (and tactical) advantages for both Buffy and Cameron. When one perplexed, nearly bitten vampire victim who is saved in a dark alley by the slayer says, "But you're just a girl," we see why he didn't recognize her as dangerous, even after she verbally taunts the vampire away from him.[5]

Likewise, Sarah Connor offers a male antagonist freedom but only after she says, "If you can get past her," ("Heavy Metal" 1.4, airdate 2/4/08), nodding toward Cameron. So he takes one look at the pretty, dark-haired girl who has been standing silently at the periphery and assumes he can escape. This female cyborg, like the vampire slayer, wields her ability to pass as a normal teenage girl to help carry out her mission of protection. What Cameron does in this regard aligns with what Donna Haraway in "A Manifesto for Cyborgs" describes as "seizing the tools to mark the world that marked [her] as other" (217). The binaries that often operate around gender and that make such marking possible speak to the depiction of the film and television cyborgs (as well as to female warriors of any kind) under discussion here. The fact that Cameron is feminine without being *feminized* (which in academic and cultural discourse is often a buzzword for disempowerment) suggests that the gendered dualisms themselves offer an opportunity to dismantle the assumptions that often underscore the relative hierarchies between women, men, and technology in sf. Ironically, the act of dismantling includes the recuperation of difference. In both *The Sarah Connor Chronicles* and *Buffy the Vampire Slayer*, we see that looking like a girl has real, tangible value.

Difference, in terms of sf's shifting characterization of the female cyborg, is legible across the screens of cinema and television when one situates Summer Glau's portrayal against previous versions. Her cyborg may be seen as the most recent evolutionary point along a trajectory that encompasses Schwarzenegger's muscular enactment through *Star Trek*'s two central female Borg (and their progression from cinema to television as outlined above). Consequently, it is through such differences that this television adaptation of the *Terminator* film narrative accents the interdependence between fictional characters and the media formats that relay them along their journey. The internal logic of the sf genre resonates with equally mimetic components. Cameron's ability to "pass" as an ordinary teenager in human society runs parallel to what J. P. Telotte has noted is sf's thematic figuring of "human doubles" (4) and also to Haraway's model in which the cyborg is the "reproduction of the self from the reflection of the other" (191). Cromartie (Owain Yeoman), the first killer cyborg to arrive in *The Sarah Connor Chronicles*, is physically depicted much like the original Terminator assassin: big, male, muscular, and just as quickly *not* able to "pass" as human once his constructed outer surface begins to break down from repeated battles. In his first encounter with John (when he poses as a substitute teacher in the classroom), he calls roll and, upon identifying his target, gouges a hidden gun out of his metallic thigh and uses it to fire at the fleeing teenager. Nineteen witnesses later report "a shooter with some kind of robot leg" ("Pilot" 1.1) that they saw clearly as he walked past them. In *T2*, Sarah Connor warns Schwarzenegger's Terminator, as he patches up the bullet holes in his torso, "If you can't pass for human, you're no good to us." The doubling motif so prevalent in sf opens up a space for the representation of unstable constructions of gendered bodies. That same instability is mapped onto the male body of the television cyborg Cromartie in his first scene, while it also points to the denatured, incoherent male warrior's body as a reflection of permeable masculinity.

The *Sarah Connor Chronicles* further interrogates the coded cultural norms of gendered identity through its study of active heroines who operate without the overt cultural signifiers of muscularity that were previously visible in both the male and female characters in *T1* and *T2*. In the episode titled "Heavy Metal" (1.4, airdate 2/4/08), Cameron engages a T-888 (combat Terminator model), first in a moving cargo truck with Sarah at the wheel and then, after shoving him through the metal siding of the vehicle, on the street. In this scene, Cameron wears dark utilitarian clothing, as is her predominant style throughout the series. Her military-style black fatigues, dark T-shirt, and black jacket reveal no sign of any musculature. She uses a metal pipe, swinging it at the triple-8 until he goes face down on the pavement, and then she bends it around his head, calling for John to bring a tool box. As she straddles the larger cyborg, crouched over him with the pipe in her hands, we see the top edge of her blue satin bra above the neckline of her T-shirt. She flips open a switchblade to access the neural chip in the Terminator's head, then asks John to hand her a pair of pliers with which she extracts it. The male cyborg's eyes flash red then go dark. Throughout this sequence, in battle and in her deployment of technological knowledge, Cameron is visually depicted as powerful, subtly feminine, and without muscular display of any kind. That this rejection of physically masculinized female warriors occurs across the bodies of both a human and a nonhuman character (Cameron and Sarah Connor) emphasizes the series' break from its cinematic and temporal origins.

Figure 6.2 Cameron (Summer Glau) defeats a Terminator to protect the teenage John Connor. Copyright Warner Bros. Television.

When *T2* was released in 1991, commentators readily addressed the hardbody physique of Linda Hamilton, who had originated the role of Sarah Connor. The discourse that followed was often through a negative framework of gender difference and its visible lack in this character. Thomas B. Byers asserts that "Sarah's excesses at once expose her shortfall in masculinity and signal her 'betrayal' of maternity" (20), whereas Susan Jeffords dismisses her physicality altogether as not enough of a "machine body" to compete with the superior (and fatherly) Terminator; Sarah is merely a "brutish" unnatural mother (163). Elsewhere, Jeffrey A. Brown describes her "symbolic cross-dressing," which goes beyond costuming and weaponry to "the realm of the body itself" ("Gender and the Action Heroine" 59), and notes that she, like Ellen Ripley of the *Alien* films, performs masculinity "as figurative males" ("Gender, Sexuality, and Toughness" 49). Linda Hamilton's portrayal of Sarah Connor also prodded Yvonne Tasker to explore what she calls "musculinity" (149) and to remark that this kind of "phallic woman" is just a "male ruse" (139). In sf contexts, Christine Cornea writes that with these new female figures, "their heroic status was written upon their bodies" through that visible musculature and their demonstrated fighting prowess, thereby breaking with "the representations of women within the conventions of science fiction cinema" that had previously inclined toward evil serial villains in the 1930s and 1940s or love interests and sidekicks for the central male characters in the 1950s (160). When the action genre infuses sf (in these iconic characters), the body has typically been seen as driving the discourse.

In Sarah Connor's crossover to television sixteen years later, the earlier interpretations of Hamilton's portrayal of the character have undergone some changes. Call it revisionism, call it fictive memory, call it nostalgia, but those muscles that used to be described as gender parody, as male drag, as a disavowal of femininity, as misogynistic and ultimately patriarchal, now seem to signify something else, at least to a new batch of critical perspectives. In remarks from the *LA Times* to the *Boston Herald* to British feminists to online fan groups, the casting of English actress Lena Headey (who played "the formidable Spartan queen Gorgo" in the film adaptation of the graphic novel *300* [2006]), caused a stir (Smith). Descriptions of her physical portrayal of the Connor character call her "a twig of an action figure" as well as "a dangerous example of the growing acceptability of emaciation and anorexia," and the most hyperbolic commentary charges that "having a toothpick-thin, feeble-looking Sarah Connor is a crime against the iconography of the character; and presenting a clearly emaciated actress is a crime against women" (Smith). Yet in the course of the series she bloodies a large police officer's nose with her elbow (while handcuffed). She walks up to a man pointing a gun at her head and disarms him with a blinding combination of elbow, fist, and knee strikes while distracting him with the query, "Have you seen a little Dachshund puppy?" In addition, the character is depicted using quick-witted and decisive battle tactics, evident in a scene in which she pursues a running Terminator by riding up behind him on a motorcycle and then laying it over on its side and jumping off in time for it to sweep his feet out from under him, a feat she recreates in "Automatic for the People" (2.2, airdate 9/15/08) but without the bike, as she rolls her body under a running human male before disabling him with high-velocity blows. One of Headey's off-screen pursuits is boxing, so she might be a featherweight, but she knows how to sell a fight on-screen. Her five-feet, five-and-a-half-inch build, while not as small as Sarah Michelle Gellar's Buffy at five feet, two inches, is appropriate to the Sarah Connor persona. Years spent on the run, incarceration in a mental institution, and fighting to protect her son against relentless killing machines with no less than the future of humanity at stake have gradually given Sarah the fine edge of a lean, predatory, constantly wary heroine. In the series, Headey conveys this anxiety and motion by turning her head slightly off-center and sliding her eyes to one side while she is speaking to others, never holding her gaze in one place for very long. Her outward momentum always seems on the verge of bursting out. What the *New York Times* calls Headey's "mad, crazy blood love" (Bellafante n. pag.) for John helps explain why this Sarah *should* seem a little hungry. Looking at bodies without really seeing them may enable dramatic pronouncements, but it creates blind spots around what could be culturally and textually productive nuances.

Although much has been written about Sigourney Weaver's Ripley from the *Alien* films as a big-screen prototype of the 1980s and 1990s sf heroine, all gun wielding and flame throwing, her physicality is most frequently fused in the discourse with that of Hamilton's Sarah Connor. In this way, these two bodies have been undifferentiated and simultaneously assessed as "tooled-up and muscled-up" (Williams 170). However, closer consideration shows that Ripley is neither excessively muscular nor hyper-masculine; she is, in fact, tall (five feet, eleven inches), thin, and lanky. Christine Cornea describes the "masculine prowess" marked on the bodies of 1990s female sf heroines as part of their "ambivalent" gender characterizations (161). This analysis raises questions. Is their gender identity perceived as ambivalent by male viewers, female viewers, or the culture at large? Does the presence of culturally coded "masculine" characteristics like physical violence and gunplay *require* the visual component of muscles when enacted by females; and if so, does that ideologically denaturalize their actions, thus restoring a patriarchal context? What might the *absence* of female muscularity convey, especially when violence or gunplay or both happen without it? I would suggest that the real transgression in *The Sarah Connor Chronicles* (for both Sarah and Cameron) lies in the series' very *lack* of gender ambivalence. As Sarah muses in voice-over that there is no shelter except in "the love of family and the body God gave us" ("Gnothi Seauton" 1.2, airdate 1/14/08), she renaturalizes and even reclaims the female warrior body from its big-screen excesses, its visible (and cultural) signifiers of muscles, and from the *T2* Sarah's truncated personal relationships.

We can see another dimension of that reclamation project in the series' treatment of another cyborg. Much like the vampire, the cyborg figure suggests the dissolution of boundaries between human and nonhuman. According to Patricia Melzer, cultural anxieties about such transgression or boundary crossing figure in the sf genre as "representations of technology [that] are ... linked to metaphors of gender: hard, muscular, armed masculine bodies oppose fluid, morphing, unstable feminine forms" (128).[6] Examining sf cinema through the lens of cyborg feminism, Melzer notes that "both woman and machine undermine the white male subject position" (110), adding that "just as racial and gender passing are threatening to the social order, technological passing undermines hierarchies and denaturalizes categories by disclosing them as constructed" (124). This undermining points up another departure in *The Sarah Connor Chronicles* from the negative cinematic characterizations of gendered technologies that Melzer describes. Late in the series' second season we learn that a female liquid metal Terminator Catherine Weaver (played with chilly Scottish precision by Garbage lead singer, Shirley Manson) is, in fact, working to assist the resistance against Skynet. We might here recall Ellis's argument about the "gaze" as "the constitutive activity of cinema" (50), a notion that leads him to suggest that our attention is too diverted in the domestic space he associates with television to truly engage with it. Yet this particular cyborg[7] offers a site at which we might point to a crossover or development in how we look at the network of screens that Ellis associates with the media landscape. Our expectation, born of prior experiences with sf cinema, is that Weaver is resolutely Other, with antagonistic opposition written on her technological (and gendered) body. Indeed, the series seems to confirm this judgment in "Goodbye to All That" (2.5, airdate 10/6/08), when she takes the form of an attractive young woman in order to seduce a nuclear plant manager outside a local tavern and then transforms her tongue into a penetrative weapon, killing him. By intensifying our mode of looking across screens that themselves culminate in the myth-building that sf television is capable of, we once again read the familiar trope of the female cyborg as sexually threatening, only to see it then deconstructed as the narrative expands. Like Sarah Connor, Weaver has been raising a "son," John Henry (Garret Dillahunt), the reprogrammed Cromartie, to learn the value of human life and morality and to help turn back the ultimate corporate takeover: Skynet versus humanity. So it is a shock when she suddenly unfolds her body, creating a shield against cyborg fire that saves the lives of Sarah and John in the series finale ("Born to Run" 2.22, airdate 4/10/09). Until this point, she has passed as human in the diegetic world and as violently alien to the television viewer, since Robert Patrick's villainous T-1000 in *T2* previously established an oppositional relationship between metal (good) and liquid (bad). In this instance too, then, the television series creator Josh Friedman has pointedly shifted the *Terminator* mythos in an unexpected direction.

We might extend Telotte's description of sf's "generic emphasis on the constructed nature of all things, including human nature" (4) to both the *Terminator* films and *The Sarah Connor Chronicles* to include the gendered bodies both media narratives put on display. The extradiegetically constructed Schwarzenegger cyborg body, when compared to the likewise constructed Linda Hamilton body in *T2*, creates a metaphor not of gender but of power relations. Christine Cornea remarks that the big-screen Sarah Connor "is placed within a hierarchy of muscularity in which the Terminator's more bulky appearance signals his superior strength and importance" (163). Therefore, as Jeffords, Tasker, and Melzer all note—in works that explore sf cinema through politics, gender, and feminism—the original, big-screen Sarah Connor can be seen as ultimately trapped in a narrative "that strongly upholds patriarchal values" (Cornea 164). But what happens when you remove the muscles? What happens when a mother, a teenage boy, and a female cyborg that can pass as an ordinary high-school girl are positioned within a pop culture narrative as the last line of defense (and even offense) in a battle for the human race? How are we to read a female cyborg that is not hypersexualized as in conventional fashion, that does not symbolically represent the threat of female sexuality through the trope of technology? Sue Short, in *Cyborg Cinema and Contemporary Subjectivity*, describes the ultimately illogical "tendency to regard technology as intrinsically patriarchal" (96) and "women with agency" as "phallic imposters" (103). This dynamic is certainly apparent in the commentary about Hamilton's portrayal of the muscular film version of Sarah Connor and Sigourney Weaver's Ripley (despite, as noted above, the dissimilarity in their body types). So if we remove a constructed patriarchy from technological, gendered bodies, then *The Sarah Connor Chronicles'* Cameron is not the traditionally threatening female cyborg, especially as she carries the legacy of Buffy Summers in her physicality and through her intertextual casting. Likewise, the television characterization of Sarah Connor is not masculinized by excessive muscular display in order to play an active sf heroine. What we thus see is a recuperation of femininity by both characters that functions to undercut accusations of gender spectacle usually associated with the female heroines of 1980s and 1990s cinema.

Yet we should acknowledge that some cross-media spectacle persists in the depiction of the female cyborg. In *Star Trek: First Contact* (1996) we are introduced to the Borg queen (Alice Krige) when her torso, trailing a sinuous metal spine, is lowered onto her mechanical body.[8] Whether due simply to the striking visual impact of this image or to the lingering media impulse toward the fragmentation of the female body, Fox resurrected and exploited it in the marketing for *The Sarah Connor Chronicles*, depicting Summer Glau similarly. Additionally, print ads used by the network starkly contrasted to the television narrative. These glossy, high-tech images eroticized, even fetishized the female cyborg, going so far as to portray her sporting tight leather, deep cleavage, and a big gun—a look never effected in the series itself. Kevin Kelly reminds us that the "android babe with wires dangling from her severed torso isn't exactly a new image in science fiction" since Francis Ford Coppola used it in *Captain EO* (1986) and it appeared in Masamune Shirow's *Ghost in the Shell* manga (1989), as well as its animated adaptation by Mamoru Oshii in 1995. Christine Cornea contrasts the physiques of sf heroines in the 1990s against 1940s female comic book superheroes whose bodies were "codified as pleasingly sexual for the male viewer" (161), anticipating that targeted demographics for action-oriented texts still run headlong into ossified industrial memes. The cultural stereotypes that persist around masculinity and technology (as well as the predominantly male spectatorship that Hollywood insists on courting for its sf products) simply continue to emerge in the bodily displays that are the visual interface of gender and genre. To gaze at the depths beneath that ephemeral, manufactured surface is like seeing behind the curtain of the Great and Powerful Oz.

It is, in fact, worth noting that both seasons of *The Sarah Connor Chronicles* repeatedly reference *The Wonderful Wizard of Oz* (1900). The hybrid human/cyborg family adopts the surname Baum. They explain their lack of paper documentation by saying there was a tornado. Sarah repeatedly calls Cameron "Tin Man." She describes the pleasures of reading the book to her son when he was a child. And we might well recall how Dorothy Gale cut a swath through Oz, where no one believed that just a girl (and a highly feminine one at that) could eliminate their two most dreaded and powerful witch villains. For the Kansas schoolgirl, the slayer, and the cyborg of today, being underestimated has its advantages—advantages effectively mobilized in the transition from cinema to television by *The Sarah Connor Chronicles* with its refiguring of the human female warrior types as evading the expected cinematic category of the spectacle, as neither hypersexual nor overtly muscular. On the first day that John Connor and Cameron start at a new school, they walk past a painting on the building's outer wall that she pronounces "a trompe-l'œil fresco" ("The Turk" 1.3, airdate 1/21/08), just before she sets off the metal detectors at the front door. John explains to security that his sister has a metal plate in her skull, prompting the guard to wand the top of her head, which launches a chorus of mechanical beeps. Then, embodying a quite literal "trick of the eye," the cyborg passes. It is this series' key "trick" as well, its passing of this difficult gender figure across big and small screens that, in the process, lets us too see behind the curtain and into the textual relays between our sf media.

NOTES

1. One element from *Terminator 3* remains: Sarah Connor's eventual (and fatal) cancer, a plot point in the TV series when John, Sarah, and Cameron jump ahead in time from 1999 to 2007, skipping over Sarah's death. Cameron also informs John (in the series finale) that his mother has lost "11% of her mass in the last six weeks" (2.22, airdate 4/10/09).
2. Casting Glau brings the sci-fi TV fandom of *Firefly* (and its big-screen sequel *Serenity*, 2005) together with that of the *Terminator* film series, linking media, narrative, and characters through this spectatorship. Carol M. Dole notes "screenwriter Joss Whedon's contention that Hollywood 'hasn't

yet figured out how to harness' the use of women in action plots" and that "[s]creenwriter, Josh Friedman" also notes that "'the flinty heroines played by Sigourney Weaver and Linda Hamilton in the Alien and Terminator movies 'were well done, but they're outdated. [. . .] I want to see women respond to danger and solve problems differently than men'" (89). Whedon was the artistic force behind *Buffy the Vampire Slayer*, and Friedman later became the creator/producer of *Terminator: The Sarah Connor Chronicles* (2008).
3. These are Xena (TV, *Xena: Warrior Princess*, 1995); Princess Leia (*Star Wars*, 1977); Wonder Woman (TV, *The New Adventures of Wonder Woman*, 1975); Trinity (*The Matrix*, 1999); Dana Scully (TV, *The X-Files*, 1993); Nyota Uhura (TV, *Star Trek*, 1966); Jaime Summers (TV, *The Bionic Woman*, 1976); Caprica Six (TV, *Battlestar Galactica*, 2004); Capt. Kathryn Janeway and Seven of Nine (TV, *Star Trek: Voyager*, 1995); Neytiri (*Avatar*, 2009); and Leeloo (*The Fifth Element*, 1997); information from the *Rankopedia* website, <http://www.rankopedia.com/Favorite-Science-Fiction-/-Fantasy-screen-heroine/Step1/20448/.htm>. Accessed 5 Nov 2010.
4. The show occasionally hints that John might have feelings for Cameron, something Sarah seems uncomfortable contemplating. In "Allison from Palmdale," (2.4, airdate 9/29/08), Cameron discovers that her exterior design was modeled on a real-life freedom fighter whom future-John trusts implicitly (and possibly loves?). The final episode, "Born to Run" (2.22, airdate 4/10/09), has a topless Cameron instruct John to lie on top of her in order to cut through her organic tissue, reach in under her metal breastplate, and ascertain if her "chip" is functioning properly. John's demeanor during this procedure indicates arousal (a scene that most fans seemed to have found awkward and forced, according to online commentary). However, this aspect of the John-Cameron dynamic does echo Susan George's analysis of *Battlestar Galactica* in which she notes that it is the younger men (Helo, Gaius) who pursue relationships with female Cylons because they do not have the same suspicion toward technology as the previous generation (Col. Tigh, Admiral Adama) (George, 169).
5. In the *Chronicles* episode "The Demon Hand" (1.7, airdate 2/25/08), a woman who has just watched Cameron kick a grown man across a ballet studio is incredulous: "You're just a girl. How did you do that?"
6. This characterization is at the center of *Male Fantasies*, Klaus Theweleit's investigation of the masculinity of the German *Freikorps* (roughly 1914-45) to whom women represented a fluid, threatening force capable of engulfing the impenetrable warrior armor of manhood (1987).
7. Even during the early arc of this character when we assume she is evil, Manson, as Catherine Weaver, is costumed in a form-fitting but conservative, even severe wardrobe, diverging from the sexually suggestive female cyborg villain in earlier media texts, as described previously.
8. This effect reappears in the TV series *Star Trek: Voyager* episode (5.15, airdate 2/17/99) "Dark Frontier, Part 1" (1999) with Susanna Thompson in the role of the Borg queen.

WORKS CITED

Bellafante, Ginia. "Running and Fighting, All to Save Her Son." *New York Times* 12 Jan. 2008. Accessed 23 May 2008. <http://www.nytimes.com/2008/01/12/arts/television/12bell.html?ref=todayspaper>.
Brown, Jeffrey A. "Gender and the Action Heroine: Hardbodies and the *Point of No Return*." *Cinema Journal* 35.3 (1996): 52–71.

Brown, Jeffrey A. "Gender, Sexuality, and Toughness: The Bad Girls of Action Film and Comic Books." *Action Chicks: New Images of Tough Women in Popular Culture*. New York: Palgrave Macmillan, 2004. 47–74.
Buffy the Vampire Slayer. Creator Joss Whedon. Perf. Sarah Michelle Gellar, Alyson Hannigan, Nicholas Brendon. Twentieth Century-Fox Television, 1997–2003.
Buttsworth, Sara. "'Bite Me': *Buffy* and the Penetration of the Gendered Warrior-Hero." *Continuum: Journal of Media & Cultural Studies* 16.2 (2002): 185–99.
Byers, Thomas B. "Terminating the Postmodern: Masculinity and Pomophobia." *Modern Fiction Studies* 41.1 (1995): 5–33.
Cornea, Christine. *Science Fiction Cinema: Between Fantasy and Reality*. New Brunswick: Rutgers UP, 2007.
Dole, Carol M. "The Gun and the Badge: Hollywood and the Female Lawman." *Reel Knockouts: Violent Women in the Movies*. Ed. Martha McCaughey and Neal King. Austin: U of Texas P, 2001. 78–105.
Ellis, John. *Visible Fictions: Cinema, Television, Video*. Rev. ed. London: Routledge, 1992.
George, Susan. "Fraking Machines: Desire, Gender and the (Post) Human Condition in *Battlestar Galactica*." *The Essential Science Fiction Television Reader*. Ed. J. P. Telotte. Lexington: UP of Kentucky, 2008. 159–75.
Haraway, Donna. "A Manifesto for Cyborgs: Science, Technology, and Socialist Feminism in the 1980s." *Feminism/Postmodernism*. Ed. Linda J. Nicholson. New York: Routledge, 1990. 190–233.
Inness, Sherrie. "'Boxing Gloves and Bustiers': New Images of Tough Women." *Action Chicks: New Images of Tough Women in Popular Culture*. New York: Palgrave Macmillan, 2004. 1–17.
Jeffords, Susan. *Hard Bodies: Hollywood Masculinity in the Reagan Era*. New Brunswick: Rutgers UP, 1994.
Kelly, Kevin. "Terminator, The Queen Borg in The Shell Chronicles." *io9*. Accessed 3 Oct. 2010. <http://io9.com/341381/terminator-the-queen-borg-in-the-shell-chronicles>.
Melzer, Patricia. *Science Fiction and Feminist Thought*. Austin: U of Texas P, 2006.
Short, Sue. *Cyborg Cinema and Contemporary Subjectivity*. Hampshire: Palgrave Macmillan, 2005.
Smith, David. "'Weedy' Action Heroine Under Fire." *Observer* 20 Jan. 2008. Accessed 16 July 2008. <http://www.guardian.co.uk/media/2008/jan/20/television.gender/print>.
Star Trek: First Contact. Dir. Jonathan Frakes. Perf. Patrick Steward, Brent Spiner. Paramount, 1996.
Tasker, Yvonne. *Spectacular Bodies: Gender, Genre and the Action Cinema*. London: Routledge, 1993.
Telotte, J.P. *Replications: A Robotic History of the Science Fiction Film*. Urbana: University of Illinois Press, 1995.
Telotte, J.P. "The Trajectory of Science Fiction Television." *The Essential Science Fiction Television Reader*. Ed. J. P. Telotte. Lexington: UP of Kentucky, 2008. 1–34.
Terminator, The. Dir. James Cameron. Perf. Linda Hamilton, Arnold Schwarzenegger, Michael Biehn. Hemdale Film, 1984.
Terminator 2: Judgment Day. Dir. James Cameron. Perf. Linda Hamilton, Arnold Schwarzenegger, Edward Furlong. Carolco Pictures, 1991.
Terminator 3: The Rise of the Machines. Dir. Jonathan Mostow. Perf. Arnold Schwarzenegger, Nick Stahl, Claire Danes. Kristanna Loken. C-2 Pictures, 2003.
Terminator: The Sarah Connor Chronicles. Creator Josh Friedman. Perf. Lena Headey, Summer Glau, Thomas Dekker. Warner Home Video, 2008-09.

Theweleit, Klaus. *Male Fantasies, Volume 1: Woman, Floods, Bodies, History.* Minneapolis: University of Minnesota Press, 1987.

Williams, Linda Ruth. "Ready for Action: *G.I. Jane*, Demi Moore's Body and the Female Combat Movie." *Action and Adventure Cinema.* Ed. Yvonne Tasker. London: Routledge, 2004. 169–85.

Part III
Case Studies

Television to Film

7 *Star Trek* and the Birth of a Film Franchise

M. Keith Booker

As the most extensive and important multimedia franchise in the history of science fiction, the *Star Trek* empire provides some especially interesting examples of the issues involved in translating content from one medium to another. With the original television series, broadcast on NBC from 1966 to 1969, as the founding text, the franchise grew through the 1970s, when the original series both went into syndication and underwent its first adaptation into another medium when converted into an animated series (*Star Trek: The Animated Series*, 1973–74), with most of the original cast providing the voices for their increasingly iconic characters. From there, talk of reviving the original series on a new television network to be founded by Paramount Studios gradually morphed into plans for a *Star Trek* feature film from Paramount, especially after the huge box-office success of the original *Star Wars* in 1977. Those plans eventually led to the release of *Star Trek: The Motion Picture* in 1979. Much maligned by critics (and many fans of the original series), this film was nevertheless a commercial success that led to the release in 1982 of a much-admired sequel, *Star Trek II: The Wrath of Khan*, then further sequels (still featuring the original series cast) in 1984, 1986, 1989, and 1991. By the time *Star Trek VI: The Undiscovered Country* was released in 1991, the *Star Trek* film sequence was clearly losing steam, although the franchise had returned to television with the premiere of *Star Trek: The Next Generation* (1987), featuring a new cast and an overall look and feel that clearly identified the series as inspired more directly by the films than by the original television series. Meanwhile, the success of this new series suggested that the *Star Trek* franchise was still far from morbidity.

Other *Star Trek* television series followed, and *Star Trek* thus became the first and only American television series to spawn a sequence of feature films that then inspired an additional sequence of television series. More films would follow, shifting to the *Next Generation* cast, along with the additional series, so that a cross-fertilization between *Star Trek* films and *Star Trek* television series became an ongoing and extremely complex intermedia conversation, augmented by the ongoing production of *Star Trek* fiction, comic books, and games, as well as an extensive online presence and various aspects of the legendary *Star Trek* fan culture.[1]

Star Trek thus offers an especially telling array of materials with which to examine the differences among different media as vehicles for the transmission of largely similar science-fiction content. As a first step toward unpacking that material, I want to focus on the relationship between the original television series and the first two feature films. These films, I would argue, are both direct adaptations of the original television series, whereas the third film (which directly continues the plot of the second) marks a point at which the film series had taken on a life of its own, complicating any discussion of the phenomenon of adaptation. I am particularly concerned with suggesting some of the reasons why the first *Star Trek* film is generally considered an unsuccessful adaptation of the television series whereas the second film is widely regarded as a successful one. I believe the most important of these reasons is that the original series and second adaptation belong essentially to the same genre (adventure/romance), whereas the first adaptation is more properly sf, at least when viewed through the lens of Darko Suvin's famous delineation of sf as a genre of "cognitive estrangement," a resource that gives the genre special utopian potential.

I will return to this generic argument (and the associated topic of utopianism) later, but first we might note some of the other reasons why the first film is considered inferior to the second as an adaptation of the original series. For example, John Scalzi sums up many criticisms of the first film when he notes that it "stank" because "while the film *did* replicate elements of the TV show, it replicated the *worst* aspects, including a plodding, obvious script, a boring 'villain' . . . and overwrought acting" (116). Although Scalzi does not say what he believes the series' best aspects were, I think these would surely involve the strong bonds of camaraderie among the members of the *Enterprise* crew, especially the three central figures of the dashing Captain James T. Kirk (William Shatner), the half-Vulcan science officer Mr. Spock (Leonard Nimoy), and the irascible ship's doctor Leonard McCoy (DeForest Kelley). These bonds are alluded to in *The Motion Picture* but do not play a major role; the highly individualized personalities of these iconic characters, developed over dozens of television episodes, are largely beside the point in the film, in which Decker emerges as the most important character, even though he is fulfilling the role of the famously expendable redshirts of the original series. And his absorption into the *Voyager* entity at the end of the film carries little emotional clout—as opposed, for example, to the emotionally powerful sacrifice of Spock at the end of the second film.

John Ellis's comments in *Visible Fictions* on the differences between television and film as media are also helpful for describing the success of the second adaptation relative to the first. Many of Ellis's comments focus on technological differences between television and film, including the fact that film images in a theater is larger than television's and that film images are generally of higher quality. Moreover, he argues that film places much more emphasis on the image itself than does television. Thus, a key difference for Ellis is that "contrasting with cinema's profusion (and sometimes excess) of detail, broadcast TV's image is stripped-down, lacking in detail" (130). This image difference is particularly crucial to the first film adaptation of *Star Trek*. The plot is based on a treatment by sf novelist Alan Dean Foster, who had become extensively involved with the *Star Trek* franchise in the 1970s by writing a series of novelizations of *Star Trek: The Animated Series*. However, the plot involves a number of "big" sf ideas (such as artificial intelligence and encounters with genuinely "other" intelligences), is fairly pedestrian, and might well have served for an episode of the original series. Moreover, the film's screenplay was written by *Star Trek* creator Gene Roddenberry, so one might expect it to adhere closely to the original series' parameters. The film also features many of the same characters (played by the same actors) as the television series; indeed, much of the film's first half involves gathering together the original key members of the *Enterprise* crew, thematically echoing the filmmakers' own casting process.

The casting, in fact, is one of the key ways this film strives for fidelity with the original series. In addition to the three central characters, secondary characters from the series, such as Sulu (George Takei), Chekhov (Walter Koenig), Uhura (Nichelle Nichols), and Nurse (now Doctor) Chapel (Majel Barrett) are present, although they have little to do and largely serve as window dressing designed to try to solidify the continuity between the series and the film. Even the chief engineer, Mr. Scott (James Doohan), who was more important in the series, is relatively unimportant in this film, which emphasizes only the three central original characters of Kirk, Spock, and McCoy.

This casting continuity enriches and personalizes the link between the universes in which both works are set, a twenty-third-century future in which the social, economic, and political problems of the twentieth century have been overcome, at least on Earth, which has created an essentially utopian (and socialist) global society that is the centerpiece of a benevolent "United Federation of Planets" that encompasses much of the galaxy, reaching out to new worlds with its message of tolerance, peace, and interplanetary cooperation. Crucial to this utopian vision of the future is a widespread affluence that has been created by highly advanced technologies, especially the replicators that are able to rearrange atoms to produce virtually any desired commodity from almost any raw material. Meanwhile, crucial to the texture of the series (and to the operations of the Federation) are the technologies that facilitate intergalactic travel and exploration: starships equipped with "warp drives" that enable faster-than-light travel, advanced communication devices like the tricorder, and the iconic transporters that are central to this future world. Also important is advanced weaponry such as phasers and photon torpedoes, despite the fact that the Federation is ostensibly devoted to peaceful exploration and to understanding and mutual respect among different civilizations and intelligent species.

Star Trek: The Motion Picture features all of these technologies but with some minor updates, which makes sense given that only a few years have passed between the narratives of the two works. However, the technologies are represented very differently in the film and in ways that speak directly to Ellis's argument about the different role of the image in film. Thus, the film features these key technologies and they now *look* more impressive, which in fact directly thematizes these differences by stipulating that the *Enterprise* (surely the most important single piece of technology in the *Star Trek* universe) has just spent eighteen months being extensively redesigned and refurbished, providing an explanation for the fact that the ship looks so much better (especially in the interior shots) than in the series.

This difference in the quality of the images of technology between the original series and the first *Star Trek* film is no doubt partly a matter of the difference in media, much along the lines indicated by Ellis. However, it is also important to note that when *The Motion Picture* was released in 1979, the sf film was itself in the midst of a technological revolution that had been triggered by the unprecedented sophistication of the special effects for *Star Wars* just two years earlier. Thus, much of the image making employed in the first *Star Trek* film would have been unavailable to filmmakers a decade earlier; it might also be noted that less than a decade later, when the *Star Trek* franchise returned to television with *Star Trek: The Next Generation*, the overall look of that new series, thanks to great advances in television-effects work, had more in common with the films than with the original series. Moreover, the spruced-up technologies represented within the first *Star Trek* film echo the recent improvements in the filmmaking process itself, the updating of the technologies available to the crew of the *Enterprise* serving as a stand-in for the improved technologies available to the makers of the film as opposed to those available to the makers of the original series.

The Motion Picture, no matter how we gauge its level of achievement, exemplifies the way in which sf films are often as much about their own real-world technological resources as they are about the fictional technologies that exist within the world of the film's narrative. It may thus be no surprise that the film, while it represents essentially the same fictional technologies as the original series, reflects a different attitude toward these technologies. The series, which uses only rudimentary special-effects technologies, seems to take its fictional technologies almost for granted. No one in the series is amazed or impressed that the *Enterprise* can travel faster than light or that transporters can instantly beam them from the ship to the surface of a nearby planet: such things are simply a normal part of everyday experience, though some characters (most notably Dr. McCoy) sometimes express discomfort with these technologies. And the series seems to expect viewers to suspend their disbelief and accept these technologies as well.

The characters in the film similarly accept the technologies that surround them, though one of the ways in which the film thematizes its differences from the series is in Captain Kirk's struggle to familiarize himself with the newly refurbished *Enterprise*, as he was not involved in refitting the ship. Meanwhile, thanks to the vastly improved special-effects technologies of the film, the advanced technologies that populate the world of *Star Trek* can be represented much more richly than in the television series. In fact, one of the most striking aspects of *The Motion Picture* is the fascinated, almost loving way in which it represents technology. Ships moving through space often seem to be moving in slow motion, which has the effect of suggesting weightlessness and also allows the camera to linger on various technological devices, showing a sense of wonder with regard to these technologies that is almost entirely missing in the original television series.

Creating this attitude, of course, is more feasible in film than in television, simply because the superior image-making technologies available to big-budget efforts like *The Motion Picture* make it possible to represent fictional advanced technologies in a more detailed and admiring way with the camera lingering lovingly on specific devices (especially the *Enterprise* itself), accompanied by a quasi-classical soundtrack that reinforces the notion of their grandeur. However, it is possible, even within the medium of sf film, to treat advanced technologies either as amazing or simply as ordinary parts of the world. We might recall, for example, how the original *Star Wars*, which clearly influenced the first *Star Trek* film, often seems fascinated with its own *special effects* technologies, but presents its *fictional* technologies in a rather blasé fashion that makes it clear that everyone in the filmic world takes these technologies for granted. No one in the original series seems amazed by the technologies available to them, nor does the camera treat them as anything more than routine.

Indeed, in scenes such as the leisurely approach of the shuttlecraft bearing Kirk and Scott to the refitted *Enterprise*, *The Motion Picture* does not resemble *Star Wars* so much as *2001: A Space Odyssey* (1968), which similarly contains numerous shots of advanced technologies that seem designed to make them appear wondrous and strange.[2] The *Star Trek* film also creates a similar effect with its representation of the huge and powerful alien entity that approaches Earth, threatening to destroy the planet. Of course, this entity turns out to be a *Voyager* space probe (two real versions of which had been launched in 1977 and were thus still topical at the time of the film), seriously souped up by the denizens of a "machine planet" and now returning to Earth on a quasi-spiritual quest to find its maker. Having achieved consciousness in the form of the pure logic Spock has long advocated, the machine finds this logic empty; and to evolve further, it seeks a higher meaning—one that it finds by joining with Commander Decker (Stephen Collins) of the *Enterprise*, thus adding a touch of human emotion to its logical matrix (and thus teaching Spock a valuable lesson as well).[3]

One of the ironies of *The Motion Picture* is that the basic premise of the film suggests the superior value of human interrelationships over machine logic, yet the strongest human emotion in the film seems to be Kirk's love for his ship, the famous camaraderie that binds the crew in the original series being almost absent in this first film adaptation.

It is in this context that Ellis's comments on the "centring" of broadcast television on domestic situations and particularly on families seems especially relevant (136). This focus, for Ellis, helps to establish an important bond between a television series and its viewers who feel that they are somehow sharing in the intimacy of its domestic focus. At first glance, the original *Star Trek* series might seem an exception to this rule as it takes place in the far-flung reaches of the galaxy rather than in the home, and families are notably absent. However, the *Enterprise* crew, as critics have often noted, functions as a sort of surrogate family with the *Enterprise* their surrogate home. By remodeling this home so as to be almost unrecognizable, and by dropping the emphasis on the interpersonal bonds among the main crewmembers, *The Motion Picture* lost much of its connection with fans of the series, giving up crucial cultural capital in the process. In fact, *The Motion Picture*'s stronger emphasis on images of technology obscures its human relations, oddly (and surely inadvertently) echoing one of the main themes of the film, in which *Voyager*, having achieved consciousness and essentially become "alive," finds its life empty precisely because it lacks meaningful connections with others.

Of course, sf has long been regarded as a genre that emphasizes thought over emotion, along the lines of Suvin's seminal suggestion that the genre's key defining characteristic is its central reliance on "cognitive estrangement" to achieve its effects. Writing specifically about literature, but in a way that has since been widely applied to all sf, he sees the genre placing its audience in a world different from their own in ways that stimulate thought about the nature of those differences and cause them to view their own world afresh. The key markers of those differences are what, following Ernst Bloch, he calls "novums," technological or other innovations that have either caused the world of the fiction to be different from our own or that suggest that difference. Suvin finds important utopian energies in these novums, which suggest the possibility of fundamental historical change in ways that encourage us to imagine (and to hope) that our own world might someday be better than it currently is. The *Enterprise* and the other "tame" technological devices deployed by the Federation serve as novums that mark the vast technological progress that separates the world of *Star Trek* from our own world, progress that has also extended into the social, political, and economic realms and establishes the basic premise of the franchise in which advanced technology has created a utopian future. Indeed, *Star Trek: The Motion Picture* ends on just such a utopian note, as Kirk commands the *Enterprise* to head "out there" in search of the new, of what Bloch would call the "not yet," followed by the on-screen notation that "the human adventure is just beginning."

Yet however much this ending might seem consistent with the series' ideology, the emphasis on the image in the lingering shots of technological devices that mark the *Star Trek* film is basically cinematic. The original *Star Trek* television series merely stipulated the utopian consequences of its high-tech equipment, without evoking the power implicit in its relatively impoverished images of that equipment. In Ellis's terms, the contrast between the original *Star Trek* television series and the first *Star Trek* film is absolutely paradigmatic of the difference between film and television as media. One reason, then, for the failure of the first film to seem an satisfying adaptation is that it relies so heavily on the resources of film, while the series is so thoroughly televisual.

However, I would also argue for a second (and possibly more important) reason for the failure of the first *Star Trek* film as adaptation, one based on the concept of cognitive estrangement. Viewed strictly through this concept as a marker of the effectiveness of sf works, we might see *The Motion Picture* as *superior* to the original series because it does seek to create a sense of potentially unsettling strangeness that could cause viewers to reconsider their views about the world and especially about the role of technology in that world. However, as I have previously argued, the original series produces little in the way of cognitive estrangement; it actually "did very little to produce the kind of troubling defamiliarization that might genuinely lead to the reconsideration of received ideas" (Booker, *Strange TV* 71). In fact, the original series is basically comforting, assuring viewers that technology will solve their problems, virtually without human intervention, whereas *The Motion Picture*, particularly in its figuration of the *Voyager* entity, acknowledges that technology can cut both ways, warning specifically of the possible dangers of technology proceeding under its own steam.

I am, in fact, tempted to posit at this point that the original *Star Trek* series is in some ways not sf at all, but rather closer to what Suvin would consider fantasy, a genre he sees as relying more on emotion than cognition. However, in this case a better designation might be, as we earlier noted, "adventure/romance."[4] Of course, the boundary between sf and adventure/romance is surely not absolute, nor is the question of whether a given work does or does not produce cognitive estrangement in its audiences one that can be simply answered in the negative or affirmative. These matters reside along a continuum, on which *Star Trek: The Motion Picture* and *2001: A Space Odyssey* would exist nearer the "science fiction" pole as works that rely on cognitive estrangement as their central strategies, whereas the original *Star Trek* series and *Star Wars* would reside nearer the "fantasy" or "adventure/romance" pole as works that create worlds of wonder and adventure that can be enjoyed by mere suspension of disbelief and that invite emotional, rather than cognitive, engagement. Following Suvin's emphasis on the utopian potential of sf, we might also distinguish these poles in terms of their different utopian energies, with sf encouraging genuine forward thinking and fantasy or adventure/romance encouraging a wish for a different future, but seldom encouraging genuine thought about what that future might entail or how it might be achieved.

What is at stake here is a distinction between different forms of utopian thinking first articulated by Friedrich Engels when he contrasted "scientific" socialism as a good form of utopianism and "utopian" socialism as a bad form because it is ahistorical and escapist (Marx and Engels 683–717). The distinction, essentially, is between bad utopian visions that lead to escapism, quietism, and ultimate acceptance of the status quo, and good utopian visions that might lead to a transformation of the existing social order. Working in this same tradition, Terry Eagleton argues that American utopianism tends toward a "bad" utopianism, or utopianism in the "subjunctive mood." Rather than providing a model for building, or at least imagining, a better future, it describes a future that is disengaged from the present because it can never be reached. This bad utopianism "grabs instantly for a future, projecting itself by an act of will or imagination beyond the compromised political structures of the present. By failing to attend to those forces or fault lines *within* the present that, developed or prised open in particular ways, might induce the condition to surpass itself into a future" ("Nationalism" 25).

This kind of utopianism, for Eagleton, can even make us miserable by causing us to "desire uselessly rather than feasibly" ("Nationalism" 25). A more useful vision, he suggests, would allow us to imagine a leap from the "eternal recurrence of new variants on persistent forms of exploitation" that Marx termed "prehistory" into the realm of history proper, "the kingdom of use value, sensuous particularity, and an endless productivity of difference" (Marx and Engels 27). I have noted elsewhere the essential Americanness of the original *Star Trek* series, and I would further add here that the utopianism of the original series is American as well, and in the very way that Eagleton notes (Booker, "Politics" 196). For example, despite its seeming espousal of a fairly straightforward technological utopianism, the original series tells us very little about how the ideal future society it posits might actually have been achieved—and provides very few details about the actual nature of that society. Indeed, most of the details about the future provided by the series are grim ones, with hints that the golden age of the twenty-third century was achieved only after much suffering and struggle.

The series also valorizes suffering and struggle in a variety of ways, sometimes by showing a strong skepticism toward the possibility of achieving a genuine utopia. Thus, though it stipulates that technology has solved Earth's social and political problems, the series consistently acknowledges the dangers inherent in overly rapid scientific advancement, frequently expressing a concern that science and technology can be utilized positively only in societies in which social and ethical development keeps pace with scientific knowledge. As a result, all Starfleet missions to less-developed worlds are strictly forbidden by the so-called "Prime Directive" from sharing technology or scientific knowledge that might lead to unnaturally rapid development.

In some episodes, the crew of the *Enterprise* encounters explicitly utopian societies in outer space, only to discover the flaws inherent in those societies. This motif sometimes figures in the tension between Kirk and Spock, with Kirk typically suspicious of utopianism and Spock supportive of it. The crucial episode here is "This Side of Paradise" (2 March 1967), in which the *Enterprise* travels to the planet Omicron Ceti III, expecting to find the Earth colonists there dead due to the effects of usually fatal Berthold radiation that has been bombarding the planet. Instead, they find the colonists not only alive, but living in unnaturally perfect health amid what seems to be a utopian paradise of peace, plenty, and tranquility. That health is due to the effects of strange plants that grow on the planet, spraying the colonists with spores that give them both a perfect physical status and mental contentment. The spores even affect Spock, causing him to relax his usual logical exterior and settle into a life of romantic bliss with a woman colonist whom he knows from a previous encounter. In fact, the spores ultimately affect the entire crew of the *Enterprise* (with the exception of Kirk), causing them to abandon their ship and join the colonists in their seemingly idyllic life. When even Kirk finally starts to succumb, he finds that his violent reaction to the thought of leaving the *Enterprise* (again his true love) negates the spores' effect and allows him to free Spock and eventually the rest of the crew from the spores' influence. And finally the colonists agree to relocate to a new planet, where they can resume their struggle to build a better new world rather than simply live in passive tranquility.

This episode again indicates how the original series tends to value struggle and strife (as opposed to acceptance of the status quo) as central to the very definition of what it means to be human. Kirk sums up this official attitude at the episode's end when he notes, "Maybe we weren't meant for paradise. Maybe we were meant to fight our way through. Struggle. Claw our way up. Scratch for every inch of the way. Maybe we can't stroll to the music of the lute. We must march to the sound of drums." On the other hand, Spock, who quite often voices a dissenting opinion, is not so sure. Dismissing Kirk's speech as so much "poetry," he points out that the situation on Omicron Ceti III was not unequivocally bad. "For the first time in my life," he notes, "I was happy."

Of course, *Star Trek* contains so many of the trappings of sf that it cannot be considered simply a work of adventure/romance, nor can it be considered simply anti-utopian. This final exchange between Kirk and Spock indicates how the original series gains energy from a tension between genres and attitudes toward utopia, particularly via the relationship between Kirk and Spock. Seen in this light, the swashbuckling and emotional Kirk functions essentially as an adventure/romance character, while the rational Spock serves as a representation of the sf mentality.[5] It is important, though, that Kirk clearly represents the favored point of view in the series, so that the adventure/romance elements of the series remain dominant over the sf ones. Thus even Spock seems most likeable when he is at his most human and emotional, as when he falls into the throes of *pon farr* in the episode "Amok Time" (15 September 1967). Here, the mindless sexual passion that periodically overtakes the otherwise hyperrational Vulcans almost proves to be Spock's undoing, until he is saved by the intervention of Kirk and McCoy and safely returns to his work aboard the *Enterprise*.

Whatever its shortcomings on its own terms (poor acting, slow and plodding plot development, lame premise), *The Motion Picture* specifically fails as an adaptation of the original series because it differs from that series in three fundamental (yet interrelated) ways. First, *The Motion Picture* relies on the richness of its cinematic imagery as its most important resource, which sets it strongly apart from the series, whose impoverished images are of little value in their own right and serve only to move forward individual episode plots. Second, *The Motion Picture* generically resides firmly within the realm of sf, making the production of a potentially unsettling cognitive estrangement in its audience a central goal, whereas the original series is more nearly a work of adventure/romance designed to entertain and to be more comforting than unsettling. Third, this generic difference produces differing utopian energies in the two works, with *The Motion Picture* striving to encourage the consideration of a genuinely different future (including fundamental changes to the human race itself), whereas the original series, though stipulating a different future, does little to encourage its viewers to think much about the nature of that future or how it might be attained.

These three differences also help to explain why the subsequent feature, *The Wrath of Khan*, seems a more satisfying adaptation of the series, for it proves more consistent with the series in all three of these ways. Visually, for example, *The Wrath of Khan* is quite impoverished in comparison with *The Motion Picture*, largely because of a substantial reduction in its production budget relative to the first film, from approximately $35 million to approximately $11 million.[6] Though imagistically richer than the series, its visual style is more in keeping with that of the original series, to which it seemingly pays homage with a number of cheap-looking sets (Styrofoam rocks, etc.) and artificial-looking painted backdrops, especially of various cosmic phenomena. And this stripped-down imagery works well because it is consistent with the essentially pulpy nature of the adventure/romance genre in which both the original series and *The Wrath of Khan* participate. Of course, that sharing of generic conventions is to be expected, given that the narrative of this film is a direct sequel (set fifteen years later) to an episode of the original series, one that is specifically suspicious of the notion, embraced by *The Motion Picture*, that technology might work positive changes in the human race itself.

That original episode, "Space Seed" (16 February 1967), is one in which the *Enterprise* crew discovers a derelict spacecraft from Earth, vintage 1990s. Aboard the craft, frozen in stasis, are a number of exiles from Earth's "Eugenics Wars," including the formidable Khan Noonien Singh (Ricardo Montalban), a genetically engineered superman who, once awakened, plans to regain the political power he once held on Earth. The *Enterprise* crew is able to thwart Khan's efforts and exile him and his followers to a barren, uninhabited planet, although he uses his considerable abilities to mount another plan of conquest from there, which results in the action that eventually leads to his death in *The Wrath of Khan*.

Montalban's over-the-top performance in both "Space Seed" and *The Wrath of Khan* makes Khan the perfect pulpy *Star Trek* protagonist, standing as a sort of evil twin to Shatner's histrionic Kirk. Also, gone in the second film are the loving shots of elegant technological devices that mark *The Motion Picture*, replaced by merely functional shots of technologies that allow the plot to take its course. Although the "genesis device" that is crucial to the film is stipulated to be wondrous, the wonders lie in its effects, not in the device itself (which is rather unimpressive looking), and even those effects are stipulated to be highly dangerous, potentially as much a curse as a boon to humanity. The device, indeed, is specifically presented in the film as both a wonder that can bring life to lifeless planets and a weapon that can wipe out planets entirely.

With the first film's confrontation between humans and an inscrutable alien intelligence replaced in the second by an essentially personal duel between Kirk and Khan, *The Wrath of Khan* is greatly reduced in thematic magnitude. Moreover, it displays significantly weaker utopian energies than its predecessor; in particular, its suggestion that genetic engineering is more likely to lead to dystopia than utopia places *The Wrath of Khan* more in the spirit of the original series than of *The Motion Picture*, which is able to imagine that a technology-fueled change in the human race might be a good thing. In accordance with the previous argument, then, *The Wrath of Khan* might be seen as a more successful adaptation of the series than *The Motion Picture* because it resides more comfortably near the "adventure/romance" pole of the genre continuum, is suspicious of utopianism, and relies more on emotion than cognition to engage its audience.

This reliance on emotion most clearly surfaces in the frenzied competition between Khan and Kirk, as well as in the subplot involving Kirk's discovery that his old girlfriend (the genesis device's creator) had borne him a son (now an adult) without his knowledge. But most important, *The Wrath of Khan* returns to the tried-and-true formula of emphasizing the relationships among Kirk, Spock, and McCoy, thus taking advantage of the long, slow development in such relationships that occur over time in a television series but that film necessarily abbreviates. The focus here, in particular, is on Spock's love for both McCoy and Kirk. As the film nears its end and as Khan lies dying, he swears vengeance and, quoting Melville's Captain Ahab (his favorite literary role model), sets off the genesis device, sending out a destructive wave that promises to obliterate all living things in its path, including the crew of the nearby *Enterprise*, which has been disabled. Spock manages to repair the engines and exposes himself to a fatal dose of radiation in the process. And while justifying his action on the basis of the logical premise that "the needs of the many outweigh the needs of the few, or the one," his sacrifice is clearly motivated more by love than logic, especially that for McCoy and Kirk. This fact is then emphasized in the film's peak emotional moment, as the dying Spock bids farewell to Kirk, noting that "I have been and always shall be your friend."

Eventually, the film ends with a somewhat tacked-on moment of hope, involving the rather heavy-handed suggestion that there might be a chance that the effects of the genesis device will somehow lead to Spock's resurrection (which, of course, occurs in the third film). However artificial, this vaguely optimistic ending carries a certain utopian energy, especially when reinforced by a recollection of Spock's belief that there are potentially positive possibilities in every situation. But this utopianism is surely weak in comparison with the first film's evident love of technology and its suggestion that technology might ultimately not only improve human life but also merge with its makers to create something superior to either humans or machines. However, this weaker utopianism fits with the adventure/romance genre of *The Wrath of Khan*, as do its reliance on an emotional, rather than intellectual, response from its audience and its relatively impoverished, almost televisual imagery. In short, *The Wrath of Khan* works as a film because all of its elements are consistent with all of its other elements, and it works as an adaptation because these elements are also consistent with those of the original series. *The Motion Picture*—whose title, seen in this light, turns out to be strikingly appropriate—does *not* work precisely because it strives to be so cinematic, as well as striving to be sf, even though it is constructed from elements that are in themselves fundamentally televisual and that reside within the generic conventions of adventure/romance.

The success (and the ending) of *The Wrath of Khan* virtually assured a sequel; however, that film, *Star Trek III: The Search for Spock* (1984), would prove unremarkable, serving largely to restore the crucial character of Spock to the *Star Trek* universe so he could be available for more sequels, plans for which could be seen in the fact that this was the first film to be released with a Roman numeral attached. The three subsequent films featuring the original cast learned their lesson from the first film's failure, remaining within the adventure/romance genre and centrally emphasizing the interrelationship among Kirk, Spock, and McCoy. But this entire sequence exemplifies a number of the issues involved in taking a well-known and much-beloved television series to the big screen, reminding us both that the process requires a careful negotiation with the demands of devoted fans for fidelity to the original and that the resources of cinema and television are quite different and inevitably play a shaping role.

NOTES

1. *Star Trek* fan culture is widely cited as one of the central examples of the general phenomenon of fan culture (see, for example, Hills or Jenkins and Tulloch). This culture famously includes an array of conventions at which actors and other personalities associated with the franchise make appearances

and mingle with fans. These fans often sport elaborate *Star Trek*-themed costumes, to the point that such costumes have also become a cultural phenomenon (see Joseph-Witham). Other aspects include fan fiction set in the *Star Trek* universe, much of it published on one of the numerous websites devoted to *Star Trek* fandom. Many "Trekkers" see *Star Trek* as the basis for a whole way of life. See, for example, Geraghty and also Stafford.
2. The visual similarities between these two films are no accident, of course, given that Douglas Trumbull headed up the special visual-effects teams on both films.
3. The weakness of this premise may help to account for the fact that the images of the alien entity seem significantly less powerful and affecting than the images of the *Enterprise* as Kirk and Scott approach it, though it is also the case that the latter gain emotional power from the way in which the loving visual embrace of the camera clearly mirrors Kirk's own genuine love for the ship he once commanded and to which he now returns. These shots, then, can be taken as a sort of science-fictional version of Laura Mulvey's "gaze," in which the strangeness of this future craft, which could not exist in our world, is mitigated by an identification with Kirk's evident feeling for this technological device.
4. The affinity of *Star Trek* with various versions of adventure/romance has often been noted. For example, see the discussion by Barrett and Barrett of the ways the spacegoing adventures of *Star Trek* are modeled on the established genre of the seagoing adventure (5, 13). *Star Trek* also has much in common with the Western (that most American of adventure/romance forms), as can be seen in the longevity of the (apparently apocryphal) notion that Roddenberry initially pitched the series as a sort of "*Wagon Train* to the stars." The emphasis on space as the "final frontier" also links *Star Trek* with the Western.
5. To round out the trio, one might see the grumpy McCoy (with his down-to-earth skepticism toward many of the high-tech devices that surround him in this world) as a character derived from realism, though he has much in common with the cantankerous sidekick of the Western as well.
6. The second film, on the other hand, grossed $79 million at the domestic box office, nearly equaling the $82 million domestic gross of the first film, despite the difference in budgets.

WORKS CITED

Barrett, Michèle, and Duncan Barrett. *Star Trek: The Human Frontier*. London: Routledge, 2001.
Bloch, Ernst. *The Principle of Hope*. 1954–59. 3 vols. Trans. Neville Plaice, Stephen Plaice, and Paul Knight. 1986. Cambridge: MIT P, 1996.
Booker, M. Keith. "The Politics of *Star Trek*." *The Essential Science Fiction Television Reader*. Ed. J. P. Telotte. Lexington: UP of Kentucky, 2008. 195–208.
———. *Strange TV: Innovative Television Series from* The Twilight Zone *to* The X-Files. Westport: Greenwood, 2002.
Eagleton, Terry. "Nationalism: Irony and Commitment." *Nationalism, Colonialism and Literature*. Minneapolis: U of Minnesota P, 1990. 23–39.
Ellis, John. *Visible Fictions: Cinema: Television: Video*. Rev. ed. London: Routledge, 1992.
Geraghty, Lincoln. *Living with* Star Trek: *American Culture and the* Star Trek *Universe*. London: I. B. Tauris, 2007.

Hills, Matt. *Fan Cultures*. London: Routledge, 2002.
Jenkins, Henry, and John Tulloch. *Science Fiction Audiences: Watching* Star Trek *and* Doctor Who. London: Routledge, 1995.
Joseph-Witham, Heather R. Star Trek *Fans and Costume Art*. Jackson: UP of Mississippi, 1996.
Marx, Karl, and Friedrich Engels. *The Marx-Engels Reader*. Ed. Robert C. Tucker. New York: W. W. Norton, 1978.
Mulvey, Laura. "Visual Pleasure and Narrative Cinema." *Visual and Other Pleasures*. Bloomington: Indiana UP, 1989. 14–26.
Scalzi, John. *The Rough Guide to Sci-Fi Movies*. London: Rough Guides, 2005.
Stafford, Nikki. *Trekkers: True Stories by Fans for Fans*. Toronto: ECW P, 2002.
Suvin, Darko. *Metamorphoses of Science Fiction: On the Poetics and History of a Literary Genre*. New Haven: Yale UP, 1979.

8 "I Want to Believe the Truth Is Out There"

The X-Files and the Impossibility of Knowing

Rodney F. Hill

One of the most successful of American sf television series, *The X-Files* (Fox, 1993–2002) centers on two FBI agents, Fox Mulder (David Duchovny) and Dana Scully (Gillian Anderson) and their investigations into paranormal activities. Their cases, collectively known as "the X-files," usually lead to findings that the FBI's bureaucracy deems embarrassing (and therefore threatening) and that often require extensive redaction to create an acceptable "official story." Yet there are forces within the FBI that support the X-files, resulting in an ongoing tension between Mulder and Scully's mandate to uncover the "truth" and a perceived need to keep that truth hidden. In the nine seasons of the television series, as well as its two adaptations to the big screen in 1998 and 2008, that "truth" takes on multiple levels of significance while—thanks to the demands of the televisual and cinematic strategies of *The X-Files*—it remains rather elusive. It is in that very tension, or truth's elusiveness, though, that we may glimpse a crucial issue in such cross-media adaptations.

A common observation among most commentators on *The X-Files* has to do with the dual nature of the show's storyline. On the one hand, over half the episodes are of a relatively freestanding nature, with Mulder and Scully investigating isolated incidents of paranormal activities ranging from witchcraft to werewolves, from vampires to a take on the two film versions of *The Thing* (1951 and 1982). These so-called "creature features" are rooted in the anthology structure of earlier sf/fantasy/horror series such as *The Twilight Zone* (1959–64) and *Tales from the Darkside* (1984–88), with the recurring investigative characters of Mulder and Scully especially reminiscent of Karl Kolchak (Darren McGavin) from *The Night Stalker* (1972, 1974–75). But in terms of their narrative structure, these "creature features"—as relatively autonomous dramatic texts offering some sense of closure and resolution—bear less resemblance to episodes of a conventional television series than to a paradigm more akin to the classical Hollywood cinema (as evidenced in their borrowing from *The Thing* and other films). Furthermore, the visual style of the entire series could be characterized as highly cinematic in nature, employing single-camera cinematography with a wide variety of shot scale, elaborate lighting setups, special effects and makeup, multiple locations, temporal elision, and strategic use of off-screen space and editing to build suspense.

On the other hand, *The X-Files* also presents an ongoing, serialized narrative throughline, involving UFO abductions and shadowy government conspiracies, in which both Mulder and Scully become involved in a direct, highly personal manner over the course of the series: both characters are abducted; both lose family members to the conspiracy; and Scully becomes impregnated with a human-alien hybrid baby, originally thought to have been fathered *in vitro* by Mulder. This extended alien-conspiracy plot, which ranges over all nine seasons of the series, largely conforms to John Ellis's theoretical model of televisual seriality, in which "segments tend never to coalesce into an overall totalizing account . . . with a continuous updating on the latest concatenation of events rather than a final ending or explanation" (120). Whenever Mulder and Scully begin to understand the full nature of these conspiracies, some new revelation indicates that their understanding is still woefully limited and that further investigation is needed (to be carried out, of course, in future episodes).

Thus, the duality of narrative approach that characterizes *The X-Files* is itself twofold, having to do not only with the two types of stories being told but also with the televisual versus cinematic modes of expression employed by the series. This problematic straddling of the two media finds its most obvious locus in the two theatrical films adapted from the small-screen series: *The X-Files* (1998, a.k.a. *The X Files: Fight the Future*) and *The X Files: I Want to Believe* (2008). The two films also play into the aforementioned duality of the televisual versus the cinematic, as the 1998 film essentially works as an extended two-hour episode that falls between the final episode of season five and the opening episode of season six, whereas the second film, released five years after the end of the series, offers a free-standing, self-contained story that features a more traditional cinematic structure, complete with Hollywood-style resolution.

As *The X-Files: Fight the Future* begins, Mulder and Scully have been reassigned to relatively mundane duties, as the X-files group had been shut down at the end of the fifth season. Their investigation of the bombing of a government building (highly reminiscent of the 1995 Oklahoma City bombing) unexpectedly leads them to suburban Texas, where an alien virus (known in the series as "black oil") has caused several deaths. When they arrive in Texas, all that Mulder and Scully find is some trace of a government cover-up, with key evidence having been removed to a desert research facility where bees are being genetically engineered as a means of delivering the alien virus to the population at large. Although Mulder and Scully manage to destroy this particular facility, and thus bring some narrative closure to the film, in the end we learn that there are perhaps dozens of such centers around the world—which leaves the larger conflict unresolved and leads into season six of the series.

Given the place of the film within the overarching mythos of the television show, this sort of ending offers perhaps the best possible compromise

The X-Files *and the Impossibility of Knowing* 117

between the demands of the cinematic form and the requirements of the ongoing, serialized *X-Files* narrative; and the strategy clearly was intended to please the film's two distinct audiences: the devoted fan base of the series and a general audience less familiar (perhaps even unfamiliar) with the show. For the former, the vast government-alien conspiracy must remain unresolved to be taken up in the show's sixth season; and for the latter, the film must deliver a satisfying conclusion, which it does to some extent. Still, *Variety*'s Todd McCarthy found the first film to be "somewhere in between standing on its own feet as a real movie worth the price of a ticket and merely being a glorified TV episode refitted for theaters." He also noted that "non-'X'-philes without a vested interest in the characters and their quixotic investigation into the unknown are unlikely to climb on board in significant numbers, since the film lacks the excitement, scope and style expected from event movies" (50).

Ten years after the first film, and six years after the end of the series (Mulder and Scully having left the FBI altogether), *The X-Files: I Want to Believe* offers a more fully autonomous plotline. An FBI agent has been kidnapped, and the agency's only lead in helping to find her is a fallen Catholic priest (Billy Connolly) who claims (not unconvincingly) to have psychic abilities. Due to the paranormal nature of the case, the FBI asks Dana Scully (now working as a staff physician in a Catholic hospital) to locate Fox Mulder and persuade him to assist in determining whether or not the priest actually is psychic. The investigation ultimately leads to an organ-harvesting ring and a horrific riff on the *Frankenstein* story, placing the film firmly in the vein of the "creature features" that formed a staple of *The X-Files* for nine years. The story has nothing to do with alien colonization or government conspiracies, and beyond solving the crime, the only other "truth" that occupies Scully and Mulder is the rather narrow question of whether or not the priest really possesses psychic abilities.

Figure 8.1 Scully (Gillian Anderson) and Mulder (David Duchovny) ponder their futures in *The X-Files: I Want to Believe* (2008). Copyright Twentieth Century-Fox.

With a production budget of $65 million, plus another $25 million for prints and advertising, *The X-Files: Fight the Future* failed to break even in its theatrical run, grossing only $83.9 million (Bart and Hontz 4). *The X-Files: I Want to Believe* similarly lost money, with a pared down budget of $30 million and a box-office gross of only $21 million. Unlike its predecessor, in the second film very little is "left hanging" in the end, save Mulder and Scully's personal relationship (fodder enough, perhaps, for the consideration of further *X-Files* movies yet to come). The case of the abducted FBI agent is solved, and even the question of the priest's psychic abilities is answered fairly conclusively. In a way, then, with its more traditionally cinematic narrative form, *The X-Files: I Want to Believe* should have been the more successful of the two films; however, its underperformance may be due to the fact that its story lies almost completely outside the overarching narrative concerns of the television series. Although a few critics praised the second film, its overall critical response was considerably less positive than that of the first film. (Based on more than 150 reviews for each of the two films, the Movie Review Query Engine rates the first film a B in terms of critical reception, and the second a solid C.) Scott Foundas of *The Village Voice* derided *The X-Files: I Want to Believe* as "just plain lousy" and "considerably more meager in its ambitions than . . . *Fight the Future*." A less scathing but more typical assessment came from Brian Lowry in *Variety*: "The problem is that the mystery isn't as compelling or satisfying as it should be." (n. pag.) In other words, without much connection to the *X-Files* mythos (which, curiously, Lowry found to be too convoluted in the first film), all that the second film has to offer is a fairly pedestrian, derivative genre story, albeit with the familiar, beloved characters of Scully and Mulder.

J. P. Telotte has suggested that the touchstone phrase of *The X-Files*, "the truth is out there" (uttered by Mulder and repeated as a tagline in the show's opening credits),

> constitutes an effective *promise/premise* for a form bound up in seriality, since it can always take us towards that "truth" and then swerve off or pull back—and indeed that swerving is what keeps the series going. Our payback for watching the show is that we might someday get to the truth or at least glimpse a portion of it (like Moses and the Promised Land). Film, however, has traditionally tried to provide a kind of fulfillment, completion, or payoff. (n. pag.)

Telotte's observations point to the crux of the problem regarding the *X-Files* films' relationship to the series: the overall impetus of *The X-Files* is to postpone any ultimate revelation of "the truth," yet Hollywood films have traditionally required that questions be answered, mysteries be solved, and truths be revealed. As Ellis points out, the "entertainment cinema" typically offers a "single, coherent text," with a tight cause-effect chain of

The X-Files *and the Impossibility of Knowing* 119

events leading to resolution and closure (echoing David Bordwell's take on the classical Hollywood cinema in which "no gap is permanent" [Bordwell, Staiger, and Thompson 41]). This cinematic mode of narration runs counter to Ellis's notion of televisual seriality, which entails

> a more dispersed narrational form: it is extensive rather than sequential. . . . Repetition in the TV narrative occurs at the level of the series: formats are repeated, situations return week after week. Each time there is novelty [as] the characters . . . encounter a new dilemma. . . . This form of repetition is different from that offered by the classic cinema narrative, as it provides a kind of groundbase, a constant basis for events, rather than an economy of reuse directed towards a final totalisation. (147)

In *The X-Files* television program, whatever "truth is out there" is deferred indefinitely, largely thanks to the aforementioned duality of the narratives. Mulder and Scully may indeed solve individual mysteries, as with the "creature feature" episodes, and they may even discover major pieces of the puzzle in terms of the alien-invasion conspiracy. However, at each level, the puzzle grows larger and larger still, and the "truth" becomes ever more elusive. Furthermore, whenever the series presents us with an inordinate level of "truth" with regard to the alien-conspiracy plotline—for instance, with a multipart season finale or season opener or both—such revelations are always set aside for several weeks as the show shifts back to the "creature feature" format for a few episodes, thereby delaying any further developments in the ongoing story. This perennial dramatic tension between "truths" that are knowable and those that stubbornly escape discovery sustained the series for most of its nine seasons; and it is perhaps the lack of such an underlying dynamic in the film versions that ultimately accounts for their failure.

Figure 8.2 The mysterious conspirator "Cigarette-Smoking Man" (William B. Davis) plots his next move in *The X-Files: Fight the Future* (1998). Copyright Twentieth Century-Fox.

"The truth is out there," as the series repeatedly assures us, but what truth does *The X-Files* seek to reveal? In any given "creature feature" episode, Mulder and Scully do eventually discover much of "the truth" behind that particular show's self-contained mystery, but their conclusions ultimately are whitewashed in official reports, for even though the powers-that-be know their findings are true, they find them unacceptable. In a first-season episode titled "Tooms," for example, Mulder and Scully's superior, FBI assistant director Walter Skinner (Mitch Pileggi) asks the mysterious "cigarette-smoking man," C. G. B. Spender (William B. Davis)—who we later learn is a top figure in the "shadow government"—whether he actually believes Mulder and Scully's stories, and Spender replies coolly, "Of course I do." This tendency continues into the eighth and ninth seasons of the series, when Mulder virtually disappears from the story and is replaced by special agent John Doggett (Robert Patrick). Yet that essential narrative dynamic persists. In the third episode of season eight, "Patience," Scully and Doggett investigate a series of killings committed by a half-man, half-bat creature right out of the headlines of supermarket tabloids. Obviously, we are back within a "creature feature" formula narrative, but now with Doggett taking on Scully's former role as the constant skeptic. Even so, when confronted with the evidence of his own eyes, Doggett has to admit that something out of the ordinary is going on, although his superior, FBI deputy director Kersh (James Pickens, Jr.), has already made it quite clear that he does not want to find any reference to the paranormal in Doggett's official reports.

In addition to the relatively limited "truths" discovered in such "creature feature" episodes, Mulder, Scully, and later Doggett also seek to unfold a larger, more complex "truth" about the government conspiracies in which they find themselves caught up. What initially seemed to be alien abductions turn out to be (at least in some cases) "disappearances" carried out by agents of the "shadow government," who are conducting various experiments on the abductees—that is, literally seeking the sort of "truths" that provide the motivation for all scientific experiments. The rather convoluted plots that result do involve aliens, but there is apparently a secret program of collaboration between the potential alien invaders and the men who run the "shadow government." And the more Mulder and Scully learn about these activities, the larger the conspiracy becomes—and ultimately, so too the more impenetrable the truth of the conspiracy, including the truth behind their own roles in it.

The fascination in American popular culture with such irresolvable conspiracy theories has its modern roots in the 1963 assassination of President John F. Kennedy, which Peter Knight identifies as "the mother-lode of [a] new conspiracy style, ... an inevitably ambiguous point of origin for a loss of faith in authority and coherent causality—the primal scene, as it were, of a postmodern sense of paranoia" (4). *The X-Files* unabashedly acknowledges its own debt to this paranoid conspiracy culture in a fourth-season episode titled "Musings of a Cigarette-Smoking Man." Melvin Frohike (Tom Braidwood), one of the "Lone Gunmen"—a trio of conspiracy-minded amateur scientists who often assist Mulder and Scully in their investigations[1]—has stumbled upon a document that is supposed to be C. G. B. Spender's secret diary. This unpublished memoir, circulated among other conspiracy theorists, posits "Cancer Man" as the assassin of JFK, Martin Luther King, Jr., and Robert F. Kennedy, and operating at the behest of powerful figures at the center of the American "shadow government." Furthermore, the episode humorously suggests that Spender also controls the outcomes of the Oscars and the Superbowl, among other things. This undercutting by exaggeration points in two directions as well: to the dissolution of all conspiracy thinking because it becomes absurd; and to the sense that, indeed, all things are actually connected, all are part of a conspiracy, all make sense when taken together and thus suggest a sort of global (or universal) logic at work. The pop-culture notion of "assassination cabals" has additional roots in the so-called "Torbitt Document," which, as Knight explains, is

> a photocopied manuscript by the pseudonymous William Torbitt, which has circulated among conspiracy researchers since the early 1970s. The Torbitt Document offers an astounding exposé of the Kennedy assassination . . . [making] links between the Mafia, NASA, . . . the FBI, and corporate interests. . . . Other parts seem to fade off into more fanciful territory, with allegations about NASA's UFO program headquartered in the notorious Area 51 in the Nevada desert. (46)

The Spender diary clearly alludes to the Torbitt Document and shares many of its conspiratorial elements: the Kennedy assassination, secret machinations of the military-industrial complex, and UFO cover-ups.

One of the long-term appeals of *The X-Files*—and a key to the television series' great success—is its ability to tap into a cultural unease over the very elusiveness of "the truth," especially as it resonated with the Kennedy assassination's status as a touchstone for widespread distrust in all that we might think of as "the official story." In a sixth-season episode titled "Three of a Kind," the Lone Gunmen trick Scully into joining them in Las Vegas to investigate an apparent plot by defense contractors. The episode begins with a haunting dream, narrated by one of the three Lone Gunmen, John Fitzgerald Byers (Bruce Harwood), about his own disillusionment— but also implicitly that of the American public—triggered by the JFK assassination. The naming of this character, along with the collective naming of the Lone Gunmen (a reference to the official, arguably absurd explanation offered in the Warren Report that Lee Harvey Oswald acted alone in killing JFK), constitutes an explicit acknowledgment that *The X-Files*, despite its fantastic elements, reflects a very real cultural phenomenon: the post-JFK erosion of trust in governmental authority as a benign source of "truth."

If such earthbound "truths" as the machinations of federal agencies and "shadow governments" cannot be known due to their sheer vastness and complexity, then some of the bigger questions raised by *The X-Files*—seeking "truths" having to do with the source of life on Earth and humanity's place in the universe—would seem to be even more elusive, rendering impossible any overall, satisfying resolution. These are the same truths perennially sought—but never fully discovered—by science as well as religious and mythological traditions; and *The X-Files* is keenly aware of those traditions and its own place within them, by way of its sf/fantasy-genre status. The series seems particularly self-aware of its own status as fantasy text and, more pointedly, of its relationship to genres of fantasy such as sf and horror. Throughout the series, various characters, even Scully, deride Mulder's theories as "science fiction," even though they are unable to proffer convincing alternative explanations. In the sixth episode of the first season, "Shadows," we find a high degree of reflexivity in its multiple references to well-known horror films: Scully jokingly observes that psychokinesis is "how Carrie got even at the prom," invoking the 1976 Brian DePalma film; and later, when Mulder suggests the possible presence of a poltergeist, Scully, in a nod to Tobe Hooper's *Poltergeist* (1982), quips, "They're here!" Similarly, a scene in which blood drains out of a bathtub offers a direct visual quotation of Alfred Hitchcock's *Psycho* (1960); Scully's mysterious pregnancy clearly echoes the demonic conception of *Rosemary's Baby* (1968); and the minor figure of a graveyard caretaker who knows about all the dead under his care descends from a long line of horror-film stock characters. Such self-awareness of fantasy genre conventions serves simply as a surface-level acknowledgment that *The X-Files* is operating not only as a genre text but also as mythology. It is self-evident that the events depicted in sf and horror texts are not "true"; yet these same texts do get at some fundamental truths about human psychology and societal ills, largely through their reliance on psychological symbolism.

Building upon its numerous direct references to science fiction and horror, *The X-Files* also frequently invokes Jungian psychology, openly inviting a consideration of such prominent archetypes as the "shadow" and the "syzygy," central to the dynamics of film genres in their function as cultural mythology. In this context, we might consider the title of the episode mentioned above, "Shadows," as well as an episode from the third season, "Syzygy," which involves a series of bizarre deaths instigated by a cosmic disturbance due to Jupiter's being in opposition to Uranus. This notion of opposition lies at the heart of Jung's conception of the syzygy—the archetypal pairing of opposites—which, together with the shadow, informs much of the symbolic dimension of *The X-Files*.

Mulder and Scully, together incarnating the show's central syzygy, represent not only male and female (the most common incarnation of the yin and yang of the syzygy) but also two different approaches to seeking the truth—or two different versions of truth—at once at odds with each other and inextricably intertwined: scientific inquiry versus a belief in the paranormal (or put another way, a belief in the unknown). Generally, Mulder is the one who "wants to believe" and Scully is the cold, analytical scientist, with both characters playing against common gender stereotypes found in the media. Yet ironically, when it comes to another sort of belief—religious faith—it is Scully who believes and Mulder who is the constant skeptic. Several episodes of *The X-Files* are, in fact, built precisely upon this sort of opposition (or syzygy) between religious faith and the scientific method. For example, "Revelations," from the third season, opens with R. Lee Ermey as an evangelist pretending to be a stigmatic, deriding the cynicism of science and proclaiming the need to believe. Similarly, a seventh-season episode, "En ami," pits religion against science as an adolescent boy's parents refuse medical treatment for his cancer on the basis of their religious beliefs. When C. G. B. Spender and his men implant the boy and cure his cancer, he mistakes them for angels. While Mulder blithely scoffs at the notion that the boy could have been healed by God, as the parents so strongly believe, he all too readily buys into the (equally derisible) notion that the boy has fallen victim to the vast government conspiracy that has so often crossed paths with the X-files. This irony points up the series' problematizing of the relationship between "truth" and belief—an ongoing postmodern dance that is epitomized in two of the show's most familiar catchphrases: "The truth is out there" and "I want to believe."

The latter phrase, expressing a desire to come to grips with the irrational and unknowable—*knowledge*, after all, circumvents the need to *believe*—also points to a similarly problematic attitude in the character of Agent Mulder, who frequently pits himself in opposition not only to Scully's levelheaded scientific approach but also against religious beliefs, yet who at the same time seems open to the sort of spiritual potentialities that manifest themselves in dreams and in mythological structures. In a third-season vampire story, "3," Mulder rails against a misguided literal interpretation of the Judeo-Christian Bible, even as he also specifically addresses myth in a positive light. Similarly, in the episode "Sleepless" (a story involving external control of brainwaves that results in hallucinations and dream manipulation), Mulder invokes the concept of the "collective unconscious," a notion central to Jung's theories of how archetypes function in our dreams and myths. Yet all the while, Mulder fails to recognize that science, religion, and myth are simply different approaches to the same big questions about the nature of the universe and humanity's place in it. Mulder's refusal "to believe" in religion, paired with his strong "faith" in psychological models, stands in almost direct opposition to Scully's scientific skepticism regarding the X-files, her own strong religious faith notwithstanding.

All of these oppositions (religion versus science, science versus the paranormal, religion versus myth) come to a head at the end of season six and the beginning of season seven, in the episodes "Biogenesis" and "The Sixth Extinction"—the very titles of which stand in opposition to each other. "Biogenesis" opens with Scully, in voice-over narration, asking "the big questions" about the source and purpose of life on Earth: "[F]or all our knowledge, what no one can say for certain is what or who ignited that original spark. Is there a plan, a purpose, or reason to our existence? Will we pass, as those before us, into oblivion? ... Or will the mystery be revealed, through a sign, a symbol, a revelation?" Here once again Scully raises the issue of "truth" and its elusiveness, even raising the question of how one can go about communicating a truth, which is, of course, a difficulty inherent in all sf texts, including *The X-Files*.

The storyline that follows involves mysterious alien artifacts bearing symbols from American Indian folklore, passages from the Judeo-Christian Bible and the Koran, and sequences from the human genome. When Mulder comes into contact with one of the artifacts, a broken piece of a larger tablet, he is thrown into what seems to be a psychotic state as his nervous system goes into overdrive—as if the human body is incapable of processing the level of "truth" that seems to be emanating from the artifacts. In "The Sixth Extinction—Part 1," Scully encounters a mysterious spiritlike African tribesman, who appears and disappears suddenly, telling her, "Some truths are not for you." Later, Scully describes the mystery as a puzzle, and she tells Mulder that "the pieces are there for us to put together." Those pieces come from various religious and mythological traditions, as well as from scientific inquiry. Taken together, Scully suggests, they represent "the key" (perhaps she should have said "the keys") to every question that has ever been asked. All these religious-mythological systems, together with science, might add up to "the truth," but each of them offers only one aspect, one angle on a larger, multifaceted truth, one pathway to illumination; and Mulder's mental state seems to suggest that "the whole truth" is beyond human capacity to understand. These episodes—and indeed *The X-Files* series in its entirety—all grapple with the same mysteries that have informed mythology for as long as humans have been telling stories. As Joseph Campbell suggests, such inquiry lies at the threshold "between what can be known and what is never to be discovered, because it transcends all human thought: the source of life. What is it? No one knows" ("The Hero's Adventure").

Such a lofty quest—to discover the eternal mysteries of the universe—stands in pointed contrast to most of Mulder and Scully's investigations, which concern themselves with the temporal machinations of greedy, power-mad men. This contrast offers yet another duality or syzygy, pointing to what Campbell posits as one of the great functions of myth: its ability to help us to reconcile the temporal with the eternal, to accept the injustices and horrors of the here and now in recognition that "the horror is simply the foreground of a wonder" ("The Message of the Myth"). Even in the midst of an alien-government conspiracy plot, then, we can find some aspect of the greater search for more fundamental truths: what Mulder, Scully, and Doggett really are seeking is a glimpse of their own places within the framework of the conspiracy—or in a conspiracy narrative. This point is made explicit in the thirteenth episode of the eighth season, "Per manum," in which Scully and Doggett suspect that they have been used as pawns in a plot involving women pregnant with alien babies. Perhaps the mythological appeal of the overarching conspiracy story is that it calls into question what role each of us is playing in the "grand scheme of things," the narrative that keeps unfolding, the total truth of which remains elusive.

In approaching the truth only to veer away from it and defer its ultimate revelation, each episode of *The X-Files* (especially those in the conspiracy storyline) itself constitutes one of the many "pieces" of the truth. Perhaps we, as viewers, find these pieces more tantalizing and more satisfying than we would find some ultimate conclusion in the series—whose very seriality runs counter to any such final resolution. In this regard, the two-hour series finale, at the end of season nine, unfortunately falls just as flat as the film adaptations in its attempt to wrap up all the loose ends and "explain" the vast government-alien conspiracy. (One is reminded of the pitiful attempt of the psychiatrist in *Psycho* to explain Norman Bates's actions.) Framed as a secret tribunal in which Mulder is put on trial for killing a high-ranking military operative (who is actually a human-alien hybrid "supersoldier," played by Adam Baldwin), the final episode offers a succession of flashbacks across all nine seasons, ineffectually trying to tie together all the "pieces" of the conspiracy, which dates back to 1947. This manifestly weak and unsatisfying end to the series stands in sharp contrast to the show's greatest strength: its ability to hint at larger ultimate truths by giving us some of the pieces, pieces that we as individual viewers must put together for ourselves, gleaning whatever symbolic truths from them that we might; for as Campbell reminds us, the "ultimate truth" can only be grasped symbolically.

This same misguided impetus toward closure and resolution marks both of the *X-Files* film adaptations and perhaps finally accounts for their relative failure. By the end of the show's fifth season, when the first movie was released, the *X-Files* mythos had grown too vast to be pinned down and resolved within the limits of a feature-film narrative. As a result, *The X-Files: Fight the Future* is too confusing for neophytes and its conclusion too pat for devoted fans. As for the second film adaptation, *The X-Files: I Want to Believe* falls entirely outside the mythos of the series, as the "big questions" raised so eloquently in the sixth-season opener have simply been abandoned, having been "answered" so unsatisfactorily in the ninth-season finale. Although the second film is passable as a freestanding sf movie, there are no more "pieces" to be offered in the puzzle that was *The X-Files*, and the film bears almost no relation to the intricate dance with "the truth" so successfully carried out in the series (at least for eight of its nine seasons).

The deferred, elusive "truth" underlying the alien conspiracy is symbolic of the truth that everyone seeks: the nature and purpose of our existence. As is the case with all mythological texts, *The X-Files* series at its best does not offer a final, literal truth (or when it attempts to do so, in the last episode or in the films, that truth rings hollow); rather, on the whole it attempts to articulate basic human truths in glimpses, partially, symbolically. Through its dual mode of cinematic and televisual narration, which perennially approaches "the truth" only to back away from it and then pursue it anew, *The X-Files* mythos follows all successful fantasy genre pieces in revisiting those mysteries of human existence, whose ultimate answers can never be known but can only be, symbolically, believed.

NOTES

1. This trio of "conspiracy geeks" often provides comic relief in *The X-Files*, and their popularity with fans led to an ill-fated spin-off series, *The Lone Gunmen* (2001), which ran for just one season (thirteen episodes).

WORKS CITED

Bart, Peter, and Jenny Hontz. "The Peddling of Paranoia." *Variety* 371.7 (1998): 4+. *Academic OneFile*. Accessed 24 Nov. 2010.

Bordwell, David, Janet Staiger, and Kristin Thompson. *The Classical Hollywood Cinema: Film Style and Mode of Production to 1960*. New York: Columbia UP, 1985.

Ellis, John. *Visible Fictions: Cinema, Television, Video*. Rev. ed. London: Routledge, 1992.

Foundas, Scott. "*The X-Files: I Want to Believe* Lacks Plot-Churning Gusto." *Village Voice* 23 July 2008. <http://www.villagevoice.com>. Accessed 27 Dec. 2010.

"The Hero's Adventure." *Joseph Campbell and the Power of Myth*. Narr. Joseph Campbell and Bill Moyers. Public Broadcasting Service, 1988. Athena, 2010. DVD.

Knight, Peter. *Conspiracy Culture: From the Kennedy Assassination to* The X-Files. London: Routledge, 2000.

Lowry, Brian. "*The X-Files: I Want to Believe*." Rev. of *The X-Files: I Want to Believe*. *Variety* 23 July 2008. <http://www.variety.com>. Accessed 27 Dec. 2010.

McCarthy, Todd. "*The X-Files*." Rev. of *The X Files: Fight the Future*. *Variety* 371.7 (1998): 50+. *Academic OneFile*. Accessed 24 Nov. 2010.

"The Message of the Myth." *Joseph Campbell and the Power of Myth*. Narr. Joseph Campbell and Bill Moyers. Public Broadcasting Service, 1988. Athena, 2010. DVD.

Movie Review Query Engine. <http://www.mrqe.com>. Accessed 27 Dec. 2010.

Telotte, J. P. "Re: X-files intro." Message to the author. 17 Nov. 2010. Email.

9   *Serenity*, Genre, and Cinematization

J. P. Telotte

Both film and broadcast television, as John Ellis has argued, typically rely upon "distinctive aesthetic forms to suit the circumstances within which" each operates (111), and that set of distinctive practices, as many of the chapters in this volume suggest, helps to explain some of the difficulties of successfully adapting across the two forms' seemingly similar screens. Yet that same notion of distinct forms might also keep us from appreciating how the very dynamic character of a form such as science fiction can also provide a potential bridge for the adaptive process. For as Ellis allows, genre identity, particularly its formulaic elements, readily "locates" a work for viewers by pointing to similarities between a particular text and others that they have previously experienced (34), thereby raising expectations of a narrative trajectory and, ultimately, of certain narrative pleasures. Drawing upon those location markers, playing upon our mindfulness of generic convention in a way that effectively transcends media, thus might help to mark off a smoother path across the screens. As an example, we might consider a pair of texts whose difficulties in finding a television audience and success as film seem almost equally connected to the workings of genre. The film *Serenity* (2005), adapted from the *Firefly* series (2002–03), garnered highly positive reviews, won several sf-related awards, and confirmed through its modest box-office and DVD success the cult following that the short-lived television show had developed.[1] And it did so, I would suggest, by elaborating on some of the very generic markers that critics contend its televisual version had downplayed.

Certainly, having the television series' creator/writer/producer/director Joss Whedon in charge of the film adaptation provided important continuity and ensured that much of the flavor of the original program would be retained. And the involvement of the entire cast of major actors from the series brought a level of understanding about the characters and their backgrounds—a sense of their *lives*—that would otherwise have been difficult to obtain. Moreover, the fact that the series had already been cancelled allowed its creators a measure of freedom not found in film adaptations done while a television series was still running (see, for example, *The X-Files* [1998]), because *Serenity*'s creative team did not have to be concerned about narrative developments—such as the deaths of several characters—that would disturb *Firefly*'s continuity in the other medium or circumscribe its narrative development.

In fact, the general plot of the film seems largely intended to round off the narrative arc described by the series' fourteen episodes, only eleven of which had aired prior to its cancellation (the remaining three episodes were first broadcast in the summer of 2003). It describes how Simon Tam (Sean Maher) had rescued his sister River (Summer Glau) from a government experimentation station and how they subsequently came to be fugitives aboard the space freighter *Serenity*. It further develops the backstory of the Reavers—the violent, cannibalistic humans who inhabit a distant section of the galaxy and raid outlying settlements—offering an explanation for how they came to be. It intensifies a key plot element of most of the television episodes, the Alliance's ongoing efforts to retrieve River, while linking her to the secret behind the Reavers. And it draws out the heroic potential of its central characters, Captain Malcolm Reynolds (Nathan Fillion) and the crew of the *Serenity*, as they wager their lives to stop the Alliance and reveal its complicity in the creation of the Reavers. For devotees of the series, the film thus managed to answer, in a satisfying way, a number of still-hanging questions, while also further sketching the potential of its diverse group of characters.

Yet what is arguably most interesting about the film version is something that hardly surfaces in *Firefly*'s relatively brief existence, for *Serenity* seems pointedly mindful of its medium in a way that we do not typically see in most television series but that has always been a defining characteristic of the best cinematic sf. As Garrett Stewart observes, the film genre, "whether through an intertextual allusion . . . or through a more generalized evocation of media as embedded mediation," seems consistently to be involved in a kind of "self-inspection" (174) that shows up in few other popular film genres. Calling attention particularly to sf films' omnipresent video screens, holograms, and other media images, he suggests that we see them as consistently reflecting "the mechanics of apparition that permit these films in . . . the first place" (161) and that that we read this form, one that is both about and sourced in technology, as almost invariably self-referential. In the ways in which *Serenity* develops this aspect of its narrative, thereby opening onto a crucial element of its genre character, I would suggest, we can see how it found one of the keys to its rare success as an adaptation.

Of course, on one rather obvious level the television series had already suggested an element of self-consciousness, that is, through its rather playful approach to generic convention. Although set five hundred years in the future after humanity has fled a polluted and burned-out Earth (what several characters refer to as the "Earth-that-was"), *Firefly* "looks like no other space show you've ever seen" (L. Wright 32). Indeed, it most often recalls—both visually and in the idiom of its central characters—the post–Civil War American West, as it sought to create a genre pastiche inflecting the Western with space opera elements. To effect that combination, it asked audiences to accept various familiar conventions of both forms. The old Firefly-class space freighter that provides the home for the show's central characters rather easily and quickly moves from planet to planet; apparently generates its own gravity; seems to use turbojet engines for both atmospheric and space propulsion; and despite its very unaerodynamic look and bulk, can fly—when it is not in danger of crashing, that is—much like a conventional airplane, even a supremely maneuverable one. Moreover, the star systems to which humanity has fled in this future seem improbably full of Earth-like planets. Yet most of those planets are distinctly frontierlike outposts of human civilization; the inhabitants most often dress in costumes that recall the Old West (linen dusters, boots, leather, and wool) and at times ride horses across sagebrush-covered landscapes; and sawn-off Winchesters and Colt six-shooters tend to be the weapons of choice, even when characters face far more advanced firepower. And in mixing these elements, Whedon seemed to revel in the editing possibilities, as when in the "Serenity" pilot episode he created a climactic cross-cut montage as a Reaver spaceship dives on the *Serenity* while several of its crew race horseback across a desert landscape. However, we accept the mixture of such elements—much as we do the language that freely combines archaic English with Chinese slang—because we understand that these *are* conventions and that conventions are important to formula narratives—in fact, that they are often key terms of meaning.

Appropriately, then, one of the first critical assessments of *Firefly* approached it from the vantage of this generic consciousness, examining

Figure 9.1 A Western-style train robbery done in space-opera fashion on *Firefly* (2002). Copyright Twentieth Century-Fox.

both its echoes of the Western and its more specific indebtedness to the classic John Ford film *Stagecoach* (1939). Drawing upon Joss Whedon's acknowledgement of that work as one of his primary models for the series,[2] Fred Erisman discusses a number of similarities: in the general context of both film and series (a post–Civil War frontier); in the larger pattern of their actions (journeying through a hostile environment); in both works' emphasis on character ensemble (the nine disparate types aboard the space transport echoing those nine on the stagecoach); and especially in their common themes (particularly their mutual skepticism about the nature of "civilization" and the importance of individual freedom). The result of these borrowings, he offers, is more than just "an extended homage to John Ford and *Stagecoach*"; it is also "a testament to the continuing vitality of the Western" (257) and, we might suppose, to its continuing ability to speak to a contemporary audience.

And yet, we have to recall that the series did not win an adequate audience, and it is to these echoes, even the very specific references to the Western, that some have turned in trying to explain that failure. Although practically everyone lays some of the blame for *Firefly*'s demise squarely on a number of ill-considered decisions by the sponsoring Fox Network,[3] Ginjer Buchanan rather peevishly suggests that part of it also falls on Whedon's misreading of "pop culture," that "he *must* have noticed that the western was . . . totally moribund" (53). Rather more stridently, Nancy Holder argues that the series was not only far too much Western but also that the decision to work within what she terms "a reactionary genre" required Whedon "to conform to the basic requirements of western-ness" and "to use clichés to stay congruent with his chosen genre" (144, 147). And John C. Wright follows this view, offering that "certain protocols" of the Western are simply "incompatible" with those of sf and that even using some of those conventions today could, and perhaps did, "alienate a large segment" of the audience (157, 166), particularly those who were simply not familiar with the Western. In sum, a number of critics, even those who profess an enormous fondness for the series (like all of those cited above), find fault with Whedon's rather self-conscious emphasis on the various conventions of the Western, not to mention the specific model of *Stagecoach*.

The film adaptation necessarily retains many of its dual generic markings, as well as the archaic speech patterns of its central characters, but it is also a work that finally seems far more intent on establishing a primary generic lineage in sf. In *Serenity*, for example, the key homage is not to a particular Western but to a classic sf film, *Forbidden Planet* (1956). The "forbidden" planet in this case is named Miranda, after the character in Shakespeare's *The Tempest* on which *Forbidden Planet* was based. The repressed "monster from the Id" that is the chief menace of the earlier film is variously translated into River Tam's repressed knowledge about Miranda, her own violent but normally repressed potential, and the monstrous Reavers who were spawned there—and whose origins the Alliance

Serenity, *Genre, and Cinematization* 131

is trying to repress. Furthermore, a key image seen at various times on Miranda is a wrecked ship bearing the number C57D—precisely the name of the rescue ship in *Forbidden Planet*. Rather more broadly, *Serenity* constantly echoes what is now one of the seminal works of sf, *Star Wars* (1977): in its ship that recalls that film's *Millennium Falcon*; in its storm trooper-like Alliance soldiers; in specific scenes, especially the space bar on Maidenhead (which, of course, also evokes an Old West saloon and thus reiterates some of that Western "baggage" that critics have decried); in its central character of Malcolm Reynolds (an obvious offspring of Han Solo (Harrison Ford); and even in various snatches of dialogue. Yet it is not simply the case that, as one critic suggests, Whedon was trying to "trash the whole Western theme" in an effort to make something "resembling a good Sci-Fi Action movie" (Tyler)—that is, that he wanted to repress his own work's not-so-secret identity. In fact, the film even offers echoes of other Westerns, most notably Ford's *The Searchers* (1956). However, in adapting *Firefly* he seems to have recognized a particular potential in the science-fictional aspect of the series that had not previously been developed and that might well have a greater cultural resonance—in fact, one that might even allow him to address some of the circumstances surrounding *Firefly*'s troubled history. In short, he realized that he might be able to explore the complex media context in which *Firefly*, *Serenity*, and indeed all of contemporary culture and its popular texts are enmeshed.

As we turn to *Serenity*, then, we might recall the point made by Garrett Stewart about the sf film's reflexive spirit and about how its generic vitality draws upon its ability to address its own nature, that of other film genres, and even of the cinema itself. Series television, with a few exceptions, does not regularly pursue this sort of self-consciousness. Although series like *Moonlighting* (1985–89), *Stargate SG-1* (1997–2007), and even *The Simpsons* (1989–) have regularly stepped outside their narrative frames, calling

Figure 9.2 River (Summer Glau) watches a hologram viewing screen in the multiply-mediated world of *Serenity* (2005). Copyright Universal Pictures.

attention to their fictional status, there remains relatively little of the sort of systemic self-reflection or the array of referential imagery that Stewart locates in sf media. Yet in *Serenity*, we find that element of self-address throughout the narrative, particularly as it emphasizes what Paul Virilio has described as the workings of "the vision machine" (*Vision* 59) that constructs much of our relationship to contemporary culture. Involving every aspect of our mediated world, but most obviously the realms of film, television and other graphic media, the vision machine is Virilio's trope for the veritable "industrialization of vision" throughout the contemporary media landscape (*Vision* 59). This invisible cultural control over how we see, he argues, results in a kind of filter of "disinformation" and "distraction" that produces "a general loss of a sense of reality that permeates all aspects of normal life" today (*Vision* 67). In effect, it creates a kind of science-fictional landscape that we all inhabit.

Thus, from its lengthy pretitle sequence (which establishes a key link to the television series), through the spectacular demonstration of River's government-programmed lethality, to the efforts by *Serenity*'s crew "to misbehave" (as Malcolm puts it) by revealing the extent of the Alliance's human manipulations, the film frames all of its action in this specifically science-fictional context. That is, all of these key scenes pointedly develop the nature and power of the vision machine, suggesting the effect that Virilio terms "cinematization" or "mediatization," and underscoring the potential he warns about, that "today it would be no exaggeration to say that, 'whenever a people can be mediatized, they are'" (*Art* 6).

The three-scene pretitle sequence, which provides deep background on the government's experiments on River Tam, immediately establishes how this process of mediatization works in this world of five hundred years in the future. A soothing voice-over accompanies a series of images summarizing the recent history of a conflict between the Alliance—"a beacon of civilization," we are told—and the "outer planets," occupied by people who "were not so enlightened and refused Alliance control." If the images and voice seem didactic, it is intentionally so, for we soon realize that we have been watching a kind of film, actually a history lesson being presented to a group of students in a futuristic classroom, set in a bright and shiny new world and surrounded by pastoral imagery. And judging from the reactions of the students, who nicely model the reaction a film audience might well have at this point, it is a persuasive presentation of a utopian situation. They cannot quite understand—just as the film's audience might not—why anyone would have resisted the "blessings" of such a civilization,[4] especially given the images of prosperity and peacefulness that have been screened for them. However, one student, River Tam, with some prescience, breaks that mediatizing spell as she notes the obvious: "People don't like to be meddled with. We tell them what to do, what to think. . . . We're in their heads." And on that note—one effectively punctuated by a match cut from the teacher (Tamara Taylor) reaching toward River's head to a doctor jabbing a needle directly into her forehead, causing her to scream in pain—we see the Alliance violently reaching into *her* head, as they set about conditioning her, transforming her, as the lead doctor offers, into "a living weapon."

The shift is certainly a rather shocking one—in time, in place, in tone—but it effectively rips away the pleasant veneer of this world, its utopian semblance, to reveal in a pointedly science-fictional way the use of technology to condition human behavior, to control human thought, and certainly with as much savage force as one might find on the Old Western frontier.[5] Yet even as this scene seems to afford a certain level of narrative truth by peeling away part of its generic trappings, those pleasant utopian images, we soon recognize that it too—or at least a good bit of it, as Simon questions Dr. Mathias (Michael Hitchcock), sets off a bomb, and then rescues his sister in the resulting confusion—is also just a film of sorts, a hologram record of all that has happened in the facility. For once again a voice-over suddenly intrudes into the narrative we are watching, commanding it to "Stop!" and then "Backtrack," causing the image first to freeze and then reverse to another moment we have already witnessed, seemingly from a privileged and private angle. That controlling voice introduces the Alliance's unnamed operative (Chiwitel Ejiofor), who then disconcertingly walks through the image of River and Simon that we have been watching, walks into—and thus reveals—the primary diegesis. In doing so, he not only lays bare the level of surveillance that marks the diegetic realm—one in which everything that has occurred in this facility has apparently been seen and recorded by cameras that are essentially everywhere—but also reaffirms the extreme level of control that attends this mediatizing, as if lives themselves were practically immaterial and could simply be stopped, actions and motivations studied clinically, intentions even reversed. And in that ability to simply walk into and exert control over what had seemed to be an autonomous world—the seemingly private, unobserved actions of Simon and River—the operative also poses the sort of extradiegetic question seldom raised on television: about our own levels of surveillance, conditioning, and control; about the extent to which, as Virilio describes the contemporary situation, we too might be "victims of the set" that the postmodern world has become (*Art* 79), and our world little more than virtual images lacking real substance.

The third scene in the opening sequence builds on the violent consequences that attend resisting this process of mediatization. After replaying for Dr. Mathias some of his interaction with Simon, the operative—again like a teacher, now instructing the doctor in how he has failed the Alliance—unleashes a quick and bloody reprisal with his samurai sword, swiftly dispatching the medical facility's imposing security guards and then "helping" Mathias to die what he terms "an honorable death." The ease with which he then turns from murderer to video researcher, demanding "all the logs" on River's conditioning sessions before returning to study the scene of Simon and River's escape, suggests his distance and detachment, his ability to stand outside of this cinematized world. He has, we note, no rank, no name; and in his cold detachment he seems to embody, even more than the teacher and doctor, the violence that is implicit, and largely unseen, in the Alliance's rule—as well as in its utopian offer, now seen in its full ironic light, to help everyone, as River's teacher soothingly articulates, "enjoy the comfort and enlightenment of true civilization."

The second major sequence to develop this focus on mediatization, River's unleashing of her weaponlike potential at the Maidenhead spaceport, confirms this sense of the power the Alliance wields while it further suggests the panoptical dimension of its utopian world. As Mal and his crew enter a bar, an establishing shot shows in the background a large video screen playing news, followed by a cut to a shot from the vantage of the screen, as if we were looking through it—or at what it is transmitting to a viewer elsewhere, for this screen apparently disguises a camera that monitors activities here, as the "Maidenhead Security Feed" and "Recording" digital stamps on the images confirm. It is an immediate reminder of what we observed in the pretitle sequence: that everything that seems to proceed from the film's own narrative consciousness might also prove to be a monitored, mediatized reality, a panoptical feed. Several cuts to action in the bar underscore this point as they are quickly followed by shots from the monitor's point of view, again showing the "Security Feed" notation on-screen, linking the movie camera's freely roving eye and the surveillance camera's equally penetrating gaze and insinuating a general suspicion about who or what controls what we see.

As River enters the bar, another series of quick cuts expands on this dual perspective by matching up subjective shots and reverse angles, as if River and the screen/security feed were looking at each other. And indeed, after a fashion they are, as each essentially constitutes not the sort of televisual "glance" that John Ellis attributes to that medium (24) but an engaged gaze of recognition. As evidence we might consider the extreme close-up of River as she looks up, the lighting on her face suddenly changes, and she mutters the word "Miranda," which heralds her transformation. Similarly, we later see the operative somewhere in a ship in deep space, staring at her image as he views that security feed, analyzing the image, then pulling up information on Mal and his crew as he springs into action. Each view constitutes a kind of shock of recognition: River as she is triggered by a program hidden in what she sees on-screen to turn into a "weapon," and the operative as he is triggered into action by seeing the goal of his searches. And those equally shocking visions thrust home the surveillance power of the Alliance, suggesting that its electronic gaze is pervasive, certainly just as prying as the eye of the narrative camera, which for all we know could be complicit in a similar programming power or coercive force over us all.

What River sees also is quite telling in this context of mediatization. What captures her attention (and her psyche) is not the news we had previously been hearing amid the background cacophony about a horrific Reaver

Serenity, *Genre, and Cinematization* 135

attack—one that she and the others escaped in the previous sequence and that might logically draw her interest—but the seemingly innocuous "Fruity Oaty Bar" commercial, an *anime*-style cartoon that effectively speaks in a slant manner about what is about to happen to her, and, we might suppose, to all of the Alliance's subjects. The lyrics tell us that "Fruity Oaty Bars make a man out of a mouse / Fruity Oaty Bars make you bust out of your blouse" as the images depict a mouse painfully and in bloody fashion ripping apart to reveal a man and then an octopus suddenly bursting from a cartoon character's dress and draping itself over several other figures. It is a curious, even dreamlike mixture, upbeat and bright animation yet with a sinister and frightening dimension, appropriately suggesting the way the Alliance works through its media powers, as it employs a seemingly innocent appearance to mask its dictates while trying to extend its bloody and tentacle-like hold over everyone.

The transformation that irresistibly follows that viewing, as the mouse-like River becomes not a man but an Alliance-trained killing machine, vividly demonstrates that mediatizing power while also further attesting to the Alliance's ability to control all that is seen. River's indiscriminate attack on everyone in the bar is subsequently played and replayed in the film—at the beginning of the next scene in the operative's ship as he views the security feed of this incident, and later as Mr. Universe (David Krumholtz) watches and relishes what he terms "the very best violence." His observation that this material has not played on the regular news opens onto his explanation that such "news" is, in any case, not real news, just "the puppet show" that the Alliance Parliament allows "a somnambulant public" to see, whereas the Maidenhead incident represents "the truth of the signal," which he with his mass of equipment is able to track down because, ultimately, "Nothing can stop the signal." It is an important bit of information, not because Mr. Universe is thus able to confirm that the forces of the Alliance are monitoring everything in an effort to find River, but because it also suggests an eventual weakness in that mediatizing process. For if, as Mr. Universe says, "the signal" is "truth," if it "goes everywhere," and if "Nothing can stop" it, then it might well be turned to a subversive use. In a comment that echoes River's encounter with the Fruity Oaty Bar commercial—or the subliminal message encoded in it—the phenomenologist Gaston Bachelard once suggested that "everything that makes us see, sees" (78). And in this observation, mutatis mutandis, there lies a note of possibility: everything that sees can also, as any good moviemaker or anyone who has sought to mobilize the cinematic "gaze" might hope, make us see as well, even help us see through the mechanism of that vision machine.

And certainly, this potential is at the core of *Serenity*'s conclusion, as Mal and the crew determine to broadcast the "truth" "everywhere" by using Mr. Universe's equipment to transmit the secret accidentally revealed to River, to send out the Alliance's own report about its failed experiment in human control on Miranda. That the ensuing fight between Mal and the operative to use Mr. Universe's transmitter is of unusual importance is quickly underscored by Mal's almost uncharacteristic assertion that he is "willing to die" to reveal "the truth that burned up River Tam's brain"; as he says, "the rest of the 'verse is going to know too, because they need to." Turning this struggle over a signal into a monumental physical effort—that is, intercutting Mal's fight with the operative with the crew's desperate efforts to fight off the Reavers, while Alliance and Reaver ships are destroying each other overhead and thousands are dying—helps to translate the cold, digital manipulations of the Alliance into stark physical terms, to link this conclusion to the earlier scenes of violence surrounding that mediatizing influence, and to suggest, through the impact of cinematic spectacle, just how much is ultimately at stake here.

The bloody, if momentary, victories that occur at various levels all fittingly culminate here in a display of video images as Mal manages to broadcast the report on Miranda. Surrounded by monitors and forced to watch, the operative must see what Mal ironically introduces as "a world without sin," the catastrophic result of the Alliance's meddling with its subjects, the human toll of its utopian planning. In a look of outward regard—a shot that we seldom see in televisual narrative—the operative stares directly into one of those monitors, but into our eyes as well, and we see a tear come down his cheek as he watches these horrors, the truth behind "the set" that he has helped erect. The point is that if these images can have, as they perceptibly do, a transforming effect on the operative, on the sort of man who, as Shepherd Book (Ron Glass) had earlier noted, "believes hard," then they can also move others throughout the 'verse—and perhaps us as well. And indeed, the operative's observations some time later that this broadcast "has weakened their regime" and that he is "no longer their man" attests to that effectiveness.

However, the operative also reminds Mal that the Alliance and its forces "are not gone" and that they "do not forget." It is an ominous note that would be most appropriate for the serial-like world of television narrative as it seems to point toward other encounters to come between the crew of *Serenity* and the government forces, continuing adventures rather than a satisfying closure—or frustrating cancellation. Of course, closure has in recent years become somewhat less fashionable in cinematic narrative too, given the vogue for and profitability of sequels. And with *Firefly* cancelled by the Fox network, perhaps this hint of a possible sequel served to offer Whedon, his coworkers, and the cult fan base of "browncoats"[6] their own path of resistance to a seemingly irresistible, network-determined fate. So that reminder takes on a rather double, if also somewhat fanciful, thrust.

Virilio fittingly strikes a similar note of compromise in his own description of the thoroughly mediated postmodern world. He suggests that today there really is no escape from the technological, no real victors, only survivors of an ongoing struggle; as he notes, "to be a survivor," like Mal and his comrades, "is to remain both actor and spectator of a living cinema"

(*War* 48), to continue to cope with the "set" in which we must all live. What we must do, though, again like the *Serenity*'s crew and like those who take the power of the media seriously, is to try to look behind the scenes. Here we see how one might—at great pain and even with great loss—sometimes turn the tables and use that very mediatizing power against those who wield it in a monolithic fashion. Everything that sees, Mal and the others now recognize, can help us and others see as well, and in seeing, to better cope with this world. And it is a lesson that, we might suppose, Whedon would hope is not lost on the seemingly captive audience of network television. There is, he might suggest, a kind of moral imperative that should attach to our viewing, a need to act as well as see—an imperative he would also develop in great detail in his *Dollhouse* series (2009–10).

It is a lesson, though, that probably could not have been easily taught within *Firefly*'s initial hybrid mixture, wherein elements of the Western often seemed to trump those of sf, perhaps taking us too far away from our own postmodern context with its inevitable awareness of our own constructedness, or as he might put it after *Dollhouse*, our own "doll"-like situation. But Whedon has observed that "when you build a show . . . you open as many doors as possible, and then don't look in all of them" ("Still Flying" 8). This pattern of gradual opening up follows, in great part, from the very nature of a series, for as he explains, a "show's going to evolve; relationships are going to evolve; storylines are going to evolve. That's the way they work" ("Still Flying" 8); other doors will open later. As a work that from its start straddled various generic boundaries, *Firefly* opened a variety of these narrative and thematic doors, ones that would lead into the rich and culturally resonant territories that attach to those generic types. And in adapting the series to film, Whedon, as these comments suggest, apparently decided to enter one of the doors that has always been central to sf cinema—the one that reflexively foregrounds the relationship between its technological concerns and the technology that makes film itself possible, that in effect explores the shared foundations of sf and cinema, and the one that brought with it the added benefit of resonating with the whole process of working within the world of network television.

In doing so, *Serenity* manages to sound a caution, not only about how our technology might be employed to "meddle with" our very being—manipulating our thoughts, conditioning our behavior (both central elements of his later *Dollhouse*)—but also about how our technologically driven media, both film and television, can conspire in that meddling by channeling our experience through the "vision machine" that they constitute. It is a good cautionary note that should inflect how we approach both network television and the cinema, and as I have hinted here, perhaps even a somewhat satisfying strike for Whedon and his colleagues at Fox's hasty cancellation of *Firefly*. *Serenity* certainly suggests there is some comfort in the notion that nothing can stop "the signal," that the technology itself is finally not in control but is just a powerful tool that we have to use properly—in this case, to make oneself heard—and to guard against others' misuse. In dealing with it, though, we are probably always going to be in for a kind of "bumpy ride," as Mal notes at the film's conclusion, when a piece of his ship—a not-very-important part, we hope—breaks off and drifts into space.

It would seem to be a bumpy ride as well for anyone who tries to adapt a television series to film. Relatively few have successfully managed it, partly because by the time a series has ended its broadcast life, audience interest has often also run its course. Then too, one has to worry about which parts might be expendable and which not, in effect, whether some of those elements that made the series work might be allowed simply to drift off. Whedon's notion of opening narrative doors, though, seems a useful guideline; it suggests that one must work from a premise that was, from the start, constructed with multiple possible doors, with the potential for opening onto not just more of the same—a direction that only leads to the empty nostalgia of adaptations like *Lost in Space* (1998) or *My Favorite Martian* (1999)—but onto still-intriguing possibilities, perhaps even onto the very nature of the form. Certainly, in adapting *Firefly*, Whedon seems to have located a door that is crucial to sf cinema, but one that also foregrounds a concern, particularly resonant today, with the sort of vision machine that conditions our media experience and thus our lives.

NOTES

1. Well aware of how unusual the adaptation of *Serenity* is, Joss Whedon readily notes, "This movie should not exist. . . . Failed TV shows don't get made into major motion pictures unless the creator, the cast, and the fans believe beyond reason" (qtd. in Russell n. pag.).
2. Whedon has described his indebtedness to *Stagecoach* in a variety of sources. He notes that what the series "set out to be was . . . a *Stagecoach* kind of drama with a lot of people trying to figure out their lives in a bleak and pioneer environment," and he explains how that film also influenced the series' style, especially the detailed treatment of the Firefly-class freighter that is its primary set: "If you actually watch *Stagecoach*, they spend a long time introducing the stagecoach, because that space is very important" ("Into the Black" 6, 10).
3. A number of reasons have been offered for the relatively short life of the television series, but most rank foremost several key decisions by executives at the Fox Network. It was promoted essentially as an adventure-comedy, given a difficult time slot, and run out of intended order. Perhaps most important, Fox insisted that the series be introduced not with the two-hour introduction that Whedon originally shot ("Serenity, Part I" [2002] and "Serenity, Part II" [2002]), but with a hastily created action-oriented episode—a move that not only created problems of narrative continuity but also made it more difficult to establish the show's characters and situation, arguably its key elements. Ginjer Buchanan also suggests that this troubled history extends beyond the problems caused by "the impatient and clueless folks at Fox" (53). She points to the "spirit of Gene Roddenberry" as responsible for "creating a science fictional future that has so much emotional power and longevity" that it has come to

dominate television viewers' visions of space and of the future in a way that makes the production of a very different view of that world difficult (52).
4. This point about the blessings of civilization that the Alliance offers is, as some might recognize, precisely the coda for *Stagecoach*: when Ringo Kid (John Wayne) and Dallas (Claire Trevor) are released, Doc Boone (Thomas Mitchell) notes that "at least they're free from the blessings of civilization." By striking this note at the beginning rather than the end of his film, Whedon not only quickly foregrounds the issue of what constitutes civilization but also links that question to the tools, particularly those media tools, that are used to support and extend this futuristic version of civilization's sway.
5. This scene especially recalls another dimension of that mediatizing process; as Virilio notes, "until the twentieth century, to be MEDIATIZED meant literally being stripped of one's IMMEDIATE RIGHTS" (*Art* 6).
6. "Browncoat" is the name given to the rebels in the series. It was quickly adopted by *Firefly*'s fans who, in their own sort of rebellion against corporate decision making, tried to save the series by taking out an ad in *Variety*, who campaigned successfully for a movie version of the series, have held their own fan convention (known as a "flanvention"), produced a documentary on the show's cult following (*Done the Impossible: The Fan's Tale of* Firefly *and* Serenity (2006), and who continue through organized letter-writing and e-mail campaigns to prod various cable channels and Whedon himself to resurrect the series or do a sequel to the film.

WORKS CITED

Bachelard, Gaston. *On Poetic Imagination and Reverie*. Trans. Colette Gaudin. Indianapolis: Bobbs-Merrill, 1971.
Buchanan, Ginjer. "Who Killed *Firefly*?" *Finding Serenity: Anti-Heroes, Lost Shepherds and Space Hookers in Joss Whedon's Firefly*. Ed. Jane Espenson. Dallas: BenBella, 2004. 47–53.
Ellis, John. *Visible Fictions: Cinema: Television: Video*. Rev. ed. London: Routledge, 1992.
Erisman, Fred. "*Stagecoach* in Space: The Legacy of *Firefly*." *Extrapolation* 47.2 (2006): 249–58.
Holder, Nancy. "I Want Your Sex: Gender and Power in Joss Whedon's Dystopian Future World." *Finding Serenity: Anti-Heroes, Lost Shepherds and Space Hookers in Joss Whedon's* Firefly. Ed. Jane Espenson. Dallas: BenBella, 2004. 139–53.
"Into the Black: An Interview with Joss Whedon." *Firefly: The Official Companion*. Vol. 1. Eds. Abbie Bernstein, Bryan Cairns, Karl Derrick, and Tara Di Lullo. London: Titan, 2006. 6–13.
Russell, M. E. "The Browncoats Rise Again." *Daily Standard*. Accessed 1 Aug. 2007. <http://www.weeklystandard.com/Content/Public/Articles/000/000/005/757fhfxg.asp>.
Stewart, Garrett. "The 'Videology' of Science Fiction." *Shadows of the Magic Lamp: Fantasy and Science Fiction in Film*. Eds. George E. Slusser and Eric S. Rabkin. Carbondale: Southern Illinois UP, 1985. 159–207.
"Still Flying: An Interview with Joss Whedon." *Firefly: The Official Companion*. Vol. 2. Eds. Abbie Bernstein, Bryan Cairns, Karl Derrick, and Tara Di Lullo. London: Titan, 2007. 6–13.
Tyler, Joshua. "*Serenity*—Review." *Cinema Blend*. Accessed 15 July 2007. <http://www.cinemablend.com/reviews/Serenity-1157.html>.

Virilio, Paul. *The Art of the Motor.* Trans. Julie Rose. Minneapolis: U of Minnesota P, 1995.
———. *The Vision Machine.* Trans. Julie Rose. Bloomington: Indiana UP, 1994.
———. *War and Cinema: The Logistics of Perception.* Trans. Patrick Camiller. London: Verso, 1989.
Wright, John C. "Just Shove Him in the Engine, or the Role of Chivalry in *Firefly.*" *Finding Serenity: Anti-Heroes, Lost Shepherds and Space Hookers in Joss Whedon's* Firefly. Ed. Jane Espenson. Dallas: BenBella, 2004. 155–67.
Wright, Leigh Adams. "Asian Objects in Space." *Finding Serenity: Anti-Heroes, Lost Shepherds and Space Hookers in Joss Whedon's* Firefly. Ed. Jane Espenson. Dallas: BenBella, 2004. 29–35.

Part IV

Issues in Science Fiction Adaptation

10 *Doctor Who*
Adaptations and Flows
Mark Bould

Doctor Who (1963–89, 2005–), the longest-running and most successful sf television show of all time (Miller), provides unique insights into how television programming has developed over the last half-century. Soon after its inception it became a multimedia franchise, with comics, books, toys, games, a rebooted series, spin-off series, interactive web content, and so on, as well as cinematic, direct-to-video, televisual, and internet/DVD pornographic film adaptations.[1] Such a proliferation of commercial texts poses particular problems—and opportunities—for adaptation studies, which hitherto has tended to concentrate on the nature of textual transformations between more-or-less canonical texts and their adaptations—a focus that typically loses sight of adaptations and their sources as commodities bound up in the realms of production and consumption. In order to comprehend the work of adaptation, we must first come to terms with the nature of the intellectual, creative labor required by both producers and consumers of textual commodities. That is, we need, as Paul Grainge suggests, to "examine the historically specific conjunctures in which interests and meanings are brought into being and actively negotiated" (8). To do so requires us to pay attention not only to "the diversity of attitudes and practices that exist among consumers, audiences and subordinate social groups," as has been common in cultural disciplines since the 1980s, but also, "with equal sensitivity to context and complexity," to "the interests and meanings worked out within the field of cultural production" (8). Thinking about adaptation therefore requires us to consider both the processes by which we make culture out of commodities, and those by which capital is made out of culture.

Because *Doctor Who* originated in early 1960s broadcasting and has virtually always existed across multiple media platforms, the notion of "flow"—developed to describe television before the 1980s and subsequently reconceptualized in media convergence studies—provides a useful framework for considering the franchise's proliferation of adaptations. In the 1970s, Raymond Williams, culture shocked by American commercial television, influentially decried the medium's "single irresponsible flow of images and feelings" (92), echoing postwar public discourses about the flood of (Americanized) mass culture threatening British cultural identity. This notion of televisual flow, later elaborated by John Ellis in the 1980s, rapidly became dominant in television studies: Jane Feuer described the medium as a "continuous, never-ending sequence in which it is impossible to separate out individual texts" (15); and John Fiske, while critical of many of the conclusions derived from this model, conceded that television's typical form was "a rapid succession of compressed, vivid segments, where the principle of logic and cause and effect is subordinated to that of association and consequence to sequence" (105). However, Fiske argued, rather than inundating viewers, this segmented flow prodded them into active meaning- and pleasure-making.

To an extent, this shift in perspective followed the transition from the era of televisual "scarcity" (often referred to as TVI) to an era of televisual "availability" (TVII), in which channels proliferated and the industry emphasis shifted from attracting mass audiences to niche marketing aimed at more affluent audience segments. The current transition to an era of televisual "plenty" (or TVIII) has been described in terms of issues of media convergence, multimedia platforms, transmedial storytelling, and the cultivation of long-term loyalty to series and channels by multiplying potential points of contact between brand and consumer. In such discussions, "flow" is still used, often without critical reflection, to describe several phenomena:

> Media companies are learning how to accelerate the flow of media content across delivery channels to expand revenue opportunities, broaden markets, and reinforce viewer commitments. Consumers are learning how to use these different media technologies to bring the flow of media more fully under their control and to interact with other consumers. The promises of this new media environment raise expectations of a freer flow of ideas and content. (Jenkins 18)

Programming, it seems, has broken its banks, becoming an inescapable *flood* of content across different media platforms as producers increasingly orient their endeavors to "the lucrative possibilities of migrating content and program repurposing" (Caldwell, "Convergence" 48). However, as William Uricchio argues, beginning with the introduction of remote control devices, the viewer began to gain some mastery over this torrent; indeed, the development of domestic and portable recording, playback, time-shifting, and space-shifting technologies has produced "the effect of enhanced viewer choice in the form of a *stream* of programming carefully tailored to the viewer's preferences, tastes, and desires" (Parks 135, my emphasis). Simultaneously, digital technologies have enabled new communities to emerge among geographically dispersed consumers and for new kinds of relationships to develop with producers, ranging from moments of co-creativity to excessive policing of intellectual property. These transformations of the media environment all have important consequences for adaptation study.

Adaptation is typically understood as "the appropriation of meaning from a prior text" (Andrew 97). Such an understanding reifies the prior text as a fixed object with a set meaning rather than treats it as an ongoing site of multiple contested meanings. Thus a conventional understanding of adaptation might, for example, limit itself to considering the relationships and variations between a seemingly bounded and fixed text, such as the second *Doctor Who* serial, the seven-parter now known as *The Daleks* (21 December 1963–1 February 1964), and similarly contained adaptations: the 1964 novelization by the series' script editor David Whitaker, *Doctor Who in an Exciting Adventure with the Daleks*,[2] and the film adapation, *Dr. Who and the Daleks* (Flemyng UK 1965), coscripted by Whitaker. However, such delimitations exclude from consideration some potentially interesting questions. For example, to what extent should an episode of serial television, predicated on principles of continuity and repetition with difference, be understood as an adaptation of the *preceding* episode? Or a serial arc be understood as an adaptation of the preceding serial arc? Moreover, if adaptation is understood in contemporary industry terms as a repurposing and migration of content, what should one make of the *TV Century 21* comic's *Dalek* strip (1965–66), scripted by Whitaker, which offers a different take on Dalek history than does the serial, novelization, or film; or of the Go-Gos' "I'm Gonna Spend My Christmas with a Dalek" (1964), the first of many *Doctor Who* tribute singles; or of the Daleks' appearances in other television shows, including a 1964 edition of *The Black and White Minstrel Show*; or of Dalek merchandizing, which in the 1960s included toys, games, badges, a PVC costume, and sweet cigarettes with collectible cards? To what extent do such texts and artefacts function as adaptations? And if one accepts that consumers also adapt texts, what should one make of the games children play with such merchandizing—or of children just playing at being Daleks?[3] Furthermore, how do all of these texts and experiences contest and transform our understanding of the "prior text," a television serial that was broadcast once and never intended to be seen again?

Although it is clearly beyond the scope of a single essay to explore all of these questions, we can begin to lay a foundation for answering them. In his work on adaptation, Robert Stam describes a text as an

> open ... structuration ... reworked by a boundless context. [It] feeds on and is fed into an infinitely permutating intertext, which is seen through ever-shifting grids of interpretation. ... All texts are tissues of anonymous formulae, variations of those formulae, conscious and unconscious quotations, and conflations and inversions of other texts. (57, 64).

This description aptly fits not only the individual episode or serial, but also the entire *Doctor Who* franchise, a vast body of material produced by so many people since 1963 that no romantic-bourgeois notion of the "author" or "original" could possibly survive intact. Even the first episode broadcast, "An Unearthly Child" (23 November 1963), cannot be treated as an "original" because it is not only a tissue of intertextual borrowings but also is itself an adaptation of prior texts—an unbroadcast pilot version and the (hastily revised) script. However, in an era in which media corporations increasingly conceptualize ownership in terms not of authorship and copyright but of reproducibility and trademarks (see Lury), both promotional material and critical commentary continue to deploy notions of authorship, canonicity, authenticity, and fidelity as tools for shaping and validating certain experiences of *Doctor Who*. Such discursive interventions demonstrate the dynamic vitality of a series and a franchise that are full of inconsistencies and variations of tone and content, that continually exceed monological control and have always done so. Restoring this sense of fluidity, of contingency and contestedness to the object of analysis, whether a prior text or its subsequent permutations, is an essential first step in considering adaptation.

One way to do this is to foreground the relationships among form, content, and the context of production and consumption. Whereas questions of form dominated early studies of televisual flow, treating the programs and genres merely as variations on the same structure, contemporary uses of flow tend to treat content as if it were separable from form (or at least reducible to trademarkable characters and story worlds). In order to reconnect form, content, and context, this chapter will begin by attempting to reconstruct and explore the experience of watching a mid-1960s *Doctor Who* serial as an example of Ellis's televisual "flow." It will then trace some elements of the franchise's transmedial flow, focusing on the first cinematic film, the 1996 television movie, and the relaunched television series.

DOCTOR WHO AND TELEVISUAL FLOW

On 22 May 1965, 10 million people watched the new episode of *Doctor Who*, "The Executioners." For many, this was already a Saturday evening habit;[4] others would have tuned in because the ending of the previous Saturday's "The Final Phase" (the conclusion of the four-parter now known as *The Space Museum* [24 April–15 May 1965], seen by 8.5 million viewers) signaled that the Daleks were returning. "The Executioners" was the seventy-second episode of *Doctor Who* and the first installment of the series two six-parter—followed by "The Death of Time," "Flight Through Eternity," "Journey into Terror," "The Death of Doctor Who," and "The Planet of Decision"—that is now called *The Chase* (22 May–26 June 1965), but was known to its makers as *Serial R* or *The Pursuers*.

With the next season's *The Savages* (28 May–18 June 1966), *Doctor Who* abandoned individual episode titles and began to identify each serial by name, but for most of its first three seasons—for 118 episodes—each story flowed into the next without the clear demarcations that serial titles would have provided. Indeed, the division of a more-or-less continuous series into a succession of more-or-less distinct serials (of between one and twelve episodes) was partly driven by production planning and budget management.[5] For example, for bookkeeping reasons, the BBC treated the four-part *Serial M*, now called *The Romans* (16 January–6 February 1965), as episodes three to six of *Serial L*, now called *The Rescue* (2–9 January 1965)—a two-parter designed to introduce Vicki (Maureen O'Brien) as a new series regular after the departure of Susan (Carole Ann Ford) at the end of "Flashpoint," the final episode of the six-parter now called *The Dalek Invasion of Earth* (21 November–26 December 1964). Although each serial achieved a relatively high degree of narrative closure, the viewer did not know in advance how many episodes a particular serial would have. Such uncertainty—and the sense of an endless sequential flow—was reinforced by the use of cliffhangers. Individual episodes featured a midpoint crisis (to aid overseas sales to commercial broadcasters who required convenient advertising breaks) and a closing cliffhanger to propel viewers into the next episode, which began by repeating the previous episode's cliffhanger ending. This was also sometimes the case with a serial's final episode, with the cliffhanger placing narrative closure under erasure by propelling the Doctor and the viewer into the next serial, which had in effect already started. This sense of seriality is strongly emphasized by *The Chase*, which takes in three different terrestrial locations and at least two other planets in quick succession, rather than being set in a single time/place.

During the 1960s, *Doctor Who* was broadcast on a 405-line VHF AM system and viewed on analog televisions in which the cathode-ray tube fired electrons at a phosphor-coated screen to form images, refreshing alternate lines every fiftieth of a second.[6] This technology made the image "curiously ephemereal, . . . half gone and fading before it [was] even completed" (8) while also creating an overwhelming sense of immediacy, as if the program was "transmitted and received in the same moment that it [was] produced" (Ellis, 132). The BBC's adoption of Ampex video tape in 1958 meant that it was no longer the case that certain kinds of programs, such as drama series, were broadcast live, but that does not seem to have diminished the sense of immediacy, in part because of the persistence of many of the production practices of live broadcasting. For example, cutting videotape was time-consuming and generally considered too expensive because the tape could not then be reused to record another program.[7] Consequently, although it was not necessary for an entire episode of *Doctor Who* to be shot as a single continuous performance, it was recorded in a multiple camera studio, with "events . . . staged in temporal sequence and picked up by a number of cameras one of whose images [would be] selected at any one moment by the director" (Ellis 149) and recorded on tape. The action was normally shot from one side (to keep other cameras out of the shot), producing a grammar (unlike that of classical continuity editing's shot/reverse-shot) that favors longer takes, does not elide "dead" time, and tends to show actions in their entirety. This practice can be seen in the contrast between a sequence in "The Ordeal," episode six of *The Daleks*, and its restaging in the film *Dr. Who and the Daleks*. In the former, Ian (William Russell) and Barbara (Jacqueline Hill), making their way with three Thals through a tunnel in the mountain behind the Dalek city, come to a precipice across which they must jump, one by one. This sequence lasts nearly eleven minutes, including an interpolated minute-long scene with the Doctor (William Hartnell) and Susan captured by the Daleks; excluding this other scene, the sequence still accounts for more than 35% of the episode's total running time. In the film, the same sequence (with one fewer Thal) takes less than five minutes, including an eighty second-long interpolated scene. This contrast in duration reflects not only the respective media's editing styles but also the economic factors affecting production.

Doctor Who's budgetary constraints—there was just one studio day to shoot each twenty-five-minute episode—are perhaps most apparent in the broadcasting of errors. For example, in *The Chase*'s "Journey into Terror," the shadows of the camera and microphone boom are visible on Ian's torso when he tries to dissuade the Doctor from entering a gothic laboratory; when we cut to a reverse shot of the action from the laboratory level, the offending camera and its operator are visible behind Ian, belatedly scooting out of shot. Such errors are quite common, especially because the series was intended to be broadcast only once: in "The Executioners," Maureen O'Brien struggles not to laugh as she delivers some absurd dialogue and tries to cover it up by playing out the rest of the scene in a mildly hysterical manner; in "The Death of Doctor Who," as the camera tracks around a group of Daleks outside the TARDIS, camera 5, which is not involved in shooting the scene, comes into view; and in "The Planet of Decision," Hartnell fluffs his line, warning Ian and Barbara that if they try to use the Dalek time machine to return to 1960s London they will "end up as a couple of burned cinders flying around in Spain . . . in space!"

Broadcasting such material as "good enough"—rather than reshooting—undoubtedly contributed to the sense of immediacy, betraying not only economic necessity but also the apparent disposability of *Doctor Who*, a program to be swept away by the flow of television, never to be seen again. This "good enough" quality is also evident when other kinds of production economy become apparent. For example, the entrance to the Dalek time machine has a dog-leg structure that is difficult for the cast to navigate but ensures that its interior is not visible from outside, thus avoiding the need to build an adjacent set. In "The Executioners" this entrance is positioned on the right of the frame so three Daleks can disappear around the dog-leg, reenter the shot from behind the camera, and board the time machine again, thus doubling the number of Daleks in the "assassination group." At the climax of "Journey into Terror," the Daleks reveal that they have constructed a robotic simulacrum of the Doctor with which to fool his companions. It is played by Edmund Warwick (who only slightly resembles

Hartnell) in long shot, miming to Hartnell's off-camera voice; and when we cut to a close up, it is of Hartnell in front of a mismatched backdrop. In the following episode, Hartnell plays the real Doctor, voices Warwick's fake Doctor, and plays the fake Doctor when extended interactions with the companions are required; and Warwick plays the fake Doctor, miming to Hartnell's off-camera voice, and the real Doctor in several long shots when his lip movements can be obscured. When the two Doctors finally confront each other, Hartnell switches between roles in a series of close-ups shot from alternating sides to create an eyeline match, which are intercut with three-shots of the companions observing the exchange as if watching a tennis match. The unintended, but also unavoidable, visibility of such production economies, generate a sense of urgent jerry-rigging rather than classical stability. This is also the case with the visual contrast between taped studio images and the occasional filmed location inserts, such as the stock footage of Manhattan used in "Flight through Eternity" or the long shots in "The Executioners" of Russell's and O'Brien's stand-ins cavorting on the dunes at Camber Sands, itself standing-in for the otherwise studio-bound desert planet Aridius.

It is difficult to judge precisely how obvious the resulting differences in image texture would have seemed,[8] but two sequences in *The Chase* particularly emphasize how "[t]elevision has always been *textually messy* . . . textural rather than transparent" (Caldwell, *Televisuality* 23). In "The Planet of Decision," the Dalek assassination group joins battle with the robot Mechonoids who have imprisoned the Doctor and his companions. This sequence begins with a zoom-in over a model of the Mechonoid city to its central plaza where three Mechonoids have gathered, then cuts to a montage of brief studio sequences that involves canted camera, zooms, extreme close-ups and multiple superimpositions of action, flames, and animated explosions. Intended to conceal that the director is working on a single set with just three Daleks and three Mechonoids,[9] this filmic montage is such a stylistically pronounced compression of time and space that it shatters any sense of continuous televisual time. A second overtly textural sequence comes at the end of the same episode with a cut from the Doctor and Vicki on the planet Mechanus—a studio set with a painted backdrop—to a filmed insert of Ian and Barbara's return to London. There follows a twenty-three-second montage, including rostrum zooms, of twenty-eight freeze-frames of Ian and Barbara larking about in Trafalgar Square, on the Embankment, and in St James's Park, a stylistic choice that resonates with both *nouvelle vague* and swinging London films—as *The Chase* was being made, The Beatles were putting the finishing touches to *Help!* (Lester UK 1965). Copying filmed freeze-frames to video for broadcast certainly complicates the distinctions Ellis draws between the transience of the televisual and the ontological weight of film's photographic material, enlivening these characters' filmic stillness with televisual immediacy, memorializing them in their departure even as this moment of loss is swept away by television's flow.

Although television's lower image-resolution and the inability to "pause" or "rewind" would have rendered production economies and errors less obvious than they now seem, they would have been as commonplace and as fleeting as the ghosting, interference, loss of vertical or horizontal synchronization,[10] and other phenomena that disrupted the experience of televisual flow while guaranteeing its transience. Although television "continues whether a particular set is turned on or not" (Ellis 138), some programs were irrecoverable, with there being "hardly any chance of catching a particular TV programme 'tomorrow' or 'next week sometime' as there is with a cinema film" (111). Word-of-mouth undoubtedly increased the audience for "The Executioners," and those who had missed the Daleks' initial reappearance at the end of *The Space Museum* were able to enjoy one of the rare opportunities to "catch next week" something whose initial broadcast had been missed, thanks to the opening repetition of the previous cliffhanger.[11] This sequence also introduces *The Chase*'s self-reflexive depiction of the audience's experience of television. After the familiar opening titles, whose distinctive visual design and soundtrack announce the program,[12] an image of advanced communications equipment fades in. The camera tracks back to allow a Dalek to enter the shot, turn, and speak into the device, reporting the departure of the TARDIS from the preceding story's planet. The camera tracks in on the wall speaker from which another Dalek voice responds, revealing that the Daleks have their own time machine with which to pursue the doctor. In the preceding episode, this was akin to a continuity announcer's end-credits verbal trailer for the next installment; here, the direct address to the audience is more urgent, setting up the narrative while delaying its start so viewers, alerted by the timeslot, title sequence, theme music, and the repeated cry of "Exterminated!" can gather around the television set.

Appropriately, the following sequence depicts just such a gathering. In the TARDIS console room, the Doctor, fiddling with the workings of a large, unfamiliar machine, chides Vicki for distracting him. She stomps off to find Ian, who is reading in his room. Her kibitzing annoys him, so she heads into Barbara's room, where she spills a tray onto the dress Barbara is making for her. This familylike group (with the Doctor as grandfather, Ian and Barbara as parents, and Vicki as bothersome teenage child) then gathers in the console room as the Doctor's hammering on the recalcitrant machine causes "an unfortunate juxtaposition of the sonic rectifier and the lineal amplifier," eliciting a high-pitched wail. Vicki, who understands the machine better than the male adult trying to fix it, explains: "anything that ever happened anywhere in the universe is recorded in light neutrons" and the time-and-space visualizer "converts neutrons of light energy into electrical impulses," enabling "you [to] tune in and see any event in history." At the Doctor's request, each companion then selects a time and place to observe: Abraham Lincoln's Gettysburg Address; the court of Queen Elizabeth I, where she urges Shakespeare to write a play about Falstaff in love

Figure 10.1 The time-and-space visualizer: television on television in "The Chase," *Doctor Who*. Copyright BBC.

and Sir Francis Bacon suggests a play about Hamlet; and a 1965 BBC1 appearance by The Beatles performing "Ticket to Ride."

In the first two cases, the camera tracks in between the pseudofamily gathered around the small screen housed in the much larger machine, and then we cut to prerecorded inserts of the action. These hypodiegetic image streams possess even more pared-down visuals and an even more exaggerated frontality than are typical in presenting the primary diegesis, suggesting a lower image resolution; and both times, horizontal lines disrupt the image before it finally disappears in a storm of interference. This sense of the world being always already part of an ephemeral televisual flow, provided you happen to dip in at just the right moment to see an event before it is lost forever, is emphasized by the visualizer's third image stream. When it proved impossible to schedule a serial based on a future Beatles concert,[13] and footage of them from *Top of the Pops* was unavailable (because the BBC routinely wiped and reused tapes of that show), the director transferred footage being shot for the 10 April 1965 *Top of the Pops* onto tape to insert into *Doctor Who*. This segment is the only surviving footage from the band's numerous appearances on *Top of the Pops*.

The visualizer's flow of discontinuous segments is, of course, not "the only thing going on" (Ellis 128) in this pseudodomestic setting, and it is interrupted by the TARDIS's arrival on Aridius. Vicki switches the machine off while the Doctor consults instruments on the TARDIS console about the conditions outside. The size of the visualizer prop has evidently made it impractical to include the console in the console room, and so the Doctor's actions are shot from the viewpoint of the console's central column. In medium close-up, Hartnell looks out of the screen, his hands working (nonexistent) controls out of shot beneath the screen, before throwing the (nonexistent) switch that opens the TARDIS's doors behind him. This unusual shot produces the peculiar sensation that the *viewer* is being switched off so that the pseudofamily can get on with their lives in the outside world.

Some time later, Barbara is disturbed by noises emanating from the TARDIS, where the visualizer is still working. Their "sporadic rather than sustained" looking returns to the device, which, like the family television, has continued to operate "in blithe ignorance of its lack of reception" (Ellis 24, 138). Indeed, it seems to wait for Barbara's entrance before tuning in on the "channel" showing the Daleks initiating their transtemporal pursuit of the TARDIS, and then to wait before giving any concrete information until Barbara has summoned the Doctor. There is a strong sense of these viewers having "delegated their look to the TV institution" (25), leaving the visualizer to watch whatever it chooses until something of interest summons them. The Doctor, fortunately, is aware that the apparent liveness of on-screen events is deceptive—as he notes, "My machine can only pick up things that happened in the past"—and sets about evading the Dalek assassins. This self-reflexive depiction of televisual flow suggests that program makers themselves might have thought in terms similar to those that would later become a dominant discourse about television.

One of the most difficult things to imagine in revisiting these early episodes is just how unstable the program actually was. Nearly cancelled in its first season, it was only rescued by the popularity of the Daleks, and it was only with the departures and replacements of Susan, Ian, Barbara, and other companions, and then the replacement of Hartnell with Patrick Troughton at the end of season four's *The Tenth Planet* (8–29 October 1966) that the absolute centrality of the Doctor was cemented, along with his nonhuman status.[14] *Doctor Who* had no overarching story arc, and events from one serial tend to be forgotten in the next. Much of the backstory and detail of *Doctor Who*'s story world that are now often taken for granted were created in an ad hoc manner, appropriate to the unrecoverable, ephemeral flow of television in the era of scarcity.

Yet *Doctor Who* was never exactly scarce.

DOCTOR WHO AND TRANSMEDIAL FLOW

In the second half of the 1980s, *Doctor Who*'s audience hovered around 5 million, dropping to an all-time low of 3.1 million for the first episode of season twenty-six's first serial, *Battlefield* (6–27 September 1989), and *Doctor Who* was cancelled when the season ended on 6 December 1989.[15] The drawn-out decline of the series across the decade is often blamed on its alienation of general viewers by becoming "aimed almost solely at its fans" through "endless attempts to fold the show in on itself by evoking its past" (Newman 5, 98). This strategy is proleptic of the television industry's current conventional wisdom: "that the cultivation of . . . story-worlds . . . is as crucial an element in its success as is storytelling" (Sconce 95). Faced with a huge archive of often contradictory material (an increasing amount of which was becoming accessible in other forms, such as novelizations, reference books, magazine articles, and videos), this attention to stabilizing continuity by emphasizing certain elements of the story world—that is, reintroducing and firming up details initially introduced on an ad hoc basis—is as understandable as it was quixotic. Neil Perryman's claim that "the majority of fans now feel that . . . ancillary additions to the franchise," such as books, comics, games, and web content, "enjoy little or no legitimacy in terms of canonicity" (23) indicates a similar desire to give *Doctor Who*'s story-world the kind of coherence typical of more contemporary franchises, such as the "Buffyverse" of *Buffy the Vampire Slayer*.

As we have noted, debates around media convergence have reconceptualized and transvalued the notion of "flow." Henry Jenkins, for example, enthuses about "the flow of content across multiple media platforms, the cooperation between multiple media industries, and the migratory behavior of media audiences who will go almost anywhere in search of the kinds of entertainment experiences they want" (2). To whatever extent such phenomena might be characteristic of the present moment, it is important to note that this is a matter of proliferation and acceleration rather than rupture. However, rather than catalog *Doctor Who*'s transmedial flow, this section will focus on three specific adaptations in relation to production and consumption contexts.

In 1964, the British production company Aaru struck a deal to adapt *The Daleks* as *Dr. Who and the Daleks*.[16] The first screen-media attempt to adapt the story world, it repurposed the serial, intended for a family audience, as a U-certificate film that children could see without an accompanying adult;[17] it was released on 23 August 1965, in the closing weeks of the school summer holiday. Whereas a family audience required "different points of entry that would attract viewers of all ages" (Leach 13), hence the age-range and gender mix of the Doctor's first companions, the film, which was adapting its source for a different audience rather than trying to establish continuity or canonicity, transformed the principal characters and their relationships. It replaced Hartnell's mysterious and cantankerous Doctor with a genial inventor, Doctor Who (Peter Cushing). Barbara (Jennie Linden) became his glamorous granddaughter, and Ian (Roy Castle) her comic-relief boyfriend. More significant, Susan (Roberta Tovey) was transformed from an older teen into an eleven-year-old of whom Doctor Who is particularly fond (the *Doctor Who* strip in *TV Comic* had already given the Doctor a pair of younger grandchildren as companions). The opening scene establishes the bond between them—and their status as identification figures for the young audience—by inverting expectations as the camera tracks from Susan reading *Physics for the Inquiring Mind*, past Barbara reading *The Science of Science*, to Doctor Who reading an issue of *The Eagle* comic. Susan's red sandals indicate a further repurposing of the story world, imbuing its science-fictional iconography with a *Wizard of Oz* sensibility, transforming the Dalek homeworld of Skaro into a vivid Technicolor fantasy space. The forest is dark and threatening—especially when Susan must run through it alone—but the soundstage walls lend it a reassuring, cartoonlike simplicity. The city sets are spacious and intriguingly geometrical, and on their walls are light fittings that look like giant crumpled sweet wrappers and surveillance cameras that suggest Dalek eyestalks. The title sequence—an abstract, not-exactly-psychedelic kaleidoscope of colors, set to fairly generic 1960s jazz-pop—would not have been out of place in a James Bond spoof, and the male Thals, with their shaved arms and chests and heavy eye makeup, look like premature glam rockers. Not uncommon for a children's fantasy film, camp and queer potentials innocently abound, addressing infantile and adolescent sexualities through visual excess in the safety of cinema's dark spaces. And significantly, the film was a success, as *Dr. Who and the Daleks* proved one of the top twenty films at the 1965 British box office and prompted a more expensive but less successful sequel the following year.[18] Both films continued to be screened at Saturday morning movie clubs for over a decade and were repeated on television far more frequently than any serial.

Throughout the 1980s, various companies expressed interest in making other *Doctor Who* films, but whereas these attempts came to nothing, television producer Philip Segal's seven-year quest to relaunch the series on a US network eventually resulted in *Doctor Who* (Sax 1996), a television movie coproduced by Universal TV, Twentieth Century-Fox Television, and BBC Worldwide for $5 million.[19] When broadcast in the UK on 27 May 1996, it attracted an audience of 9.08 million. In the US, Fox premiered it during the May sweeps period—when Nielsen conducts detailed ratings surveys and thus when network competition is most intense—opposite a major baseball game and an episode of the hit comedy series *Roseanne* in which Dan (John Goodman) has a heart attack. With only 5.5 million viewers (a smaller audience share than usual for Fox's Tuesday night movie), Fox did not exercise its option to make a second television movie. In his analysis of the television movie's cultural and ideological transformations of *Doctor Who*, Peter Wright attributes this poor performance to its adoption of "non-controversial content, a bland homogeneity that will offend no one and appeal in some, relatively superficial, way to everyone" (Fiske 319, qtd. "Intertextuality" 85). But this decision should also be understood in the context of the challenges facing US networks in this period, when cable television was depleting audience size and thus advertising revenues.

Television movies were themselves a product of mid-1960s primetime competition, becoming a standard feature of network programming that was used to build audiences during sweeps periods through star casting and topical content. The most successful example was *The Day After* (Meyer 1983), which attracted one hundred million viewers when ABC premiered it during November sweeps. However, television movies were usually independent productions, that is, properties the network did not own and thus could not fully exploit. By 1996, with audiences fragmenting and the cost of marketing one-off programs escalating, the network television movie was in decline, soon to disappear and to be reinvented by cable channels not as event programming but as resolutely ordinary television (see Perren), returned to the flow from which it once stood out. Cable had already taught the networks "that the real programming game in town was [no longer] about initial air-dates, but about syndication rights" (Caldwell, "Convergence" 47). Because the *Doctor Who* television movie was not commissioned as a series pilot or approached as a potential "back-door" pilot, its ratings would have had to be remarkable for it to lead to further production, not least because Universal was "pushing the reorder of more episodes of *Sliders*. They owned 100 per cent of that show and had only a 50 per cent stake in *Doctor Who*, so you can pretty much figure out which one they really intended to support" (Segal with Russell, 144–45).

The *Doctor Who* television movie was caught between the desire to maintain continuity (another aspect of "fidelity") with the series and the need to significantly repurpose it to attract funding. Despite major revisions suggested by John Leekley's series "bible," created when Segal was developing the project as a potential series for Amblin (reprinted in Segal with Russell), the movie that was eventually produced emphasized continuity with the BBC series by casting the seventh Doctor, Sylvester McCoy, in an opening sequence that culminates in his regeneration as Paul McGann's eighth Doctor. On the one hand, this link prompted fans to expect the movie to conform to the series, as did the scattering of iconic props—a nine-hundred-year diary, a sonic screwdriver, a yo-yo, jelly babies—associated with earlier Doctors. On the other hand, it signaled a failure fully to reimagine *Doctor Who* for the industrial, social, and cultural contexts in which it was produced and consumed: Fox had built its reputation on narrow casting and counterprogramming so as to attract the lucrative eighteen-to-thirty-four-year-old male demographic, an audience unlikely to be familiar with the BBC series. This attempt to address a distinct audience resulted in a movie that introduced too much of the story world for new viewers, while its efforts to render unfamiliar content comprehensible and palatable—such as making the Doctor half-human so he could enjoy a conventional romance with Grace Holloway (Daphne Ashbrook)—alienated many who expected a "faithful" continuation of the series.

The relaunched *Doctor Who* television series (2005–) has proved more successful in managing the tension between continuity and radical revision, enjoying the space permitted by series (rather than one-off) production to carefully reveal the extent of its revisions to, and selective continuities with, the earlier series and the television movie. This dynamic is signaled by the decision not to regenerate Sylvester McCoy or Paul McGann into Christopher Eccleston, but to launch the viewer, along with Rose Tyler (Billie Piper), the new companion-to-be, into the middle of an adventure in which the Doctor is already involved; and by incrementally unveiling a tidied-up story world in which the Daleks and Time Lords eradicated each other in the Time War (except, of course, for those who later turn out to have survived), and the Cybermen are confined to a parallel universe from which they cannot venture into our own (except, of course, when they can). Series production also enabled the Doctor's romantic and/or sexual involvement with his companions—studiously ignored as a possibility in the classic series—to be cast as a series of variations on the reluctant romance narrative made familiar to contemporary television by such series as *Moonlighting*, *Remington Steele*, *Cheers*, and *The X-Files*. His involvement with Rose is eventually resolved by sending an accidentally produced human version of himself to join her in the alternative universe in which she now lives. The real Doctor, mourning her loss, does not really notice how smitten with him her successor, Martha Jones (Freema Agyeman), is until she returns to her life on Earth rather than waiting for him to reciprocate her feelings; and while the Doctor and Donna Noble (Catherine Tate) become close, their relationship is never romantic. The romance between Captain Jack Harkness (John Barrowman) and the Doctor was thwarted—before the events of the series—when he became immortal, a fixed point in the timeline, and thus someone to whom the Doctor could not be close for long. Although the latest companion, Amelia Pond (Karen Gillan), expresses her sexual interest in the Doctor as clearly as does Captain Jack, she has a fiancé, Rory Williams (Arthur Darvill), whom she marries and whom the Doctor accepts as a TARDIS regular.

As this array of relationships suggests, the new *Doctor Who* participates in television drama's adaptation of soap opera techniques, ranging from the psychologizing of character and emphasis on affect to the privileging of close-ups to convey emotion and emotionality. As Glen Creeber suggests, this turn need not be understood "as a move away from the 'social' and the 'political' and towards the 'personal' and the 'trivial,' but as a gradual progression towards newer forms of representation which offer a more contemporary articulation of present social experience" (13); but it must also be understood in terms of an industry emphasis on a property's "emotional capital," that is, the "consumers' emotional investment in media content" that can be manipulated in order to "increase the brand's worth" (Jenkins 279). This logic also underpins the turn to high-concept narratives; to spectacular CGI effects; and to the luminous cinematography and production design's emphasis on large blocks of primary color (plus yellow and purple); and to Murray Gold's semiotically thin, filmic scoring that connotatively "stresses melodrama *not* science fiction, fantasy-horror *not* science fiction, and action-adventure *not* science-fiction" (Hills, *Triumph* 179)—all of which target a general audience that might not normally be interested in sf and whose attention might wander. The new format of standalone and multiepisode stories with season-long narrative arcs, which gradually emerge as hints and rumors are released (in the series as well as its publicity and online extensions [see Perryman]), is designed to reward both casual and attentive viewers. The guiding principles, however, are always the exploitaton of a multimedia property and the audience's affective investments in it. For example, one of the most recent adaptations is *Doctor Who: The Adventure Games*, available free in four downloadable installments from the BBC website. Piers Wenger, the series' new executive producer, boasted that "[t]here aren't 13 episodes of *Doctor Who* this year, there are 17—four of which are interactive. Everything you see and experience within the game is part of the *Doctor Who* universe" ("BBC Unveils *Doctor Who*"). In the same press release, other BBC executives emphasized the integration between the televisual and interactive episodes, with the latter "defining the look and feel of future TV episodes" ("BBC Unveils *Doctor Who*"). However, such statements are a bit misleading. The four interactive episodes, which link together like a miniseason, do not "weave exciting narrative strands" with the television episodes they were developed "alongside" ("BBC Unveils *Doctor Who*"), but exist parallel to them, playing no part in the season's narrative arc. But in addition to producing additional points of contact with the franchise/brand, the interactive episodes' ambiguous relationship to the television series permitted the reintroduction of the classic series' Cybermen to the story world (in the second episode, "Blood of the Cybermen").[20] Whether this interweaving will lead to genuine transmedial storytelling is unclear, but the suggestion that *The Adventure Games* will influence "the look" of the television episodes at least hints that the classic series' Cybermen might return to the series. More likely, it is an attempt to continue to exploit the Cybermen, even though the series' own story logic prevents them from reappearing, while offering fan and older audiences what might be dubbed "narrow-cast affective content."

The same press release conjured the image of families "gather[ing] round the PC or Mac in the same way they do the television" ("BBC Unveils *Doctor Who*"). This image returns us once more to the importance of consumption contexts in understanding adaptations. Like "The Chase," the new *Doctor Who*—often credited with reconstituting a seemingly irremediably fragmented primetime family audience—self-reflexively depicts its heterogeneous audience (and, less consciously, its own contradictory attitude toward them as consumers). For example, in "The Runaway Bride" (25 December 2006), when the abducted Donna must leap from a speeding cab to the TARDIS hovering alongside, two children watch through the rear window of a car, as rapt by the action as the viewing audience, urging her to jump and celebrating when she makes it. In contrast, minutes later,

Donna has no idea what the Doctor is talking about when he mentions a giant spaceship over London, featured in the previous year's "The Christmas Invasion" (25 December 2005), because she "had a bit of a hangover" and thus missed both the event itself and its media coverage. Between the children's immediate, visceral response and Donna's inattentiveness, the show sketches a range of alternatives. "The Voyage of the Damned" (25 December 2007) introduces Bernard Cribbins as Donna's grandfather Wilfred Mott, who still finds joy in contemplating the wonders of the night sky—a piece of sentimental casting, reminding older viewers of their own engagement with children's television when young.[21] Fans and other migratory audiences who pursue their interest across media are figured by the group of gentle misfits who become friends while searching for the truth about the Doctor in "Love & Monsters" (17 June 2006), and by Clive (Mark Benton) in "Rose" (26 March 2005), who is compiling a dossier on the mysterious Doctor who reappears throughout history just before catastrophes strike. A genial figure, enjoying the amused tolerance of his wife and son, he nonetheless embodies a stereotypical middle-aged, overweight, and slightly creepy fan; but even as it denigrates fandom, Clive's brief appearance includes a nod to the fans—a photo of the Doctor in Dealey Plaza on the day before the very first episode of *Doctor Who* was broadcast. "Blink" (9 June 2007) features Larry Nightingale (Finlay Robertson), a video store clerk obsessed with DVD easter eggs in which the Doctor directly addresses the camera, as if in conversation with an unheard interlocutor; and Sally Sparrow (Carey Mulligan) who, after interpolating (and interpellating) herself into this conversation so as to learn how to avoid

Figure 10.2 Easter egg: the Doctor on DVD on television on television in "Blink," *Doctor Who*. Copyright BBC.

the threat of the Weeping Angels and rescue the Doctor, becomes obsessed with tracking him down. They are mutually redeemed from potentially dangerous obsessions by the flourishing of their relationship.

However, one of the episode's recurring images is of the Doctor's direct-address exhortation to the diegetic viewer, repeated as a coda to the extradiegetic viewer: "Don't blink. . . . Don't turn your back. Don't look away. And don't blink." In "the era of [the] permanent *marketing* campaign, where the selling of an entertainment environment is ongoing, an activity punctuated by commodity texts" (Acland 77), even a critically and commercially successful flagship television program, it seems, must demand our attention in order to reinforce viewer commitment while simultaneously working to sweep us up in the channel's flow of subsequent programs. The new *Doctor Who* desires the attentive cinematic gaze, but it also must allow for the distracted glances of viewers who might otherwise disperse, refragmenting the family audience it managed to stick back together. Yet it also wants this dispersal to occur, for family members to engage with migrated content and ancillary products, with the property's transmedial flow, so as to ensure they return next week, every week.

Adaptation studies has long recognized that adaptations may take a variety of approaches to their sources. Michael Klein and Gillian Parker, for example, divide adaptations between those that "give the impression of being faithful" (9), those that retain "the core . . . narrative while significantly reinterpreting . . . the source" (10), and those that regard "the source merely as raw material, as simply an occasion for an original work" (10). Dudley Andrew and Geoffrey Wagner offer similar tripartite schemes, and likewise privilege source over adaptation. The example of *Doctor Who* should begin to indicate how, and to what extent, such approaches are inadequate to the media environment we now inhabit. As Robert Stam argues, adaptation studies must rid itself of deeply rooted cultural prejudices about the superiority of older and linguistic arts over newer and visual ones, but it must also go further than that. It must pay greater attention to production and consumption contexts and more fully embrace the range of adaptations across media forms and such social practices as play. And in order to address this plenitude, it must develop a more fluid and flexible critical vocabulary, one that might include not only such terms as cover versions, renditions, permutations, iterations, supplements, remediations, and reboots but also, perhaps, reversed polarities and regenerations.

I would like to thank David Butler for his comments on a draft of this essay.

NOTES

1. *Summoned By Shadows* (Baggs 1992) and its sequels are the most notable fan-produced DTV movies, *Abducted by the Daleks* (Nowicki 2005) and

Doctor Loo and the Filthy Phaleks (Gee 2005) the best-known pornographic adaptations.
2. Only two further serials were novelized in the 1960s, *The Web Planet* (13 February–20 March 1965) as Bill Strutton's *Doctor Who and the Zarbi* (1965) and *The Crusade* (27 March–17 April 1965) as Whitaker's *Doctor Who and the Crusaders* (1966); but Target Books reissued them in 1973 as the first titles in a series that would adapt over 150 serials by 1994.
3. For comprehensive details of *Doctor Who* tribute records and books, see the websites *The Millenium Effect* (<http://www.millenniumeffect.co.uk/audio/tributes/index2.html>) and *Timelash* (<http://www.timelash.com/tardis/items.asp?books>), respectively. For critical analyses of Dalekmania, merchandizing, consumption, and play, see Bignell, "Space" and "The Child"; and Bignell and O'Day 61–64; and on novels, comics, audio adventures, and online adjuncts, see Perryman.
4. In its first three seasons, *Doctor Who* ran for an average of forty-one consecutive weeks per year with average viewing figures of 8.7 million, peaking at 13.5 million for "The Web Planet," the first episode of *The Web Planet* (13 February–20 March 1965), and dropping to 4.3 million for the first episode of *The Savages* (28 May–18 June 1966), the first time the audience was smaller than the 4.4 million who watched *Doctor Who*'s very first episode.
5. In the 1970s, the format eventually settled down into a combination of (mostly) four-parters and six-parters (or two- and three-parters when season 22 [1985] experimented with forty-five-minute episodes).
6. In 1964, BBC2 was launched using the 625-line PAL UHF color system developed for Western Europe, but it would be five years until BBC1 and ITV switched to this higher-definition system. Because older television could not receive such broadcasts, and because national coverage was legally mandated, programming was rebroadcast in 405-line monochrome until 1985.
7. A tape cost approximately £100; *Doctor Who* was budgeted at just £2,300 per episode, increasing to £2,750 by the end of season three.
8. The episodes from this period available to viewers are either video or DVD releases struck from original tapes or kinescopes/telerecordings (the latter produced for export by filming a monitor showing the taped show, with the camera synchronized to the monitor's scan rate), which may or not have been "cleaned up" (to varying degrees), and most likely watched on either 625-line analog or 1080-line digital televisions (the latter have an image resolution of 1925 pixels per line, which are reproduced exactly time after time, whereas the former have the equivalent of 704 pixels and imperfect reproduction). Such downgradings and upgradings of the image and soundtrack ensure that we can never experience them as originally broadcast.
9. In *The Daleks* and *The Dalek Invasion of Earth*, the problem of persuading viewers that the Daleks pose a numerical threat was addressed by including life-size cardboard cutouts in the background of several scenes. *The Dalek Invasion of Earth* also relies on the Daleks' cheaply costumed, mostly nonspeaking Robomen and cheap-looking Slyther monsters to swell their ranks. *The Chase* borrowed several of the Daleks made for *Dr. Who and the Daleks*, which finished production just before studio work on the serial began. Motionless—and thus presumably unoccupied—Daleks appear in the background of several scenes.
10. In "The Watcher," the first episode of the four-parter now called *The Time Meddler* (3–24 July 1965), the Doctor's impatient explanation of the TARDIS controls to new companion Steven (Peter Purves) includes a small metaleptic joke: looking out of the screen and pointing upward and to his right,

where some television sets would have had their controls, he says, "and that over yonder is the horizontal hold."
11. The relatively casual viewing of this audience segment is matched by the Daleks themselves, who apparently missed the end of *The Dalek Invasion of Earth* and the following twenty episodes, thus causing the robot Doctor to betray its identity by mistakenly calling Vicki "Susan."
12. To the sound of BBC Radiophonic Workshop's electronic title music, a white line rises like a rocket up the middle of the black screen, unzipping it and opening it out into Rorschach-like mirrored patterns of white light in the middle of which, courtesy of vision mixing from another camera, a white title fades in, then recedes from us as if down a low-budget version of the stargate tunnel of light in *2001: A Space Odyssey* (Kubrick UK 1968). This is not a spurious connection: Kubrick's office did contact the BBC to discover how a zero-gravity effect was achieved in the twelve-parter now known as *The Daleks' Master Plan* (13 November 1965–29 January 1966). On the Radiophonic Workshop's contribution to *Doctor Who*, see Barron; Donnelly; and Niebur.
13. "The original script was about the fiftieth anniversary of their TV debut, a concert in 2012, and the Beatles were to have been made up as old men. Later drafts said that it was 1994, and that they were appearing on 3D BBC TV in colour" (Wood and Miles 174).
14. For the first three seasons, no one seemed entirely certain whether the Doctor was human or alien. The Time Lords would not be mentioned until Troughton's final serial, *The War Games* (19 April–21 June 1969), which came after six seasons and nearly 250 episodes.
15. Cancellation did free *Doctor Who* from "budgetary constraints, intermittently poor direction, often pantomimic acting, occasionally juvenile scripting, and the BBC's own inconsistent attitude towards it," enabling the "programme's true potential" to begin "to be realised" (Wright, "Shared World" 78) when Virgin Books launched its *Doctor Who—The New Adventures* in 1991. This series of sixty-one novels, continuing the story of the seventh doctor (Sylvester McCoy), was joined in 1994 by *The Missing Adventures* series, featuring the various Doctors in thirty-three adventures interpolated between television serials. When the BBC decided not to renew Virgin's license, Virgin published twenty-three novels featuring the *New Adventures* companion Bernice Summerfield, who has continued to appear in stories, novels, and audio dramas from Big Finish Productions. Between 1997 and 2005, the BBC then published seventy-five *Eighth Doctor Adventures* (1997–2005) featuring the television movie's Doctor (Paul McGann), and seventy-six *Past Adventures* featuring the other Doctors. On the *New Adventures*, also see Smith; on Big Finish audio adventures, see Hills's "Televisuality."
16. Earlier that year, Disney approached the BBC about an adaptation of the seven-parter now known as *Marco Polo* (22 February–4 April 1964), but this project seems to have gone no further than an initial enquiry.
17. Since 1912, all films have had to obtain a certificate from the British Board of Film Censors (now the British Board of Film Classification) before they could be exhibited in the UK. From 1951–70, there were three kinds of certificate available: U (suitable for children); A (children must be accompanied by an adult); and X (suitable only for those older than sixteen).
18. Arguably, this failure resulted from the proliferation of potential identification/entry points that diminished the centrality of Susan and the Doctor. Producer Milton Subotsky abandoned plans for a third film, probably an adaptation of *The Chase* or *The Keys of Marinus* (11 April–16 May 1964).

19. On failures to make a *Doctor Who* film and on the development and production of the television movie, see Lofficier; and Segal with Russell.
20. In the classic series, the Cybermen came from the planet Mondas; in the new series they were the invention of a mad scientist on an alternative Earth in a parallel universe that is now completely inaccessible.
21. In addition to appearing as a companion in the second *Doctor Who* film, *Daleks—Invasion Earth 2150 A.D.* (1966), Cribbins narrated *The Wombles* (1973–75), voiced numerous other children's animations, and was a recurring storyteller on *Jackanory* (1965–96).

WORKS CITED

Acland, Charles R. *Screen Traffic: Movies, Multiplexes, and Global Culture.* Durham: Duke UP, 2003.
Andrew, Dudley. *Concepts in Film Theory.* Oxford: OUP, 1984.
Anon. "BBC Unveils *Doctor Who—The Adventure Games.*" BBC press release 8 Apr. 2010. *BBC.com.* Accessed 12 Nov. 2010. <http://www.bbc.co.uk/pressoffice/pressreleases/stories/2010/04_april/08/doctor_who.shtml>.
Barron, Lee. "Proto-Electronica vs. Martial Marches: *Doctor Who, Stingray, Thunderbirds* and the Music of 1960s' British SF Television." *Science Fiction Film and Television* 3.2 (2010): 239–52.
Bignell, Jonathan. "The Child as Addressee, Viewer and Consumer in Mid-1960s *Doctor Who.*" *Time and Relative Dissertations in Space: Critical Perspectives on Doctor Who.* Ed. David Butler. Manchester: Manchester UP, 2007. 45–55.
———. "Space for 'Quality': Negotiating with the Daleks." *Popular Television Drama: Critical Perspectives.* Ed. Jonathan Bignell and Stephen Lacey. Manchester: Manchester UP, 2005. 76–92.
Bignell, Jonathan, and Andrew O'Day. *Terry Nation.* Manchester: Manchester UP, 2004.
Caldwell, John Thornton. "Convergence Television: Aggregating Form and Repurposing Content in the Culture of Conglomeration." *Television After TV: Essays on a Medium in Transition.* Ed. Lynn Spigel and Jan Olsson. Durham: Duke UP, 2004. 41–74.
———. *Televisuality: Style, Crisis, and Authority in American Television.* New Brunswick: Rutgers UP, 1995.
Creeber, Glen. *Serial Televisions: Big Drama on the Small Screen.* London: BFI 2004.
Donnelly, Kevin J. "Between Prosaic Functionalism and Sublime Experimentation: *Doctor Who* and Musical Sound Design." *Time and Relative Dissertations in Space: Critical Perspectives on Doctor Who.* Ed. David Butler. Manchester: Manchester UP, 2007. 190–203.
Ellis, John. *Visible Fictions: Cinema, Television, Video.* Rev. ed. London: Routledge, 1992.
Feuer, Jane. "The Concept of Live Television: Ontology as Ideology." *Regarding Television: Critical Approaches.* Ed. E. Ann Kaplan. Frederick: University Publications of America, 1983. 12–22.
Fiske, John. *Television Culture.* London: Routledge, 1987.
Grainge, Paul. *Brand Hollywood: Selling Entertainment in a Global Media Age.* London: Routledge, 2008.
Hills, Matt. "Televisuality Without Television? The Big Finish Audios and Discourses of 'Tele-centric' *Doctor Who.*" *Time and Relative Dissertations in*

Space: Critical Perspectives on Doctor Who. Ed. David Butler. Manchester: Manchester UP, 2007. 280–95.

———. *Triumph of a Time Lord: Regenerating Doctor Who in the Twenty-First Century*. London: I. B. Tauris, 2010.

Jenkins, Henry. *Convergence Culture: Where Old and New Media Collide*. New York: New York U P, 2006.

Klein, Michael, and Gillian Parker, eds. *The English Novel and the Movies*. New York: Frederick Ungar, 1981.

Leach, Jim. *Doctor Who*. Detroit: Wayne State UP, 2009.

Lofficier, Jean-Marc. *The Nth Doctor*. London: Virgin, 1997.

Lury, Karen. *Interpreting Television*. London: Hodder Arnold, 2005.

Miller, Liz Shannon. "'Doctor Who' Honoured by Guiness." *Variety* 26 July 2009. *Variety.com*. Accessed 12 Nov. 2010. <http://www.variety.com/article/VR1118006512?refCatId=14>.

Newman, Kim. *Doctor Who*. London: BFI, 2005.

Niebur, Louis. "The Music of Machines: 'Special Sounds' as Music in *Doctor Who*." *Time and Relative Dissertations in Space: Critical Perspectives on Doctor Who*. Ed. David Butler. Manchester: Manchester UP, 2007. 204–14.

Parks, Lisa. "Flexible Microcasting: Gender, Generation, and Television-Internet Convergence." *Television After TV: Essays on a Medium in Transition*. Ed. Lynn Spigel and Jan Olsson. Durham: Duke UP, 2004. 133–56.

Perren, Alisa. "Whatever Happened to the Movie-of-the-Week? (The Shocking True Story of How Made-For-TV Movies Disappeared from the Broadcast Networks)." *Convergence Media History*. Ed. Janet Staiger and Sabine Hake. London: Routledge, 2009. 161–70.

Perryman, Neil. "*Doctor Who* and the Convergence of Media: A Case Study in 'Transmedia Storytelling.'" *Convergence: The International Journal of Research in New Media Technologies* 14.1 (2008): 21–39.

Sconce, Jeffrey. "What If? Charting Television's New Textual Boundaries." *Television After TV: Essays on a Medium in Transition*. Ed. Lynn Spigel and Jan Olsson. Durham: Duke UP, 2004. 93–112

Segal, Philip, with Gary Russell. *Doctor Who Regeneration*. London: HarperCollins, 2000.

Smith, Dale. "Broader and Deeper: The Lineage and Impact of the Timewyrm Series." *Time and Relative Dissertations in Space: Critical Perspectives on Doctor Who*. Ed. David Butler. Manchester: Manchester UP, 2007. 263–79.

Stam, Robert. "Beyond Fidelity: The Dialogics of Adaptation." *Film Adaptation*. Ed. James Naremore. London: Athlone, 2000. 54–76.

Uricchio, William. "Television's Next Generation: Technology/Interface Culture/Flow." *Television After TV: Essays on a Medium in Transition*. Ed. Lynn Spigel and Jan Olsson. Durham: Duke UP, 2004. 163–82.

Wagner, Geoffrey. *The Novel and the Cinema*. Rutherford: Fairleigh Dickinson UP, 1975.

Williams, Raymond. *Television, Technology and Cultural Form*. London: Fontana, 1974.

Wood, Tat, and Lawrence Miles. *About Time: The Unauthorized Guide to Doctor Who, 1963–1966, Seasons 1 to 3*. Des Moines: Mad Norwegian, 2006.

Wright, Peter. "Intertextuality, Generic Shift and Ideological Transformation in the Internationalising of *Doctor Who*." *Foundation* 92 (Autumn 2004): 64–90.

———. "The Shared World of *Doctor Who*: From *The New Adventures* to *The Regeneration*." *Foundation* 75 (Spring 1999): 78–96.

11 Déjà Vu All Over Again?
Cowboy Bebop's Transformation to the Big Screen

Michelle Onley Pirkle

Every television episode of the Japanese *anime* series *Cowboy Bebop* (1998–99) begins with the same jazz piece that sets the tone and serves as a kind of mission statement for the show. In this introduction, the saucy notes of "Tank" (performed by The Seatbelts) weave in and out among the fragmented images that splash and slide across the screen. Layered within the images of the main characters and their spacecraft are fleeting lines of text that flash across the screen multiple times, often broken into snippets. When pieced together, those lines describe a modern movement in jazz that started at Minton's Playhouse in Harlem in 1941. The artists there began a creative competition in an attempt to play jazz "freely," and this competition resulted in the development of bebop. The opening text links this bebop movement to the exploits of the Bebop crew (and presumably the creators of *Cowboy Bebop*) who are playing "freely" or experimenting without "fear of risky things" in the hope of creating a "new genre".

This innovative jazz style certainly embodies the synergy of the *Cowboy Bebop* television series, for the series is offering a new take on genre, not by creating unique images and sounds, but by playing "freely" with, "remixing," or adapting the images and sounds of other familiar genres in a dynamic way. This artistic technique of "remixing" has become an important part of our culture, according to Anne-Marie Boisvert, because it reflects the way we experience the world today. When flipping through channels or surfing the web, consumers are constantly "selecting, cutting up, editing, and manipulating the tide of images and sounds" (Boisvert). For remix artists such as nightclub DJs, "originality lies in having transformed pre-recorded works and transmitting devices [. . .] into means of artistic creation" (Boisvert). As a result, the typical issue of "originality" involved in so much discussion of art moves from the end product to the process itself—fearlessly playing with familiar bits and pieces in a way that produces new meaning. Inspired by this process of the bebop musicians, the creators of *Cowboy Bebop* tried to blaze new trails with their animated television series by freely remixing familiar genres to produce new meaning; however, when in 2001 they adapted the series to the big screen, this

Déjà Vu All Over Again? 165

Figure 11.1 Opening credits of the *Cowboy Bebop* series with fragments of the "mission statement." Copyright Sunrise/Bandai.

direction was largely abandoned in favor of following the well-beaten path of traditional Hollywood live-action cinema.

In the *Cowboy Bebop* television series, intertextuality layers meaning, characters, sounds, images, and genres. This practice works to "unhinge" the narrative structure of the film and series, just as Umberto Eco argues that such intertextuality disrupts the flow of films like *Rocky Horror Picture Show* and *Casablanca* (68). In fact, Eco uses the term "déjà vu" to describe the emotion evoked by the recognition of archetypes or commonly repeated textual situations in such works. A similar sense of "déjà vu" is experienced by viewers of *Cowboy Bebop*, and we find it mirrored by the character Spike in the series. In the last episode ("The Real Folk Blues [Part 2]"), Spike admits to his partner, Jet, that because of an earlier eye replacement, he has been constantly seeing the past in one eye and the present in the other. This strange double experience leads Spike to question what is real and wonder if, at times, he is simply dreaming. For viewers, the double experience of seeing *Cowboy Bebop* while simultaneously "seeing" its intertextual references unhinges the narrative, allowing viewers to break it into pieces that can be connected to their network of memories. In contrast, the film would prove to be far less "unhinged," partly because it lacks the remixing of genres so prevalent in the series. Instead of broken fragments, the film features longer scenes that flow together fluidly, so the overall effect is more contemporary Hollywood in style, despite the fact that the story is animated. Although *Cowboy Bebop: The Movie* (a.k.a. *Knockin' on Heaven's Door*) transforms the series by restructuring the narrative format and increasing the cinematic quality of the visuals, the film does not add significantly to the character arc of the series or, more important, continue to break new ground through remixing after the pattern of the television series.

Cowboy Bebop was immediately popular as an animated sf series when first aired in 1998. In 1999, the twenty-six original episode series appeared in the United States on video, and Cartoon Network selected *Cowboy Bebop* as the first Japanese animated series to be featured on "Adult Swim," a special late-night programming block with little or no editing of content that is aimed at older audiences. Due to *Cowboy Bebop*'s popularity in Japan and the following it quickly developed in the United States, director Shinicohirô Watanabe adapted the series into a feature-length film in 2001. He created the film largely as an extension of the television series' narrative arc, situating its events between those of episodes twenty-two and twenty-three of the series. *Cowboy Bebop: The Movie* premiered in the United States in 2002 and was released on DVD the following year. The English dubbings of both the series and the film feature the same actors: Steve Blum (Spike Spiegel), Beau Billingslea (Jet Black), Wendee Lee (Faye Valentine), and Melissa Fahn (Edward). Such consistency in voice casting is important in the adaptation of animated series to the big screen, much like the consistency in casting original actors is for live-action works, as seen with the success of the early *Star Trek* adaptations.

Of course, when a television series crosses over from the small screen to the big screen, viewers do expect some changes. Ina Rae Hark argues that Hollywood has not always appreciated the importance of meeting these audience expectations and notes that it was a sf series with a cult following that "taught Hollywood a lesson" concerning how to "remake" television programs for the big screen, rather than simply to "transfer them" (177). When *Star Trek: The Motion Picture* was released in 1979, the series had been off the air for more than a decade. Because film changes as technology changes (especially in the case of sf), fans of the series were greeted with substantial innovations in the film's mise-en-scène. Even the Klingons' look had been updated due to advances in makeup techniques. Hark explains that *Star Trek*'s adaptation to the big screen tried "balancing" the changes in mise-en-scène through continuities in character and narrative structure (177). In his discussion of television and film as distinct forms, Noël Carroll discusses the importance of those expectations we bring to the different media. For example, he suggests that a film is "supposed" to have a smooth flow, complete narrative, and more intricate mise-en-scène due to a visual privileging (Carroll 17). Such expectations, of course, are based on live-action television and films in the United States. In the case of *Cowboy Bebop*, both series and film are Japanese animation, or *anime*, and that form invokes a different set of expectations.

Anime has a well-established tradition in Japan, and that tradition is different in form and content from American animation, as well as live-action sf. Carroll's discussion of television and film highlights a few of the differences we might consider, especially in terms of narrative structure. He explains how American television series are typically experienced as "fragments," intermixed with commercials, and how, with every episode implying that the story will be continued, the series "potentially" becomes a "never-ending story" (19). Televised *anime* is similarly fragmented, but even though most episodes hold the promise of a continuing story, most series are created with a predetermined length. Thus they have a defined and delimited narrative arc, as is the case with *Cowboy Bebop*.

Director Watanabe originally designed the series to fit within a twenty-six-episode arc. The first episode begins in a noirish flashback, revealing fragments of Spike Spiegel's history that haunt the protagonist until an uneasy resolution is reached in the series' last moments. Spike lives with Jet Black on the spacecraft *Bebop* while they work as bounty hunters, known as "cowboys" in the year 2071. Later, Spike and Jet are joined by one canine and two females, all of them wanted but none of whom the men ever turn in for rewards: Ein, a technologically savvy corgi escaped from a lab; Faye Valentine, a young gambler plagued by debt; and Edward (Ed), a child hacker. Each human's history becomes the subject of a dramatic episode near the end of the series, and Spike's story provides the narrative with anchoring endpoints. Precisely because of the way it frames the entire arc, Spike's storyline carries the most narrative weight.

Predictably, individual episodes of the series revolve around various bounty-hunting efforts; however, when viewed as a whole, the series arc is shaped by all four main characters as it recounts how they join the *Bebop* crew and eventually face their troubled pasts. Along with Spike, Jet is the other original crew member—a cyborg who formerly worked with the interplanetary police force. Over the course of the series, he determines that his police partner was responsible for the attack that damaged his body and led him to strike out on his own. When Spike and Jet first encounter Faye, she has only recently been reanimated after being cryogenically frozen, and she still suffers from memory loss and gambles recklessly in an attempt to win the huge sum she owes the cryogenic company. She eventually recovers her memory and confronts her past, but when she discovers her family and friends are all gone, Faye returns to her new family aboard the *Bebop*. Ed is the genius child of a scatterbrained scientist who left her at an orphanage and promptly forgot its location. When the rest of the crew unknowingly tracks her father down as a bounty assignment, Ed recognizes him. In episode twenty-four, she leaves the group to join him in his work, accompanied by the dog Ein. Spike is a former member of the Syndicate, a mafia-type group that he abandoned when his fellow member and friend, Vicious, became power hungry and betrayed him. Leaving the Syndicate also meant leaving Julia, Spike's soul mate who was too frightened to leave with him. In episode twenty-five, Spike is reunited with her, but instead of fleeing, the two join the Syndicate in its fight against Vicious, and Julia is killed in the battle. Episode twenty-six concludes in a duel between Spike and Vicious in which Spike is victorious, although he collapses in apparent death. As he dies, Spike remembers his final words to Julia which reassure her it is all "just a bad dream."

This dream element is one of the main threads of the series that the creators pull into its big screen adaptation.

In designing the film, Watanabe situated his plot late in the series' storyline (as noted, between episodes twenty-two and twenty-three), as the *Bebop* crew attempts to prevent the devastation of the transplanted Martian population by the bioterrorist Vincent. Spike remains the real protagonist supported by his crewmates as well as a new character, Electra, an undercover military member. As with the series, much of the film further develops the characters' backstories, but in this case the new characters' histories actually occupy the most screen time. Flashbacks and voice-overs reveal that Vincent was the subject of a military experiment, testing a vaccine against nanomachine viruses. The vaccine made him immune, but it also took away his memory and caused perpetual hallucinations of golden butterflies. Vincent became convinced that the golden butterflies were a sign that he was simply dreaming, and thus he began searching for ways to awaken. Electra was Vincent's lover before the experiment, but he does not recognize her until the end of the film when he lies dying from her bullet. Only when it is too late does Vincent realize that he has not been dreaming after all. Although the adaptation picked up this dream thread from the series, the film's emphasis on these additional characters and closed ending keep that thread from capturing the ambiguity or sense of déjà vu created through Spike's double experience and final dream commentary.

Paul Wells argues that, starting with Disney's full-length films, animation "borrowed" the "conventional ethos of storytelling . . . from the classical live-action tradition" (206). Perhaps this direction was taken in order to meet viewers' expectations for feature films and for the pleasures associated with them. Although the *Cowboy Bebop* film does adopt a version of the typical Hollywood arc, the television series clearly was working differently as the form of the episodes shaped the narrative structure. The typical episode lasts approximately twenty-two minutes, with a couple of minutes dedicated to the jazzy introduction, bluesy closing credits, and a preview of the next episode. The twenty or so minutes between the introduction and closing credits are always broken into two parts that allow for commercial breaks. A cliffhanger is usually crafted in part A, and the break, climax, and resolution fall near the end of part B; the only real exceptions occur in episode 1, which includes a prologue before the opening, and episode twenty-five, which sets up the last episode. In contrast, the film's narrative is structured over almost two hours—an unusually long time for an animated film. Generally, Hollywood films are divided into three acts, and *Cowboy Bebop: The Movie* follows this pattern, providing viewers with a setup, rising action, and climax. Even the ending of the film fits into this live-action tradition. In the closing moments of the cinematic release, the villain is stopped, and just before dying he realizes that he has not been living in a dream—a contrast, as we have noted, with the series' concluding suggestion that the preceding turmoil has simply been the protagonist's own "bad dream." Consequently, the cinematic version meets audience expectations by standing complete as a closed narrative. Moreover, because of the lengthening of most scenes, particularly ones that emphasize character and plot development, the story flows more smoothly than the series, with little in the way of those "unhinging" disruptions and fragments that made it so stylistically distinctive.

Reviews of *Cowboy Bebop: The Movie* reflect viewers' reactions to the pacing and flow of its scenes. Lisa Schwarzbaum of *Entertainment Weekly* admits that as a "nonscholar" she enjoys the "inevitable ramping up of typical action-thriller showdowns" in the film, but she "feel[s] lost" when the characters "stand still, chirping their strangely stilted, dubbed talk" (127). In a later review for the same magazine, Marc Bernardin explains that "*Bebop* is a movie that is in no rush to get to its conclusion, and so the occasional, very well done action sequences are spaced out by languorous stretches of . . . story," which he sees as a "welcome change indeed" for *anime* (119). In *The Magazine of Fantasy and Science Fiction*, Kathi Maio admits that she is not surprised that the film "drags a bit in the middle" because viewers "expect" that from a film based on a television series, but she still insists that it is a "very pleasant diversion for anyone who enjoys animation and science fiction" (96–97). In *Sight & Sound*, Andrew Osmond contends that the film's "pace is diluted by extraneous scenes featuring the supporting cast, presumably to satisfy fans of the original series," yet overall it "*succeeds* as a stylish, enjoyable blend of genres and formats" (45). Most critics agreed with Osmond's assessment: that the cinematic adaptation "*succeeds*" in meeting general viewers' expectations.

However, the fans of the series are the ones who generally felt unsatisfied by the film's narrative. One reason may be that the film was squeezed into the midst of the series' narrative and character arc after the series was already completed. But what other choice did the creators have? Fans certainly desired to see all four of the main characters in the film, but if its story was situated after the twenty-sixth episode, the ambiguity of Spike's death scene would have to be resolved. The only real question, then, was where to fit the film into the preexisting series. The creators chose a spot near the end, after the characters were well developed but before Ed left the group in episode twenty-four. And because the main characters' backstories and futures had already been fully developed over the course of the series, the film had to focus most tightly on the new characters, Electra and Vincent. Although both are ultimately sympathetic characters, fans may have felt disappointed not to learn more about the original figures to whom they had grown attached during the series' twenty-six episodes.

Like the narrative structure of much *anime*, the visuals of *anime* deserve some explanation for their function in the adaptive process. Susan Napier argues that the visual style of *anime* with its "distinctive cuts" (20) is influenced by the narrative techniques of the *manga* form (Japanese comic books). Dani Cavallaro has listed some of the specific methods that create *anime*'s customary visual style: "sliding," when a frame slides across the plane of vision; "panning," where the camera stays in one spot while turning horizontally; and "tilting," like panning, except with the camera moving vertically (16). Cavallaro explains that Japanese animators employ these methods to enhance their limited animation style, thereby creating the "illusion of movement" with an economy of frames (16). In fact, *anime* artists have adapted a wide range of camera operations from live-action television and film. In her discussion, Cavallaro lists over twenty common borrowings in *anime*'s visuals, from "shifts of focus" to "oblique-angle" shots (16–17). She also describes typical backgrounds found in *anime* as "intricately detailed" and "painterly," and she describes the artists' approach to production as "meticulous" (15). Overall, *anime*, whether created for the big or small screen, attempts to produce the "illusion" of cinematic narrative through the use of camera movement and detail.

The *Cowboy Bebop* television series is no exception. Susan Napier describes the series as "sophisticated animation—employing unusual angles, emphasizing the contrast between light and shade" and featuring a "unique mise-en-scene" (135). In an article for *Animation Magazine*, Fred Patten contends that the series displays "theatrical-quality cartoon animation, smoothly blended with stunning CGI visuals" (45). Although the prologue for the series is distinctive, it provides a useful example of the visual intricacy exhibited throughout the various episodes. This prologue is a flashback that begins in dramatic black-and-white. The screen fades in from black, revealing the top of a tower in an oblique-angle shot as a bell tolls ominously in the distance. The camera slowly tilts down to the gray street as silvery raindrops fall soundlessly on the European-style cityscape and on a tall man (Spike) leaning hunched along a wall. As the haunting melody of a music box replaces the bells, the camera cuts to a close-up of the lower half of Spike's face, a cigarette dangling from his lips, the collar of his trench coat swept up against the rain, and only a tuft of his rowdy mane visible in the shot. His eyes are lost in shadow as he removes the cigarette and drops it among the others that litter the sidewalk where he has been standing, clearly for some time. This third shot reveals more than the pile of cigarettes and shape of his shoes: light and shadow play on the wet pavement, reflecting the steel gray of the sky and inky darkness of the encroaching buildings. The camera cuts to an extreme low and oblique-angle shot of Spike's back as he slowly walks away, a soggy bouquet of flowers dangling at his side. A moment passes and the camera cuts to a puddle of water as Spike ambles by. His full face and chest are revealed for the first time, but only in dim reflection as rain droplets disrupt the surface of the watery mirror. Just as he passes, a dusky rose falls into the puddle, apparently lost from Spike's bouquet. As the camera zooms in almost imperceptibly on the abandoned flower, several angled shots of an intense gun battle are quickly intercut, until slowly the rose warms to red to match the dripping blood in the intercut shots. The last shot is a refrain of Spike's first close-up; this time his lower face is framed by a stained-glass window at the site of the gunfight. As blood trails from his mouth, he manages an audacious smile. Through a dazzling array of visual techniques, noirish and gothic styles have been interlaced with a horror-film edginess to set the strangely mixed tone for the entire series.

Despite this intricate imagery that marked the series, *Cowboy Bebop: The Movie* did meet the expectations of moviegoers on one level—by improving on the television show's visuals. The film utilizes the stockpile of camera operations familiar from the series, but it adds other techniques like the rack focus (when the camera shifts depth of focus within the frame) to its arsenal. Spike's initial confrontation with Vincent provides several interesting examples of complexity in the film overall. The scene takes place within a suspended monorail train as it glides above the Martian city and out over the sea on a bright afternoon. A string of gun barrel close-ups and cool verbal taunts (like the squint, reminiscent of *Dirty Harry*) are followed by a particularly cinematic sequence of slow-motion shots. The scene slows down for a straight-on close-up of Spike's face and gun barrel, but then slides to the right, shifting focus to Electra running toward the bounty hunter who is unaware of her presence. The next low-angle shot frames only the barrel of a gun as Vincent switches his target. The camera returns to its last position, Spike still blurry in the foreground as Electra, in sharp focus, approaches. A straight-on close-up of Vincent and his pistol captures the moment of gunfire. The bullet is tracked from the side as it whizzes past the blur of train windows and Spike's face. An oblique close-up of Electra's face exhibits her surprise as the bullet apparently enters her body. A low-angle medium shot shows her slow fall from the side. The scene then returns to full speed and the techniques typical of the television series. The use of slow motion with a sliding shot and simultaneous shift of focus turns the somewhat normal *Cowboy Bebop* action scene into a cinematic showpiece, after the fashion of a shootout in a Sergio Leone spaghetti Western. Although the complexity of this sequence is fairly unique in the film, several scenes contain intriguing shifts of focus and most make use of the wider screen size, as the film seems intent on improving upon the already high visual style of the television series. The colors seem richer and provide a convincing sense of depth. Every movement blends sleekly into the next without any jerky or awkward stops and starts.

And yet, as I have already noted, even with such efforts the adaptation did not satisfy fans of the television series. Certainly, fitting the film into the preestablished narrative and character arc of the series restricted the development of the main characters and in that regard disappointed fans. More important, it conformed in various ways to the norms of the classical live-action tradition, whereas the series was anything but conformist. Unlike the flood of sf Japanese anime series that have appeared on Western television, such as *Appleseed*, *Dragonball* (and *Dragonball Z*), or *Macross*, *Cowboy Bebop* did not simply follow their tradition but was noted for its "originality" and "freshness" (Napier 135). And much of that "originality" comes not from new ideas but from a remixing of styles, motifs, and genre elements. Consider the title: *Cowboy Bebop*. Both words allude to uniquely American forms, the Western and jazz music. Combining these forms obviously layers the experience of watching the show, but the series synthesizes other traditions as well. In terms of film genre, the prologue's dark, drizzly cityscape is only the first of many echoes of film noir. Urban gunfights, a brooding voiceover, and femmes fatale are mainstays of both that genre and the series. But just as obviously, sf themes and aesthetics play an important role as a significant portion of most episodes takes place aboard the *Bebop* and in outer space. When Spike uses his body as a weapon, his moves recall martial arts films and particularly the work of Bruce Lee. Action movies influence the flashy style and traditional weapon choice of the main characters. In 2071, Spike may travel by spacecraft, but he still uses a semiautomatic pistol when he's on the ground. In fact, every episode of the television series remixes these and various other genres and genre elements in ways that challenge our conventional experience of these elements.

Like the series, *Cowboy Bebop: The Movie* also relies heavily on the action genre, particularly for the suspended monorail gunfight scene. With gun barrels dominating the camera and a heavy dose of fatalistic bravado, images of *Dirty Harry* seem to shadow Spike and Vincent, creating a doubling effect. When the two meet for their last battle, the rain, gunplay, and physical combat mix together film noir and martial arts action. Despite these connections, much of the film has a Moroccan tone (in an interview with *Animation Magazine*, Watanabe describes the influence of his visit to Morocco on the writing of the screenplay; Ball).

Figure 11.2 Spike investigating Rasheed in the Moroccan district on Mars in *Cowboy Bebop: The Movie*. Copyright Sunrise/Bones/Bandai.

This tone seems unfamiliar compared to the more traditional genres referenced by the series. The "newness" of the film does not layer the viewer's experience because most viewers have no previous experiences with this strangely mixed style. Instead of the layered experience of seeing the film and their memories simultaneously, viewers are generally having one experience. So while the series is fragmented by its television narrative structure and multiple intertextual references, the film flows seamlessly for long periods of time as a single, almost immersive experience.

As with the various referenced film genres, the music of *Cowboy Bebop* brings its own multiple character. Both the series and film feature the original orchestrations of Yoko Kanno performed by The Seatbelts. The band's music weaves in and out of every episode, setting the tone and shaping the very texture of each story. Most episodes feature a particular song or genre of music, as demonstrated by a few of their titles: "Bohemian Rhapsody," "Mushroom Samba," "Boogie Woogie Feng Shui," "Heavy Metal Queen." Not only does every episode begin with the same jazz piece ("Tank"), thereby coloring the mood of the entire series, but jazz itself suggests the synergy of *Cowboy Bebop*. The film tries to transfer this musical experience of the whole series through its inclusion of a variety of music genres. However, as I have noted, because the film aims for a rather seamless feel throughout, the music does not shape the texture of the film in the same way it does for the series. In fact, the film often seems to resist that musical influence, except when it employs music to set the Moroccan mood for certain scenes and an urban vibe for the rest. Although jazz does find a small place in the story, it does not hold a prominent position and thus does not exercise the same guiding influence. In fact, the film does not even include "Tank," the jazz opening that is essentially the musical signature of the series.

The creators of *Cowboy Bebop: The Movie* certainly made significant changes in order to adapt the series to the big screen. They structured a closed narrative that features almost two hours of seamless flow and drew upon a wide range of cinematic techniques to heighten a drama of, at times, highly realistic visuals. However, many fans were unsatisfied with the film, largely because it did not develop the series' four main characters or recapture the sense of celebration invoked by its many intertextual references. This dissatisfaction has led many fans simply to ignore the film's existence (like Blue Rose's *Cowboy Bebop* fan site, active since 2002) or to compare the two as if they were opposing versions of the story matter instead of parts of a whole, as in a December 2009 poll on *Cowboy Bebop*'s *Fanpop.com* website that asked participants which they prefer: 100 percent reported preferring the series. Whether animation or live action, transforming a series from the small screen to the big screen is especially complicated if it has an ardent following. Early *Star Trek* movies, for example, were able to achieve an effective balance of changes and continuities, but those films also recast the original actors from the series (Hark 177). The most recent addition to that series, the attempted reboot *Star Trek* (2009), also disappointed many fans by—inevitably—casting new actors in the roles of James T. Kirk and Spock, among others. Of course, the creators had little choice because the story is a prequel to the television series, so Kirk and Spock appear as younger than William Shatner and Leonard Nimoy were when they first played those parts in 1966. And although the reboot might lack the balance achieved by earlier adaptations, it has effectively brought in fans who are new to the films and perhaps even unaware of the foundational television series. It thus reminds us that film creators who want to cross over from the small screen not only have to balance change and continuity; they must also appeal to old and new fans as well.

If film creators wish to meet the desires of a series' fans—whether the series is animated or live action—they might focus less on changing the narrative, characters, and visuals to fit the big screen and more on why the show attained a following in the first place. While describing how film and television are essentially different, Noël Carroll also asserts that the line between the two is not "impenetrable" and that he expects the two to "continue to converge" until they eventually "become amalgamated" in the future (27). Approaching this issue from an opposite direction, Blair Davis, in her discussion of the made-from-TV movie, explains how film and television were not always segregated (198). During the 1950s, as she notes, previously aired episodes from television shows (like *Superman*) were edited together and released with some success in movie theaters (Davis 214). Critics might argue that today's cinema audience is too sophisticated to watch television episodes in the theater, but today's television series—as well as their devoted audiences—have obviously increased in sophistication too. A work like *Cowboy Bebop* begs the question of whether television series really need to change so much when they cross screens. In fact, many fans might argue that they are less interested in seeing their television series transformed for a new medium and more interested in experiencing déjà vu, or as in the case of *Cowboy Bebop* fans, déjà vu all over again.

WORKS CITED

Ball, Ryan. "Space Cowboys." *Animation Magazine* 17.2 (2003): 44.
Bernardin, Marc. "*Cowboy Bebop: The Movie* (Film)." *Entertainment Weekly* 716/717 (2003): 119.
Blue Rose: A Cowboy Bebop Fan Site. 3. 2002. http://bebop.roses-thorns.com. Accessed 3 Jan. 2011.
Boisvert, Anne-Marie. "On Bricolage: Assembling Culture with Whatever Comes to Hand." *HorizonZero Issue 08: REMIX. Banff New Media Institute* and *Culture.ca Gateway*, 16 Aug. 2007. http://www.horizonzero.ca/textsite/remix.php. Accessed 10 Dec. 2010.
Carroll, Noël. "TV and Film: A Philosophical Perspective." *Journal of Aesthetic Education* 35.1 (2001): 15–29.

Cavallaro, Dani. *Anime and the Art of Adaptation: Eight Famous Works from Page to Screen.* Jefferson: McFarland, 2010.
Cowboy Bebop Fan Club. 2010. http://www.fanpop.com/spots/cowboy-bebop. Accessed 3 Jan. 2011.
Davis, Blair. "Made-From-TV Movies: Turning 1950s Television into Films." *Historical Journal of Film, Radio, and Television* 29.2 (2009): 197–218.
Eco, Umberto. "*Casablanca*: Cult Movies and Intertextual Collage." *The Cult Film Reader.* Ed. Ernest Mathjis and Xavier Mendik. New York: MacGraw-Hill, 2008. 67–75.
Hark, Ina Rae. "The Wrath of the Original Cast: Translating Embodied Television Characters to Other Media." *Adaptations: From Text to Screen, Screen to Text.* Ed. Deborah Cartmell and Imelda Whelehan. New York: Routledge, 1999. 172–84.
Maio, Kathi. "Cult Status isn't Good Enough." *The Magazine of Fantasy and Science Fiction.* 105.3 (Sept. 2003): 94–98.
Napier, Susan. *Anime from* Akira *to* Howl's Moving Castle: *Experiencing Contemporary Japanese Animation.* New York: St. Martin's, 2005.
Osmond, Andrew. "*Cowboy Bebop: The Movie.*" *Sight & Sound* 13.9 (2003): 44–45.
Patten, Fred. "Anime Goes Mainstream with *Cowboy Bebop.*" *Animation Magazine* 13.9 (1999): 45.
Schwarzbaum, Lisa. "Animania." *Entertainment Weekly* 706/707 (2003): 127.
Wells, Paul. "'Thou Art Translated:' Analyzing Animated Adaptation." *Adaptations: From Text to Screen, Screen to Text.* Ed. Deborah Cartmell and Imelda Whelehan. New York: Routledge, 1999. 199–213.

12 Fan Films, Adaptations, and Media Literacy

Chuck Tryon

When *Star Wars Uncut* (2009), a fan-produced remake of *Star Wars: A New Hope* (1977), won an Emmy in the recently created Interactive Media category, it was celebrated as a powerful expression of the potential of fan filmmaking and social media. This "film," produced for the computer screen, compiles hundreds of short segments, or clips, created by fans in a scene-by-scene remake of the original film. Following up on past winners, such as *The Lost Experience* (2006) and *The Heroes Digital Experience* (2007), both of which were sanctioned extensions of popular sf television series, *Star Wars Uncut* seemed to offer new evidence of the power of fan-created content. However, little attention has been directed to the fact that *Star Wars Uncut* is also an adaptation; it is both a translation of the *Star Wars* saga into a new medium—web video—and a collective reinterpretation of the film. But far from simply imitating the source film, *Star Wars Uncut* retells the original through the collaborative efforts of literally hundreds of participants. Although the number of participants is itself noteworthy, *Star Wars Uncut* is also the latest in a long line of fan productions that take existing popular culture texts and adapt them into new media, often with the goal of commenting on the original.

Fan films have a much longer history, but *Star Wars Uncut*, with its dazzling mosaic of fan-produced clips, gleefully displays its collaborative and amateur origins. It offers us a new way of thinking about the film on which it is based, reminding viewers not only of their enjoyment of *Star Wars* but also of the diverse ways in which Lucas's swashbuckling space epic has influenced a generation of popular culture producers and consumers. Drawing on this example, this chapter looks at a special case of cross-screen adaptation: films produced and distributed by fans, specifically as those forms are gaining new visibility and even new storytelling techniques through the use of social media and online video. By looking at fan practices through the lens of adaptation theory, we can get a better sense of the critical-thinking skills and interpretive practices fans use when they cross these new screens to make a fan "film"—as we might continue to call it. And by examining adaptation theory through such fan productions, we can better understand adaptation as a process, one that demands the media literacy skills of reading and retelling a popular story.

In addition, this chapter examines how social-media tools have been used to rethink the nature of the fan film. Although fan films have circulated via official and unofficial channels for decades, often playing at fan events such as the annual Comic-Con, fans have begun to use social-media tools not only to share films but also to create new storytelling methods, such as those used in *Star Wars Uncut*, which would have been impossible to produce otherwise. Further, these social-media tools position fan films more squarely within the public media cultures where films and TV series exist as objects of discussion or analysis. These practices are a form of what Jason Mittell refers to as "participatory fandom," a practice in which fans collectively organize—across a variety of screens—around their shared enthusiasm for a popular-culture text. Although Mittell focuses primarily on the creation of fan-produced wikis, such as *Lostpedia*, he points out that like fan films, "all fan wikis can be considered *paratexts*, independent cultural works that exist in relationship to other texts" (Mittell's emphasis). These paratexts often comment upon, annotate, or reimagine the original text, thereby contributing to what John Ellis refers to as the "social discourse" of a wider media community (282). By examining this relationship between intertextuality and participatory fandom, this chapter will explore the phenomenon of digital fan adaptations, as well as their role in a wider transmediated participatory culture, and make the argument that fan adaptations contribute to an evolving media literacy, one that allows fans to actively shape the meaning of popular films and television shows.

RETHINKING ADAPTATION

To understand how these participatory cultures engage in processes of interpretation, we need to reconsider traditional notions of adaptation. As Thomas Leitch notes, adaptations have most often been evaluated based on their fidelity to the source text, with the implication that the adaptation is secondary or derivative. This comparison, Leitch observes, inevitably privileges the source, for example, as critics are quick to announce of literary adaptations that "the book is better" (16). However, instead of looking at adaptation in terms of a product (the "derivative" texts spawned by a source), Leitch invites us, instead, to look at the *process* of adaptation, the motivations behind revising or reimagining an existing text. Rather than criticize an adaptation for omitting material or going outside of the source's boundaries, Leitch argues that we should understand adaptation as a creative act and concludes that adaptations are an important reminder that "source texts must be rewritten; we cannot help rewriting them" (16). In this sense, adaptation becomes a form of commentary or critical engagement, a practice central to fan activity.

Like many adaptations, fan films are usually dismissed as inferior and seen as borrowing from the popularity of the source text without adding anything original. Even in one of the most enthusiastic accounts about fan films, Clive Young glibly asserts that "the average fan film stinks. The acting is lousy, the story is slow, the comedy isn't funny, and yet the drama is hysterical" (1). Similarly, Jane Graham suggests of fan films that "many still regard them as flatulent waste products of the socially deficient unemployed-layabout community." However, this focus on a specific realist aesthetic often obscures some of the critical practices that are involved in adapting a text from one medium into another. Further, as Linda Hutcheon points out, adaptations allow us to rethink the prior text, creating what she calls "an engagement with the original text that makes us see that text in a different way" (16). In other words, an adaptation is an interpretation that offers a new reading of the source text. Curiously, Hutcheon brackets off fan fiction and excludes it from her definition of adaptation, arguing that "there is a difference between never wanting a story to end . . . and wanting to retell the same story over and over in different ways" (9). Hutcheon's dismissal of fan fiction seems to privilege officially produced adaptations because after all, many contemporary adaptations—including the dozens of film-to-video-game adaptations—do not simply retell the original narrative. Instead, they expand, amplify, and recast elements of the story world, pushing well beyond the boundaries of the original narrative. The practices of adaptation are also informed by a recognition that texts are always embedded in a larger textual system, as Jonathan Gray points out in his discussion of movie trailers and other paratexts. For example, we don't encounter a movie like *Avatar* (2009) in isolation. Instead, we become aware of it and begin interpreting it through a series of paratexts, whether trailers, advertisements, or talk-show interviews with the stars or with the director. Some may see a television program that discusses the film's use of special effects or 3-D technology, whereas others may read about the film's depiction of the military or environmental politics on a political blog. Later, movie reviews and fan parodies reframe the film in new ways, shaping whether we choose to see the film and even how we watch it. In all cases, texts are constantly interacting, shaping how we interpret and understand them.

INTERTEXTUALITY

These forms of creativity emerge from the recognition that all texts—films, television shows, video games, etc.—build upon, incorporate, allude to, or rework even older texts through the process of intertextuality. As Roland Barthes observes, every text is "a tissue of quotations drawn from the innumerable centers of culture" (146). These references and citations remind us of the permeable boundaries of any work, as all texts respond to or rework prior texts; and when they are cited or adapted, they begin to "live through" those texts (Gray, *Watching* 26). Intertextuality also allows us to make sense of the ways in which texts overlap, intersect, quote, and rework each other. In fact, if we begin to recognize the deeply sedimented layers of meaning and reference embedded in any fan film, we can also begin to recognize similar processes of intertextuality operating even in the projects of professional filmmakers. As *Film Threat* founder Chris Gore asks, "Considering the number of influences from fantasy and science fiction contained in the original *Star Wars*, from *Flash Gordon* to Buck Rogers to Westerns and war movies, didn't George Lucas just make one big-budget fan film?" (xiii).

These references help to make films and TV series intelligible for audiences who consume them, allowing those texts to participate in a wider conversation. As John Ellis observes, broadcast television in particular "has an intellectual and emotional importance in society because it admits ideas and individuals, whether in dramatic scenarios or in factual programming, into the general social discourse of the nation" (282). Although Ellis is more focused on an older broadcast model, in which three or four major networks dominated the attention of a national audience, television and movies remain a crucial means through which audiences can establish common ground. Ellis was writing at the moment when VCRs were first promoting a "greater sophistication in viewing habits" for movie and TV audiences, enabling consumers to review segments much more easily than in the past. At the same time, access to a vast archive of images makes it easier for fan filmmakers to learn from and build upon existing texts, allowing them to use techniques of adaptation to participate in a wider social discourse.

As Leitch observes in his "grammar" of adaptation, there are a wide range of such techniques that adapters can use, spanning from the most faithful "curatorial" approaches to radical reinterpretations and parodies that significantly rewrite the original (97–119). Notably, many fan films operate through parody, tweaking the original text by mocking conventions of plot, character, or genre, often through forms of genre mixing. Parody is, in fact, a privileged form of intertextuality, with pop-culture-savvy filmmakers demonstrating not only their visual storytelling skills but also their knowledge of the source texts. Thus, parody, like other forms of adaptation, allows adapters to offer a rereading of the source text. Therefore, fan films, whether using parody or other forms of commentary, often require significant cultural literacy at the level of both production and consumption. These questions of engagement are a crucial element of fan films and have been throughout the history of the form.

VIDDING AND FAN FILMS

We should acknowledge that fan-produced films and videos have circulated for decades, well before they became widely visible through video-sharing sites such as *YouTube* and *Vimeo*. Clive Young's *Homemade Hollywood* navigates a long history of fan filmmaking, one that can be traced back to hobbyist filmmakers working in the 1920s and 1930s. Young highlights one of the earliest known fan films, the 1936 film *Tarzan and the Rocky Gorge*, produced by a Connecticut family, demonstrating that even in the earliest days of amateur moviemaking, aspiring filmmakers often borrowed from or mocked the movies they saw in theaters (16–23).

Although Young's historical account grounds fan-film production in enjoyment, many early productions took a more ambivalent stance toward their source text. As Francesca Coppa reminds us, practices such as vidding, in which fans "use music in order to comment on or analyze a set of preexisting visuals," can be traced back to the earliest stages of *Star Trek* fandom in the early 1970s. In her discussion of early vidders, Coppa argues that feminist fans of *Star Trek* often used musical cues and painstakingly reedited clips to comment on the "representational tensions" within the show's depictions of gender and technology. As a result, vids did not offer straightforward affirmations of the television shows they represented. Instead, they were often involved in negotiating meanings and making arguments about gender and racial representation, especially as those questions were articulated through the ambiguous half-human, half-Klingon character of Spock.

To be sure, television and film producers often enlisted these fan practices in order to sustain a television show with mediocre ratings or to provide leverage for a movie deal. As Coppa points out, Gene Roddenberry actively supported the *Star Trek* fan base because he was aware that a visible, energized fan base would allow him to demonstrate that there was an audience for a *Star Trek* movie. These fan practices continue to be encouraged by some within the entertainment industry. George Lucas, for example, has worked to incorporate fan practices into his sprawling *Star Wars* empire by sponsoring an annual contest, the Official Star Wars Fan Film Awards, eventually renamed the Star Wars Fan Movie Challenge. Winning films have played on the website *AtomFilms.com*, as well as on specials screened on the SciFi/Syfy Channel and, later, on Spike TV (Young 205–06). More significant, as Henry Jenkins points out, by sponsoring these contests and endorsing favored fan films, especially parodies and documentaries, Lucasfilm has been shaping how *Star Wars* is interpreted by fans, imposing constraints that might limit such genres as vidding or fan fiction (*Convergence Culture*, 158–59).

Thus, although vidding and fan films have existed for some time, *YouTube* and other video sharing sites have made these practices more visible. More crucial to the phenomenon, fan film creators and viewers have created an infrastructure that allows the films to circulate. Websites such as *TheForce.net* and *FanFilms.net* archive fan films and encourage commentary about them. This visibility has also helped contribute to the circulation and institutionalization of different forms of fan adaptation. If *Star Wars* and *Star Trek* serve as influential films that have shaped fan behavior, then popular fan films themselves can be seen as having a significant influence on fan practice. For example, the editing techniques of vidding continue to shape fan films, with the editor being reimagined as a kind of author who rewrites or adapts the original text. In addition, fans who appreciate the humor of a "crossover" film, such as Kevin Rubio's *Troops* (1998), create other films that use parody as a creative form of commentary. Finally, as digital cinema tools make it easier for fans to contribute to a single project, even when at a physical distance, fan films begin to offer new forms of collaboration, making it possible for them to work together to produce engaging stories, convincing special effects, and even seamless editing.

THE EDITOR AS AUTHOR

Although fans are often seen as blindly devoted to the text they choose to adapt, retelling a source text can often take a resistant or oppositional stance as well. In fact, as Jenkins argues fan films often spring from a "mixture of fascination and frustration," given that favorite films sometimes fail to conform to audience expectations ("Reception Theory"). As an example, we might consider one of the most commonly cited reasons for the critical and popular failure of *Star Wars: The Phantom Menace* (1998), the presence of the computer-generated character Jar Jar Binks. As Will Brooker points out, the film's sluggish narrative and the presence of Jar Jar Binks led to the "harsh voice of criticism directed personally at George Lucas as director, and a general sense of distrust about his ability to handle the mythos" (90). As a result, a number of fans sought to rewrite, or even remake, *The Phantom Menace* in order to make it more consistent with what they regarded as the true spirit of the *Star Wars* universe. To express their frustration, fans produced films with titles such as *The Phantom Edit*, which sought to revise the original, whether through carefully editing out Jar Jar Binks or through redubbing his voice, transforming him from a naïve, childlike character into a sage.

In the most familiar version of *The Phantom Edit* (2000), a then-anonymous fan who identified himself as "the Phantom Editor"—later identified as Mike J. Nichols, a professional editor and postproduction supervisor working in Hollywood—reedited *The Phantom Menace* to remove virtually all scenes depicting Jar Jar Binks. These edits are visible from the opening crawl, itself a sequence that invites verbal play. *The Phantom Edit* dispenses with Lucas's detailed introduction to establish a fan's discontent: "Being someone of the 'George Lucas Generation,' I have reedited a standard VHS version of 'The Phantom Menace,' into what I believe is a much stronger film by relieving the viewer of as much story redundancy, Anakin action and dialog, and Jar Jar Binks as possible." Ultimately, *The Phantom Edit* trimmed approximately twenty minutes from the theatrical release version, turning the Phantom Editor into what *Salon* critic Daniel Kraus described as a "revisionist filmmaker," one who is steeped in the grammar of adaptation. At the same time, his work was highly influential in helping to spawn a number of responses, as other editor-critics sought to use cheap editing software to register their commentaries on the film as well. Thus, rather than using the techniques of juxtaposition and montage often associated with vidding, the Phantom Editor intervened in the source text by trimming it significantly. Although these changes may seem superficial—especially given that the Phantom Editor produced no new material—they emphasize the degree to which the editor can function as an author, or adapter, of an earlier text; and in subsequent projects, including a reedit of *Star Wars Episode II: Attack of the Clones* (2002), Nichols even added a commentary track to illustrate and explain the task of the editor. In fact, as Walter Murch insists, film editing might also be considered as "film construction," given the degree to which editors have license to reassemble the fragments of a film narrative in order to create new meanings (qtd. in Hutcheon 80). The power of the editor to create new meanings is crucial to the work of vidders and other remix artists, but in the case of *The Phantom Edit*, eliminating selected scenes also served to express the contested meanings of the *Star Wars* story world, turning it into one of the more creative modes of adaptation deployed by digital filmmakers.

EXPANDING THE STORY

Whereas reediting an existing film can serve as a powerful form of commentary, other fans have emulated the industry practice of transmedia storytelling by expanding their story world, either by exploring characters or embellishing plot details. One of the most common of such practices involves creating new characters, whether to develop existing characters' motivations or to supplement plot details. In other cases, textual expansions involve "crossover" narratives that bring together characters, settings, or plot techniques from several media texts, such as Julian Bane's *Doctor Who: Alternate Empire* (2009–), a web series in which Bane plays a noncanon Doctor Who, who through the magic of time travel, winds up in the *Star Wars* galaxy. In these texts, fan filmmakers can demonstrate both their knowledge of a text like *Star Wars* or *Doctor Who* and their creativity in linking it with other texts, producing intertextual references that can be used to comment on the source texts, often quite humorously, through a creative superimposition of seemingly unrelated texts.

A prominent example of this sort of intertextual creativity is Kevin Rubio's *Troops*, a ten-minute *Star Wars* parody that places the narrative structure and visual style of an episode of the reality TV show *Cops* (1989–) onto a climactic scene on the planet Tatooine. *Troops* follows a pair of storm troopers over the course of their day as they police the Tatooine neighborhood near the Skywalker ranch. Rubio's film displays

Fan Films, Adaptations, and Media Literacy   183

Figure 12.1 A group of (action-figure) storm troopers patrol Tatooine in Kevin Rubio's *Cops/Star Wars* crossover, *Troops*.

an astute understanding of both texts. The film opens with the familiar "Bad Boys" theme from the television series and then depicts one of the two storm troopers describing his daily routine—all shot with a handheld camera that is a common feature of the show. But *Troops* also demonstrates that it is conversant with the world of *Star Wars*, in part because it makes the unexpected move of exploring the personalities of the normally inscrutable storm troopers, turning them into regular guys who are just doing a job. In addition, *Troops* fleshes out one of the most dramatic scenes from *Star Wars: A New Hope*, explaining action that takes place off-screen, namely, the destruction of the Skywalker homestead and the deaths of Uncle Owen and Aunt Beru. As Brooker notes, *Troops* transforms Luke Skywalker from a central character into an incidental one; Luke's "is not even a walk-on part," but our awareness of what happens to him becomes the subject of a number of knowing references (186). For example, when the storm troopers attempt to resolve what appears to be a typical domestic dispute (at least as we might view it through the lens of television documentary), they are actually describing Luke's plans to become a Jedi. After the "domestic dispute" between Owen and Beru ends tragically, one of the storm troopers comments in passing that they will look for their nephew "and make sure he's okay," echoing the often artificial closure of the television show while also parodying the fact that the storm troopers will be pursuing Luke throughout the rest of the film.

Star Wars Uncut

Many of these practices come together in the fan-produced *Star Wars Uncut*, a scene-for-scene remake of the original *Star Wars: A New Hope*. The project was initiated by twenty-six-year-old web developer Casey Pugh, who cut the film into 475 fifteen-second chunks and invited fans to sign up to remake any segment they wanted and, once approved, in whatever style they chose. The result was fan-produced segments built upon a variety of animation, stop-motion, and live-action techniques. Pugh then allowed participants to vote on the "best" version of each scene and created an algorithm that automatically compiled the highest-rated scenes into a completed film, available for free online viewing through *Vimeo*. Moreover, the film could change in real time as audiences voted for different scenes to be included, making *Star Wars Uncut* a truly dynamic text, one that exists as a film, a website, and a database of clips that can potentially constitute other versions of the film. Even without these changes, fans can watch all versions of a specific segment and imagine how the film might have turned out differently or, in some cases, enjoy the cleverness with which a group of fans quote, or remake, a specific scene. In fact, the *Star Wars Uncut* website specifically caters to this impulse by listing multiple versions of the "cantina scene" in one of the sidebars. Pugh's ultimate intention is to produce a more seamlessly edited final version of the film with the official soundtrack superimposed, and as of this writing, he is negotiating with Lucasfilm to obtain rights to the soundtrack. However, the existing rough cut helps to reinforce the film's intertextual structure, as well as the enthusiasm of the fans who participated in this adaptive activity. As Pugh observes in an interview with *New York Times* reporter Brian Stelter, the

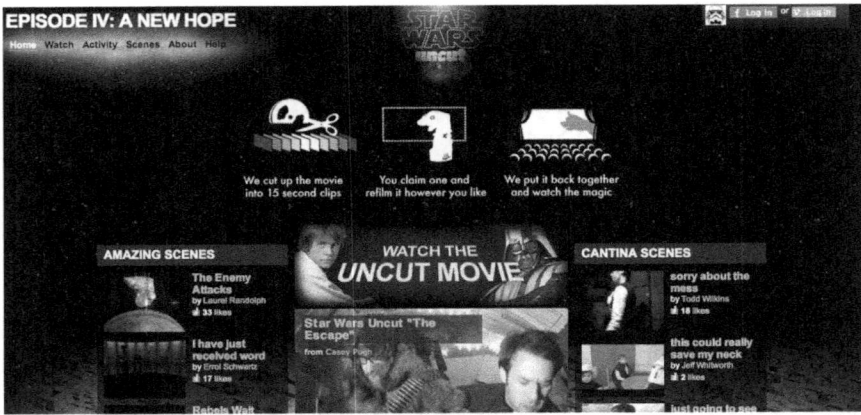

Figure 12.2 The *Star Wars Uncut* website invites users to participate in "remaking" the original film.

reward for participating in *Star Wars Uncut* was simply to be involved with the project of producing one of the most ambitious fan films ever.

Because of this dynamic construction, *Star Wars Uncut* is impossible to reduce to a single meaning. Instead, it offers a mosaic of different styles, aesthetics, and stances toward its cinematic text. Some clips feature highly stylized animated sequences designed to display the creator's skill as an animator or effects designer. Others use stop-motion animation of *Star Wars* action figures, Legos, and other materials to depict an action—a technique borrowed from past filmmakers. Finally, others show human actors, often in costume, performing the assigned scenes. The performers range from groups of college students to families, often parents with young children. In the latter case, the performances serve as a means for parents to share their enjoyment of *Star Wars* with their children. In fact, the film is saturated in nostalgia, not merely for the original *Star Wars*, but also for the pleasures of the original viewing experience and of seeking to recreate that experience through various forms of play. Remaking *Star Wars* in this way allows fans to collectively share in this enjoyment. In her discussion of DVD consumption practices, Barbara Klinger touches on this effect, as she compares the practice of repeat viewing to "nostalgic pleasures" and describes rewatching movies as "a particularly vivid, tangible means of returning to the past" (175). This "return to the past" connects the nostalgia already inherent in the *Star Wars* narrative to the desire to recapture the excitement and innocence of watching the film.

Star Wars Uncut brings together the pleasures of production and consumption in other ways as well. Pugh's canny decision to break the film into fifteen-second chunks foregrounds its citability—the practice of quoting, paraphrasing, or reworking part of an earlier text. The movie's basis in the social media where it was planned and executed is emphasized from the very opening scene, with the phrase, "a long time ago, in a galaxy far, far away" appearing as a status update, or "tweet," on the movie's Twitter page. The famous introductory scroll not only offers a plot description but also includes tweets by participants in *Star Wars Uncut*, again reminding us that the film is a collaborative project, one built upon the shared enthusiasms for the *Star Wars* films and for fan filmmaking as an activity. The use of these tweets tells us that this is not (just) George Lucas's *Star Wars*. It is a project conceived and produced by fans, one that embraces the original but also reimagines it.

Star Wars Uncut also reminds us that the act of reading often incorporates the intersection between texts. This idea is particularly illustrated in the cantina scene, a moment in the source movie that has often inspired repeat viewings, citations, and reinterpretations. During one animated clip, the camera seems to pan across the Mos Eisley Cantina, arriving at a shot of Moe Szyslak, the notoriously prickly proprietor of Moe's Tavern in the animated series *The Simpsons* (1989–). Although the *Simpsons* reference is initially startling, *Star Wars Uncut* is loaded with such references that extend well beyond the already expansive *Star Wars* universe (or at least galaxy), helping to underscore Hutcheon's reminder that all texts are ultimately "mosaics of citations" (21). Similarly, during one of the chase scenes, Han Solo, wearing a New York Rangers hockey jersey, complains, "I'm not even supposed to be here today," a line that evokes Kevin Smith's *Clerks* (1994), which is itself steeped in *Star Wars* fandom; the clip is shot in black-and-white like *Clerks*, furthering the connection. During a subsequent clip, another actor playing Han Solo comments, "I hate snakes," linking the scene to Harrison Ford's Indiana Jones character. Thus, in addition to displaying their expertise and investment in *Star Wars*, the fan producers also show their intertextual knowledge by drawing connections to other movies and television shows. In fact, Brooker, in his analysis of ritual movie-watching, observes that such line quoting can serve to reinforce community, even while the participants seek to demonstrate their cleverness (58–60). Although many of these verbal jabs will disappear from the planned final version of the film, because of its timing to the original *Star Wars* soundtrack, the visual jokes will continue to be an important part of the film, as the cross-screen version celebrates not only *Star Wars* itself, but also the transformative potential of collective filmmaking.

POLITICIZING ADAPTATION

In addition to commenting on popular culture, audiences have also activated such cross-screen adaptations as an element in political struggle. Perhaps the most compelling example of this attempt to reactivate the meaning of an sf film or television show in a new context is the use of James Cameron's superficially anticolonialist fable, *Avatar* (2009), by Palestinian and Israeli activists to challenge settlement construction on the West Bank. *Avatar* depicts the struggles of an indigenous group known as the Na'vi as they fight back against the humans who have colonized their planet, Pandora, in order to mine its resources. The blue-skinned Na'vi are loosely modeled on Native Americans and other indigenous tribes who have been colonized by Europeans, and the film's plot revisits the killing and forced migration of a number of Native American tribes.

This critique of colonization provided the Palestinian and Israeli activists with an allegorical structure they could use to express opposition to the Israeli occupation of the West Bank. In the protest, the activists painted themselves blue to resemble the Na'vi while wearing the traditional keffiyeh, marched through the village of Bil'in, which was occupied by the Israeli Army, and recorded their activities. They then edited footage of the protest with pivotal scenes from *Avatar* to highlight similarities between the experiences of the Na'vi and the Palestinians. After the protest, the group posted the videos on *YouTube* and used social media-tools to ensure the story would circulate as widely as possible, generating discussion and debate. As Henry Jenkins argues in an editorial published in *Le Monde diplomatique*, "the event is a reminder of how people around the world are mobilizing icons and myths from popular culture as resources for political speech," a practice he describes as "Avatar activism" ("Avatar"). Thus, whereas the film offered a simplified account of the history of colonialism—a fact noted by many of the film's conservative critics, as John Nolte's review for Big Hollywood suggests—the protesters were able to identify relationships between the film's narrative and the situation in Bil'in. As Jenkins is quick to point out, the video is no substitute for understanding the complex history of the Israel-Palestine conflict, but it illustrates the potential of such adaptive filmmaking to comment on vital social issues. In this sense, the interpretive practices of fan adaptations, rather than simply commenting on texts, become aligned with the political aims of the fan producers, taking a familiar narrative and using it to redirect energy toward a chosen political cause.

Although these examples illustrate the role of fan adaptations in fostering critical skills in visual and textual literacy, it is important to resist what Jonathan Gray punningly describes as a "'You-topian' rhetoric" that merely celebrates the power of the consumer to rewrite or reimagine material produced by the media industries (*Show Sold Separately* 163). The ability to create fan films typically depends upon access to equipment such as a digital video camera or an editing suite, as well as a high-speed internet connection. But more crucial to the process, intellectual property laws provide copyright holders with quite a bit of control over the content of media franchises like the *Star Wars* films and *Star Trek* series. Lucasfilms, for example, has famously policed what videos are allowed to circulate, and works that violate what Lucas defines as the "spirit" of the *Star Wars* saga are often threatened with being taken down from websites like *YouTube* (Gray, *Show Sold Separately* 165). Also, fan films, as a complement to the film industry, may reinforce traditional gender and racial stereotypes rather than challenge them.

Although fan films are often dismissed as a peripheral aspect of the media industry, they just as often demonstrate a profound understanding of the processes of intertextuality and adaptation, an awareness of how texts speak to and through each other and across the various screens that increasingly surround us. These fan productions draw on the principles of adaptation not simply to tell new stories but to use those stories to engage a wider public. The ability of fan filmmakers to add to or comment on a larger narrative leads to an expansive transmediated storyworld in which fans increasingly fashion themselves as participants in, rather than mere consumers of, a wider audiovisual culture. Thus, we must reconsider definitions of textuality and authorship as audiences continue to retell and rework popular stories. Although fan films have long participated in the process of engaging with issues of representation and meaning, they have become embedded in a wider culture of social media and video sharing, pushing these forms of critique from the margins toward the mainstream. As a result, fan films are becoming a crucial part of the ongoing transformation of the film and television industries, one that is dependent upon and revitalized by what John Hartley refers to as "the creativity and imagination of its viewers" (10). Fans have always been involved in the production of meaning, and digital adaptations such as those discussed here serve to highlight the ways in which fan filmmakers have embraced the storytelling techniques of sf while adapting those techniques to engage with or participate in a wider social discourse. In some cases, such as the example of "Avatar activism," fans can even use the imaginative narratives of sf to comment on vital social and political issues.

WORKS CITED

Barthes, Roland. *Image Music Text*. Trans. Stephen Heath. New York: Hill and Wang, 1977.
Brooker, Will. *Using the Force: Creativity, Community, and* Star Wars *Fans*. New York: Continuum, 2002.
Coppa, Francesca. "Women, *Star Trek*, and the Early Development of Fannish Vidding." *Transformative Works and Cultures* 1 (2008). Accessed 30 Nov. 2010. <http://journal.transformativeworks.org/index.php/twc/article/view/44/64>.
Ellis, John. *Visible Fictions: Cinema, Television, Video*. Rev. ed. London: Routledge, 1992.
Gore, Chris. "Introduction." *Homemade Hollywood: Fans Behind the Camera*. New York: Continuum, 2008.
Graham, Jane. "The New Wave of Fan Films." *Guardian* 13 May 2010. Accessed 30 Nov. 2010. <http://www.guardian.co.uk/film/2010/may/13/fan-films-wes-anderson-spiderman>.
Gray, Jonathan. *Show Sold Separately: Promos, Spoilers, and Other Media Paratexts*. New York: New York UP, 2010.
———. *Watching with* The Simpsons: *Television, Parody, and Intertextuality*. London: Routledge, 2006.
Hartley, John. *Television Truths*. Malden: Blackwell, 2008.
Hutcheon, Linda. *A Theory of Adaptation*. London: Routledge, 2006.
Jenkins, Henry. "Avatar Activism." *Le Monde diplomatique* Sept. 2010. Accessed 30 Nov. 2010. <http://www.monddiplo.com/2010/09/15avatar>.
——— *Convergence Culture: Where Old and New Media Collide*. New York: New York UP, 2006.
———. "Reception Theory and Audience Research: The Mystery of the Vampire's Kiss." *Henry Jenkins' Official Website*, n.d. Accessed 30 Nov. 2010. <http://web.mit.edu/cms/People/henry3/vampkiss.html>.
Klinger, Barbara. *Beyond the Multiplex: Cinema, New Technologies, and the Home*. Berkeley: U of California P, 2006.
Kraus, Daniel. "The Phantom Edit." *Salon* 5 Nov. 2001. Accessed 30 Nov. 2010. <http://www.salon.com/entertainment/movies/feature/2001/11/05/phantom_edit>.
Leitch, Thomas. *Film Adaptation and its Discontents: From* Gone with the Wind *to* The Passion of the Christ. Baltimore: Johns Hopkins UP, 2007.
Mittell, Jason. "Wikis and Participatory Fandom." *Just TV* 18 Sept. 2010. Accessed 30 Nov. 2010. <http://justtv.wordpress.com/2010/09/18/wikis-and-participatory-fandom/>.

Nolte, John. "Review: Cameron's 'Avatar' Is a Big, Dull, America-Hating, PC Revenge Fantasy." *Big Hollywood* 11 Dec. 2009. Accessed 1 Dec. 2010. <http://bighollywood.breitbart.com/>.
Stelter, Brian. "An Emmy for Rebuilding a Galaxy." *New York Times* 27 Aug. 2010. Accessed 15 Nov. 2010. <http://www.nytimes.com/2010/08/28/arts/television/28uncut.html>.
Young, Clive. *Homemade Hollywood: Fans Behind the Camera*. New York: Continuum, 2008.

Contributors

M. Keith Booker is the James E. and Ellen Wadley Roper Professor of English at the University of Arkansas. He has authored or edited more than thirty books on literature, film, and television, including *Monsters, Mushroom Clouds, and the Cold War: American Science Fiction and the Roots of Postmodernism, 1946–1964* (2001), *Strange TV: Innovative Television Series from* The Twilight Zone *to* The X-Files (2002), *Science Fiction Television* (2004), *Alternate Americas: Science Fiction Film and American Culture* (2006), *Postmodern Hollywood* (2007), and, with Anne-Marie Thomas, *The Science Fiction Handbook* (2009).

Mark Bould is Reader in Film and Literature at the University of the West of England and co-editor of *Science Fiction Film and Television*. He is the author of *Film Noir: From Berlin to* Sin City (2005) and *The Cinema of John Sayles:* Lone Star (2009), co-author of *The Routledge Concise History of Science Fiction* (2011), and co-editor of *Parietal Games: Critical Writings by and on M. John Harrison* (2005), *The Routledge Companion to Science Fiction* (2009), *Fifty Key Figures in Science Fiction* (2009), *Red Planets: Marxism and Science Fiction* (2009), and *Neo-Noir* (2009). He is currently writing *Science Fiction: The Routledge Film Guidebook* (2012). He is an advisory editor for *Extrapolation*, *Historical Materialism*, *Paradoxa* and *Science Fiction Studies*.

Gerald Duchovnay, Professor of English and Film at Texas A&M University-Commerce, has published numerous articles on literature, film, and media. His books include *Humphrey Bogart: A Bio-Bibliography* (Greenwood, 1999) and *Film Voices* (SUNY Press, 2004), and he is the founding and general editor of *Post Script: Essays in Film and the Humanities*.

Mary Pharr is Professor Emeritus of English at Florida Southern College. She has edited two collections of criticism on fantastic literature: *The Blood Is the Life* (co-edited with Leonard G. Heldreth) and *Fantastic Odysseys*. She has published extensively on fantastic film and fiction, including articles on David Cronenberg, Stephen King, and epic mythology in contemporary forms. Her essay, "A Paradox: The Harry Potter Series as Both Epic and Postmodern," appears in the anthology *Heroism in the Harry Potter Series* (Berndt and Steveker, 2010).

Rodney F. Hill, Assistant Professor of Film at Georgia Gwinnett College, holds a Ph.D. in Theatre & Film from the University of Kansas and an M.A. in Communication Arts from the University of Wisconsin–Madison. He is co-author of *The Francis Ford Coppola Encyclopedia* (Scarecrow, 2010) and *The Encyclopedia of Stanley Kubrick* (Checkmark, 2002), co-editor of *Francis Ford Coppola: Interviews* (UP of Mississippi, 2004), and a contributor to several other books, including *The Essential Science Fiction Television Reader* (UP of Kentucky, 2008) and *The Stanley Kubrick Archives* (Taschen, 2005). His essays have appeared in *Film Quarterly*, *Cinema Journal*, *Literature/Film Quarterly*, *Post Script*, and elsewhere.

Cynthia J. Miller, a cultural anthropologist specializing in popular culture and visual media, is Scholar-in-Residence at Emerson College and Associate Editor of *Film & History: An Interdisciplinary Journal of Film and Television Studies*. She has published extensively on the B-movie and exploitation film genres in a range of journals and edited volumes, including: *Why We Fought: War in Film, Television, and History* (UP of Kentucky, 2008), *Tracing an Indian Diaspora: Contexts, Memories, Representations* (Sage, 2008), *Heroes of Film, Comics, and American Culture* (McFarland, 2009), *Cultural Adaptation in American History, Literature, and Film* (Edward Mellen, 2009), *Sounds of the Future: Essays on Music in Science Fiction Film* (McFarland, 2010), *James Bond: The Films Are Not Enough* (Cambridge Scholars, 2010), *Télévision: le moment expérimental* (INA/Apogee, 2010), and several forthcoming volumes, including *Learning from Mickey, Donald, and Walt: Essays on Disney's Edutainment Films* (McFarland, 2011) and *Birthplace and Commemoration in American Public Memory* (U of Massachusetts P, 2011). She is currently completing *Too Bold for the Box Office: A Study in Mockumentary* (Wayne State UP) and *The Encyclopedia of B Westerns* (Scarecrow).

Lorrie Palmer is a Ph.D. candidate in Film and Media at Indiana University, immersed in the swirling seas of gender and genre. She has published widely on cinema (Harold Lloyd, Will Smith, Australian film) and on television (*Angel*, *Supernatural*, *Star Trek*) in such journals as *Camera Obscura*, *Cinema Journal*, *Extrapolation*, *Film & History*, *Velvet Light Trap*, *Senses of Cinema*, *Journal of Popular Film & Television*, *Bright Lights*, and in several edited collections. She also hopes one day to visit Istanbul.

Contributors

Michelle Onley Pirkle is a doctoral candidate in film studies at Texas A&M University-Commerce, where she teaches literature and composition. With a certificate in Children's and Adolescent Literature and Culture, she focuses her research on the cinematic depiction and construction of the child's perspective.

J. P. Telotte is a Professor of Film and Media and Chair of the School of Literature, Communication, and Culture at Georgia Tech, where he teaches courses in film history, film genres, and film and television. Author of more than 100 articles on film, television, and literature and co-editor of the journal *Post Script*, he has published numerous books, the most recent of which are *The Mouse Machine: Disney and Technology* (Illinois, 2008), *The Essential Science Fiction Television Reader* (Kentucky, 2008), and *Animating Space: From Mickey to WALL-E* (Kentucky, 2010).

Chuck Tryon is an Assistant Professor in the English Department at Fayetteville State University, where his teaching and research focus on various aspects of digital cinema, documentary studies, political video, and technology in the language arts classroom. He is the author of *Reinventing Cinema: Movies in the Age of Media Convergence* (Rutgers UP, 2009). He has published essays on film and media culture in *Film Criticism*, *The Journal of Film and Video*, *Popular Communication*, and in the anthologies *The Essential Science Fiction Television Reader* and *Flow TV: Television in the Age of Media Convergence*. He is currently working on a book about the effects of online distribution on the entertainment industry.

Sherryl Vint is an Associate Professor in the Department of English at Brock University, the author of *Bodies of Tomorrow* (2007) and *Animal Alterity* (2010), and co-author of *The Routledge Concise History of Science Fiction* (2011). She has co-edited the collections *Fifty Key Figures in Science Fiction* (2009), *The Routledge Companion to Science Fiction* (2009), and *Beyond Cyberpunk* (2010), and she is a founding co-editor of the journal *Science Fiction Film and Television*.

Selective Filmography/Videography

S=source   A=adaptation

(S) *Captain Video and His Video Rangers* (1949–55). Dumont. Scientific action-adventure. Producers: James Caddigan, Frank Telford, Olga Druce. Cast: Richard Coogan, Al Hodge, Don Hastings, Hal Conklin, Stephen Elliott, Ben Lackland.

(A) *Captain Video, Master of the Stratosphere* (1951). Columbia Pictures. Scientific action-adventure serial in 15 chapters. Directors: Spencer Gordon Bennet, Wallace Grissell. Writers: Royal K. Cole, Sherman L. Lowe, Joseph L. Poland. Cast: Judd Holdren, Larry Stewart, George Eldredge, Gene Roth.

(S) *Cowboy Bebop: Remix* (1998–99). Sunrise/Bandai. Animation/action/adventure. Director: Shinicohirô Watanabe. Writer: Keiko Nobumoto. Creator: Hajime Yatate. Producers: Masahiko, Kazuhiko Ikeguchi. Cast: Steve Blum, Beau Billingslea, Wendee Lee, Melissa Fahn.

(A) *Cowboy Bebop: The Movie*, a.k.a. *Knockin' on Heaven's Door* (2001). Sunrise/Bones/Bandai. Animation/action/crime. Director: Shinicohirô Watanabe. Writer: Keiko Nobumoto. Creator: Hajime Yatate. Producer: Takayuki Yoshii. Cast: Steve Blum, Beau Billingslea, Wendee Lee, Melissa Fahn. DVD.

(S) *Firefly* (2002). Twentieth Century-Fox Television/Syfy Channel. Space travel/adventure. Creator/Writer/Executive Producer: Joss Whedon. Cast: Nathan Fillion, Gina Torres, Alan Tudyk, Morena Baccarin, Adam Baldwin, Jewel Staite, Sean Maher, Summer Glau, Ron Glass.

(A) *Serenity* (2005). Universal/Mutant Enemy. Director: Joss Whedon. Writer: Joss Whedon. Producer: Barry Mendel. Cast: Nathan Fillion, Gina Torres, Chiwetel Ejiofor, Alan Tudyk, Morena Baccarin, Adam Baldwin, Jewel Staite, Sean Maher, Summer Glau, Ron Glass.

(S) *Logan's Run (1976)*. MGM. Director: Michael Anderson. Writer: David Zelag Goodman. Based on the novel by William F. Nolan and George Clayton Johnson. Producer: Saul David. Cast: Michael York, Jennie Agutter, Richard Jordan, Farah Fawcett-Majors, Peter Ustinov.

(A) *Logan's Run (1977–1978)*. MGM Television/CBS. Executive Producers: Iva Goff and Ben Roberts. Producer: Leonard Katzman. Story Editor: D. C. Fontana. Cast: Gregory Harrison, Heather Menzies, Donald Moffat, Randy Powell.

(S) *Stargate* (1994). Canal+. Military space adventure. Director: Roland Emmerich. Writers: Dean Devlin and Roland Emmerich. Producer: Cast: Kurt Russell, James Spader, Alexis Cruz, Jaye Davidson.

(A) *Stargate SG-1* (1997-2007). MGM/Showtime/SciFi Channel. Creators: Brad Wright and Jonathan Glassner. Key Directors: Peter DeLuise, Martin Wood, Andy Mikata. Key Writers: Jonathan Glassner, Brad Wright, Robert C. Cooper,

Joseph Mallozzi, Paul Mullie. Cast: Richard Dean Anderson, Michael Shanks, Amanda Tapping, Christopher Judge, Don S. Davis, Ben Browder, Claudia Black.

(S) *The Terminator* (1984). Helmdale Film/Orion Pictures Corporation. Director: James Cameron. Writers: James Cameron, Gale Anne Hurd, William Wisher, Jr. Producers: John Daly, Derek Gibson, Gale Anne Hurd. Cast: Arnold Schwarzenegger, Linda Hamilton, Michael Biehn, Paul Winfield, Lance Henriksen, Earl Boen.

(S) *Terminator 2: Judgment Day* (1991). Carolco Pictures/TriStar Pictures. Director: James Cameron. Writers: James Cameron, William Wisher, Jr. Producers: James Cameron, Gale Anne Hurd, Mario Kassar. Cast: Arnold Schwarzenegger, Linda Hamilton, Edward Furlong, Robert Patrick, Joe Morton, Earl Boen.

(A) *Terminator: The Sarah Connor Chronicles* (2008-09). Bartleby Company/C2 Pictures/Warner Bros. Television. Action/sf/thriller. Creator: Josh Friedman. Producers: Josh Friedman, Mario Kassar. Cast: Lena Headey, Thomas Dekker, Summer Glau, Richard T. Jones, Brian Austin Green, Garret Dillahunt, Dean Winters, Shirley Manson.

(S) *The X-Files* (1993–2002). Twentieth Century-Fox Television/Ten Thirteen Productions/X-F Productions. Sf/mystery/drama. Creator/Producer/Writer/Director: Chris Carter. Producers: Paul Rabwin, Kim Manners, Vince Gilligan, Frank Spotnitz. Directors: Kim Manners, Rob Bowman, David Nutter. Cast: Gillian Anderson, David Duchovny, Mitch Pileggi, Robert Patrick, Tom Braidwood, William B. Davis, Bruce Harwood, Dean Haglund, Nicholas Lea, Annabeth Gish, James Pickens, Jr.

(A) *The X-Files*, a.k.a. *The X-Files: Fight the Future* (1998). Twentieth Century-Fox Film Corporation/Ten Thirteen Productions. Director: Rob Bowman. Writers: Chris Carter, Frank Spotnitz. Producers: Chris Carter, Daniel Sackheim. Cast: David Duchovny, Gillian Anderson, John Neville, William B. Davis, Martin Landau, Mitch Pileggi, Jeffrey DeMunn, Blythe Danner.

The X-Files: I Want to Believe (2008). Twentieth Century-Fox Film Corporation/Ten Thirteen Productions/in association with Dune Entertainment III/Crying Box Productions. Director: Chris Carter. Writers: Frank Spotnitz, Chris Carter. Producers: Chris Carter, Brent O'Connor, Frank Spotnitz. Cast: David Duchovny, Gillian Anderson, Amanda Peet, Billy Connolly, Alvin "Xzibit" Joiner, Mitch Pileggi.

Bibliography

Abbott, Jon. *Irwin Allen Television Productions, 1964–1970: A Critical History of* Voyage to the Bottom of the Sea, Lost in Space, The Time Tunnel *and* Land of the Giants. Jefferson: McFarland, 2006.
Anderson, Christopher. *Hollywood TV: The Studio System in the Fifties.* Austin: U of Texas P, 1994.
Barrett, Michèle, and Duncan Barrett. Star Trek: *The Human Frontier.* London: Routledge, 2001.
Beeler, Stan, and Lisa Dickson. *Reading* Stargate SG-1. London: I. B. Tauris, 2006.
Bernardi, Daniel L. Star Trek *and History: Race-ing Towards a White Future*: New Brunswick: Rutgers UP, 1998.
Bignell, Jonathan, and Stephen Lacey, eds. *Popular Television Drama: Critical Perspectives.* Manchester: Manchester UP, 2005.
Bluestone, George. *Novels into Film: The Metamorphosis of Fiction into Cinema.* Berkeley: U of California P, 1957.
Booker, M. Keith. *Science Fiction Television.* Westport: Praeger, 2004.
———. *Strange TV: Innovative Television Series from* The Twilight Zone *to* The X-Files. Westport: Greenwood, 2002.
Bould, Mark. "Film and Television." *The Cambridge Companion to Science Fiction.* Ed. Edward James and Farah Mendlesohn. Cambridge: Cambridge UP, 2003. 79–95.
Brooker, Will. *Using the Force: Creativity, Community, and* Star Wars *Fans.* New York: Continuum, 2002.
Brosnan, John. *The Primal Screen: A History of Science Fiction Film.* Boston: Little, Brown, 1991.
Bukatman, Scott. *Matters of Gravity: Special Effects and Supermen in the 20th Century.* Durham: Duke UP, 2003.
Butler, David, ed. *Time and Relative Dissertations in Space: Critical Perspectives on* Doctor Who. Manchester: Manchester UP, 2007.
Buxton, David. *From* The Avengers *to* Miami Vice: *Form and Ideology in Television Series.* Manchester: Manchester UP, 1990.
Caldwell, John Thorton. *Televisuality: Style, Crisis, and Authority in American Television.* New Brunswick: Rutgers UP, 1995.
Carroll, Noël. "TV and Film: A Philosophical Perspective." *Journal of Aesthetic Education* 35.1 (2001): 15–29.
Cartmell, Deborah, and Imelda Whelehan, eds. *Adaptations: From Text to Screen, Screen to Text.* New York: Routledge, 1999.
Castleman, Harry, and Walter J. Podrazik. *Watching TV: Four Decades of American Television.* New York: McGraw-Hill, 1982.

Caughie, John. *Television Drama: Realism, Modernism and British Culture.* Oxford: Oxford UP, 2000.
Cavallaro, Dani. *Anime and the Art of Adaptation.* Jefferson: McFarland, 2010.
Chapman, James. *Saints and Avengers: British Adventure Series of the 1960s.* London: I. B. Tauris, 2002.
Cline, William C. *In the Nick of Time: Motion Picture Sound Serials.* Jefferson: McFarland, 1984.
Cornea, Christine. *Science Fiction Cinema: Between Fantasy and Reality.* Edinburgh: Edinburgh UP, 2007.
Creeber, Glen. *Serial Television: Big Drama on the Small Screen.* London: BFI, 2004.
Dixon, Wheeler-Winston. *Lost in the Fifties: Recovering Phantom Hollywood.* Carbondale: Southern Illinois UP, 2005.
Dunleavy, Trisha. *Television Drama: Form, Agency, Innovation.* Basingstoke: Palgrave Macmillan, 2009.
Edgerton, Gary R. *The Columbia History of American Television.* New York: Columbia UP, 2007.
Ellington, Jane Elizabeth, and Joseph W. Critelli. "Analysis of a Modern Myth: The *Star Trek* Series." *Extrapolation* 24.3 (1983): 241–50.
Ellis, John. *Seeing Things: Television in the Age of Uncertainty.* London: I. B. Tauris, 2000.
———. *Visible Fictions: Cinema, Television, Video.* Rev. ed. London: Routledge, 1992.
Elsaesser, Thomas, Jan Simons, and Lucette Bronk, eds. *Writing for the Medium: Television in Transition.* Amsterdam: Amsterdam UP, 1994. 91–97.
Espenson, Jane, ed. *Finding Serenity: Anti-Heroes, Lost Shepherds and Space Hookers in Joss Whedon's* Firefly. Dallas: BenBella, 2004.
Fiske, John. *Television Culture.* London: Routledge, 1987.
Foucault, Michel. *Language, Counter-Memory, Practice: Selected Essays and Interviews.* Ed. Donald F. Bouchard. Ithaca: Cornell UP, 1977.
Frayling, Christopher. *Mad, Bad and Dangerous? The Scientist and the Cinema.* London: Reaktion, 2005.
Friedberg, Anne. *The Virtual Window: From Alberti to Microsoft.* Cambridge: MIT P, 2006.
Geraghty, Christine, and David Lusted, eds. *The Television Studies Book.* London: Edward Arnold, 1998.
Geraghty, Lincoln. *American Science Fiction Film and Television.* Oxford: Berg, 2009.
———, ed. *Channeling the Future: Essays on Science Fiction and Fantasy Television.* Lanham: Scarecrow, 2009.
———. *Living with* Star Trek: *American Culture and the* Star Trek *Universe.* London: I. B. Tauris, 2007.
Gitlin, Todd. *Inside Prime Time.* Rev. ed. London: Routledge, 1994.
Goldwyn, Samuel. "Hollywood in the Television Age." *Hollywood Quarterly: Film Culture in Postwar America, 1945–1957.* Ed. Eric Smoodin and Ann Martin. Berkeley and Los Angeles: U of California P, 2002. 199–204.
Gunning, Tom. "The Cinema of Attractions: Early Film, Its Spectator, and the Avant-Garde." *Film and Theory: An Anthology.* Ed. Robert Stam and Toby Miller. Malden: Blackwell, 2000. 229–35.
Hawes, William. *Live Television Drama, 1946–1951.* Jefferson: McFarland, 2001.
Hills, Matt. *Triumph of a Time Lord: Regenerating* Doctor Who *in the Twenty-First Century.* London: I. B. Tauris, 2010.

Hoesterey, Ingeborg. *Pastiche: Cultural Memory in Art, Film, and Literature.* Blomington: Indiana UP, 2001
Hutcheon, Linda. *A Theory of Adaptation.* London: Routledge, 2006.
James, Edward. *Science Fiction in the Twentieth Century.* New York: Oxford UP, 1994.
Jameson, Fredric. "Towards a New Awareness of Genre." *Science-Fiction Studies* 9 (1982): 322–34.
Jenkins, Henry. *Convergence Culture: Where Old and New Media Collide.* New York: New York UP, 2006.
Jenkins, Henry, and John Tulloch. *Science Fiction Audiences: Watching* Star Trek *and* Doctor Who. London: Routledge, 1995.
Johnson, Catherine. *Telefantasy.* London: BFI, 2005.
Johnson-Smith, Jan. *American Science Fiction TV: Star Trek, Stargate and Beyond.* Middletown: Wesleyan UP, 2005.
Kinnard, Roy. *Science Fiction Serials.* Jefferson: McFarland, 1998.
Kittler, Friedrich. *Optical Media: Berlin Lectures, 1999.* Trans. Anthony Enns. Cambridge: Polity, 2010.
Klinger, Barbara. *Beyond the Multiplex: Cinema, New Technologies, and the Home.* Berkeley: U of California P, 2006.
Knight, Peter. *Conspiracy Culture: From the Kennedy Assassination to* The X-Files. London: Routledge, 2000.
Krantz, David L., and Nancy C. Mellerski, eds. *In/Fidelity: Essays on Film Adaptation.* Newcastle-on-Tyne: Cambridge Scholars, 2007.
Kuhn, Annette, ed. *Alien Zone.* Ed. Kuhn. London: Verso, 1990.
Lahue, Kalton, C. *Continued Next Week: A History of the Moving Picture Serial.* Norman: U of Oklahoma P, 1964.
Lavery, David, Angela Hague, and Marla Cartwright, eds. *Deny All Knowledge: Reading* The X-Files. Syracuse: Syracuse UP, 1996.
Leitch, Thomas. *Film Adaptation and Its Discontents: From* Gone with the Wind *to* The Passion of the Christ. Baltimore: Johns Hopkins UP, 2007.
Lury, Karen. *Interpreting Television.* London: Hodder Arnold, 2005.
Mellencamp, Patricia. *Logics of Television: Essays in Cultural Criticism.* London: BFI; Bloomington: Indiana UP, 1990. 1–13.
Melzer, Patricia. *Science Fiction and Feminist Thought.* Austin: U of Texas P, 2006.
Morton, Alan. *The Complete Directory to Science Fiction, Fantasy, and Horror Television Series: A Comprehensive Guide to the First 50 Years, 1946 to 1996.* Peoria: Other Worlds, 1997.
Naremore, James, ed. *Film Adaptation.* New Brunswick: Rutgers UP, 2000.
Phillips, Mark, and Frank Garcia. *Science Fiction Television Series: Episode Guides, Histories, and Casts and Credits for 62 Prime Time Shows, 1959 through 1989.* Jefferson: McFarland, 1996.
Pierson, Michele. *Special Effects: Still in Search of Wonder.* New York: Columbia UP, 2002.
Potter, Tiffany, and C. W. Marshall, eds. *Cylon in America: Critical Studies in Battlestar Galactica.* New York: Continuum, 2008.
Presnell, Don, and Marty McGee. *A Critical History of Television's* The Twilight Zone, *1959–1964.* Jefferson: McFarland, 1998.
Rose, Brian G., ed. *TV Genres: A Handbook and Reference Guide.* Westport: Greenwood, 1985.
Rovin, Jeff. *The Great Television Series.* Cranbury: Barnes, 1977.
Sconce, Jeffrey. *Haunted Media: Electronic Presence from Telegraphy to Television.* Durham: Duke UP, 2000.
Sobchack, Vivian. *Screening Space: The American Science Fiction Film.* New York: Ungar, 1987.

Sontag, Susan. "The Imagination of Disaster." *Against Interpretation*. New York: Dell, 1966. 212–28.
Spigel, Lynn, and Jan Olsson, eds. *Television After TV: Essays on a Medium in Transition*. Durham: Duke UP, 2004.
Staiger, Janet, and Sabine Hake, eds. *Convergence Media History*. London: Routledge, 2009.
Stanyard, Stewart T. *Dimensions Behind* The Twilight Zone. Toronto: ECW, 2007.
Stedman, Raymond William. *The Serials: Suspense and Drama by Installment*. Norman: U of Oklahoma P, 1971.
Stewart, Garrett. "The 'Videology' of Science Fiction." *Shadows of the Magic Lamp*. Ed. George E. Slusser and Eric S. Rabkin. Carbondale: Southern Illinois UP, 1985. 159–207.
Storm, Jo. *Approaching the Possible: The World of* Stargate SG-1. Ontario: ECW, 2005.
Suvin, Darko. *Metamorphoses of Science Fiction: On the Poetics and History of a Literary Genre*. New Haven: Yale UP, 1979.
Telotte, J. P., ed. *The Essential Science Fiction Television Reader*. Lexington: UP of Kentucky, 2008.
———. *Replications: A Robotic History of the Science Fiction Film*. Urbana: U of Illinois P, 1995.
———. *The Science Fiction Film*. Cambridge: Cambridge UP, 2001.
Tulloch, John. *Television Drama: Agency, Audience, and Myth*. London: Routledge, 1990.
Virilio, Paul. *A Landscape of Events*. Trans. Julie Rose. Cambridge: MIT P, 2000.
———. *The Lost Dimension*. Trans. Daniel Moshenberg. New York: Semiotext(e), 1991.
———. *The Vision Machine*. Trans. Julie Rose. Bloomington: Indiana UP, 1994.
Wagner, Geoffrey. *The Novel and the Cinema*. Rutherford: Fairleigh Dickinson UP, 1975.
Warren, Bill. *Keep Watching the Skies! American Science Fiction Movies of the Fifties*. Jefferson: McFarland, 2010.
Welsh, James M., and Peter Lev, eds. *The Literature/Film Reader: Issues of Adaptation*. Lanham: Scarecrow, 2007.
Westfahl, Gary. *The Mechanics of Wonder: The Creation of the Idea of Science Fiction*. Liverpool: Liverpool UP, 1999.
Whitfield, Stephen E., and Gene Roddenberry. *The Making of* Star Trek. New York: Ballantine, 1968.
Wilk, Max. *The Golden Age of Television: Notes from the Survivors*. New York: Delacort, 1976.
Williams, Raymond. *Television*. London: Routledge, 2003.
Wingrove, David, ed. *The Science Fiction Film Source Book*. Essex: Longman,1985.
Young, Paul. *The Cinema Dreams Its Rivals: Media Fantasy Films from Radio to the Internet*. Minneapolis: U of Minnesota P, 2006.

Index

Please note: all **bolded** numbers refer to illustrations.

A
Aaru 153
Abbott, Jon 47
Abbott, L. B. 38, 44, 56
ABC 5, 42, 45, 63, 155
Abyss, The (film) 81n
Academy Award xxviii n, 55, 58
Academy of Science Fiction, Fantasy, and Horror Films 55
Acland, Charles R. 159
Adams, Nick 42
adaptation xiii, xxiii, xxiv, 3, 35, 42, 43, 45, 46, 48, 63–64, 73, 81, 143; and nostalgia xiv, 138; fidelity issue xv, xx, xxviiin, 68, 78, 127, 159, 177; adaptation studies xix–xx, xxvii, xxviiin, 143, 145–146, 159, 176, 117–178, 182; and film studies xx–xxi; and genre issues xx, xxi, xxiii, 102, 107, 109, 110, 111, 111n, 113n, 122, 126, 127, 128–130, 133, 138n, 156–157, 160n, 164–165; as cross-media issue xx–xxi, xxiv, xxvii, 53, 68, 102, 103, 107, 110, 112, 115, 125, 144, 156, 157, 159, 166, 169, 171, 174, 176–189; as pastiche xxi-xxii, 78–79; and liminality xxii; gender issues in xxvi, 84; and fan culture 101, 106, 112n–113n, 117, 125, 139n, 158, 169, 171, 174, 178, 180–81; and cult activity xxvii, 136; in animation xxvii, 101, 166; and serials 9–10, 15–16; and media specificity 68–69; and technology 102, 102, 104–105, 137–38; and cognitive estrangement 107, 110; as commodity 143, 145, 153, 157, 159, 160n, 161n; politicizing 186–87; Baudrillard on 8; and postmodernism 78–79
Agutter, Jenny 55
Agyeman, Freema 156
A.I.: Artificial Intelligence (film) xvi
Albert, Eddie 41, 42
Alfred Hitchcock Presents (series) 21
Alias (series) 88
Alien (films) xvi, 84, 91, 92, 96n
Alien Nation (series) xxiii
Allen, Irwin xxv, 36, 37, 39, 40, 41, 45, 47, 48, 54, 56, 59; and spectacle 35, 43–44, 47, 48; and disaster films 36, 48; awards 36; pseudoscience of 37–38, 45; as showman 42; as formulaic filmmaker 43, 44, 46, 47
Allen, Rex 18n
Altman, Robert 62
American Cinematographer (magazine) 56
American Weekly (magazine) 12
Anderson, Christopher 32
Anderson, Gillian 115, 117
Anderson, Michael 54
Anderson, Richard Dean 72, 81n
Andrew, Dudley 145, 159
Andrews, Dana 7
Andromeda (series) 80
Andy Hardy films 27–28, 29, 33n
Animation xxvii, 162n, 168, 169, 170, 173, in *Serenity* 135; and special effects 184, 185. *See* anime
anime xxvii, 95, 166–67, 168
anthology series 9
Anthony Adverse (novel) xiii

Anwar, Gabrielle 88
Area 51 121
Ash, Jerry 9
Ashbrook, Daphne 155
Ashes to Ashes (series) xvi
Asimov, Isaac 80
auteurism xx, 37, 47, 62
Autry, Gene 5, 18n
Avatar (film) xvi, 96n, 178, 186–87

B

B-film xxv
Babylon 5 (series) 69, 79
Bachelard, Gaston 135
Backer, Ron 15, 17n, 18n
Bacon, Sir Francis 151
Baldwin, Adam 125
Bane, Jullian 182
Barbour, Alan 17n
Barrett, Duncan 113n
Barrett, Majel 103
Barrett, Michèle 113n
Barron, Lee 161n
Barrowman, John 156
Bart, Peter 118
Barthes, Roland 178
Basehart, Richard 41, 42, 45, 46
Bassior, Jean-Noel 12, 13, 18n
Batman (series) 47
Battlestar Galactica (original series) 60 (new series) xvi, 67, 81n, 86, 96n
Baudrillard, Jean 8, 78
BBC 147, 151, 154, 155, 157, 160n, 161n
Beatles, The 149, 151, 161n
Becker, Christine 6, 7, 17n
Bellafante, Ginia 92
Bennett, Charles 37
Bernardin, Marc 169
Best Years of Our Lives, The (film) 7
Billingslea, Beau 166
Bionic Woman, The (series) 62, 96n
Black, Claudio 80
Black and White Minstrel Show, The 145
Blade Runner (film) xxii, xxiii
Block, Ernest 106
Bluestone, George xx
Blum, Steve 166
Blu-ray 53
Boisvert, Anne-Marie 164
Bocher, Christian 76
Bond, James 54

Booker, M. Keith xxvi, 8, 21, 73, 80, 107, 108
Bordwell, David 119
Bould, Mark xxvii
Boxleitner, Bruce 79
Brahm, John 22
Braidwood, Tom 121
Brick Bradford (film) 15
British Board of Film Censors 161n
British Board of Film Classification 161n
Brooker, Will 181, 183, 186
Brooks, Avery 79
Brooks, Maurice C. 16
Brosnan, John 58
Browder, Ben 79, 80
Brown, Jeffrey A. 91
Brown, Les 63
Buchanan, Ginjer 130, 138n
Buck Rogers (film) 7, 15, 63, 179
Buffy the Vampire Slayer (series) xxvi, 84, 87–88, 89, 92, 94, 96n, 153
Bukatman, Scott xvii
Burn Notice (series) 88
Butler, David 159
Buttsworth, Sara 87, 88
Byers, Thomas B. 91

C

cable television xiii, xvi, xxviii n, 58, 68
Caldwell, John T. 69, 144, 149, 155
Cameron, James 86, 89, 186
Campbell, Joseph 124, "The Hero's Adventure" 124; "The Message of the Myth" 124
Captain EO (film) 95
Captain Midnight (radio) 16
Captain Satellite (series) 17n
Captain Video (series) xiv, xxv, 7, 9, 12, 16, 17n, 18n, 63; as film serial xiv, 9–10; budget for 10; and product tie-ins 11–12, 13. See serials
Captain Z-Ro (series) 7, 8, 12, 17n, 18n
Carlson, Richard 42
Carroll, Noël 53, 166–67, 174
Carson, Rachel 36
Cartoon Network 166
Casablanca (film) 165
casting 62, 103, 155, 156, 158, 166, 174
Castle (series) 88

Castle, Roy 153
Castleman, Harry 42, 45
Cavallaro, Dani xxvii, 169–179
CBS xiii, 5, 33n, 42, 45, 58, 62, 63
censorship 161n
CGI 69, 70, 71, 81n, 156, 170. *See* special effects
Charlie's Angels (series) 59
Cheers (series) 156
Christie, Dorothy 5
Cinefantastique (magazine) 58
classical cinema xxiii, xxvi
Clemens, George T. 22
Clerks (film) 186
Cline, William C. 17n
Close Encounters of the Third Kind (film) 58, 63, 81n
cold war 38, 44
Collier's Magazine 12
Collins, Stephen 102, 105
Colliver, Tim 41
Columbia Pictures 15, 17n
Comic Con 177
comic books 68, 81n, 101, 95; influence on science fiction television 14, 15, 16; and Japanese *manga* 95, 169
Commando Cody (series) 9, 12, 17n
Connolly, Billy 117
Constellation Award 82n
convergence: media xv, xxi, xxviii n, 15, 20, 21, 32, 143, 144, 153; as style 23; culture of 33
Coogan, Richard 9, 10, 18n
Coppa, Francesca 180
Coppola, Francis Ford 63, 94–95
Cops (series) 182, 183
Corman, Roger 36
Cornea, Christine 86, 91, 92, 94, 95
Cowboy Bebop (series) xxvii, 164–165; "The Realy Folk Blues, [Part 2]" 165; cult following 166
Cowboy Bebop: The Movie (film) xxvii, 164–65, 166, 168–69, 171, 172, 173
Coyle, Jack 18n
Crabbe, Buster 15
Creeber, Glen 68, 156
Cribbins, Bernard 158, 162n
Crichton, Michael 58
cult television xvi
Cushing, Peter 153
cyborg figure 83, 84, 85, 86–87, 89, 90, 93–95, 96n, 167

D

Darvill, Arthur 156
David, Saul 54, 56, 57, 59
Davis, Blair 174
Davis, William B. 119, 120
Day After, The (series) 155
Day After Tomorrow, The (film) 82n
Death by Television (film) xxiii
DeForest, Kelley 102, 103, 104, 110, 111–12, 113n
Dekker, Thomas 86
DeLuise, Michael 74, 75, 76
DePalma, Brian 122
Desk Set (film) 39
Destination Moon (film) 7
Dick Tracy (radio) 16
digital media xiv
Dillahunt, Garret 93
Dirty Harry (film) 171, 172
disaster films 27, 36, 48
Disney, Walt 32, 37, 45, 46, 161n, 168
Doctor Who: (series) xix, 143–63; serial format xxvii; adaptations 159n–60n, 182; *Doctor Who: The Adventure Games* (game) 157; *Daleks Invasion Earth 2150 A.D.* (film) 162n; *Doctor Who and the Daleks* (film) 145, 148, 153, 154, 160n; flow in 146, 152; novelizations of 145, 160n; *Doctor Who: Alternate Empire* (web series) 182; pornographic adaptations of 159n–60n. Episodes: "Battlefield" 13; "Blink" 158; "Blood of the Cybermen" 157, 162n; "The Chase" 151; "The Christmas Invasion" 158; "The Dalek Invasion of Earth" 147, 160n, 161n; "The Daleks" 145, 153, 160n; "The Daleks' Master Plan" 161n; "The Death of Doctor Who" 146, 148; "Death of Time" 146; "The Executioners" 146, 148, 149, 150; "The Final Phase" 146; "Flashpoint" 147; "Flight Through Eternity" 146, 149; "Journey into Terror" 146, 148; "The Keys of Marinus" 161n; "Love and Monsters" 158; "Marco Polo" 161n; "The Ordeal" 148; "The Planet of Decision" (aka "The Chase," "Serial R," and "The

Pursuers") 146, 148, 149, 150, 151, 157, 160n, 161n; "The Rescue" 147; "Rose" 158; "The Runaway Bride" 157; "The Savages" 146, 160n; Serial L 147; Serial M (aka "The Romans") 147; "The Space Museum" 146; "The Tenth Planet" 152; "The Time Meddler" 160n; "An Unearthly Child" 146; "Voyage of the Damned" 158; "The War Games" 161n; "The Watcher" 160n; "The Web Planet" 160n
Dole, Carol M. 95n–96n
Dollhouse (series) xxviii n, 137
Domeier, Doug, 59
Done the Impossible: The Fan's Tale of Firefly *and* Serenity (film) 139n
Donnelly, Kevin J. 161n
Donner, Richard 22, 23
Doohan, James 103, 105
Duchovnay, Gerald xxvi, 8, 35, 37
Duchovny, David 115, 117
Dumont television network 5
Duncanson, Herbert 75, 80
Dunn, Michael 47
Duval, Robert 42

E
Eagleton, Terry 108
Eastwood, Clint 62
Eco, Umberto 165
Edgerton, Gary 62
Ehrlich, Paul 55
Ejiofor, Chiwitel 133
Elizabeth, I, Queen 150
Ellis, John xxiv–xxvii, 6, 10, 23, 55, 68, 93; and the television image xxv, 20, 53; and segmentalisation 7; and television aesthetics 20–21, 31, 42, 46, 69, 72, 127, 147, 149; and the glance 23, 33n, 69, 85–86, 134; on niche programming 81n; interdependence of film and television 85–86; television vs. film image 102–03, 104, 107; on audience 106, 177, 179; and televisual flow 116, 118–19, 144, 146, 150–51, 152
Ellison, Harlan 44
Elsaesser, Thomas 7
Emmerich, Roland 67, 70, 82n
Emmy Award 75, 176

Engels, Friedrich 108
Enterprise (series) xxviii n4
Enterprise (starship) 102, 103, 104, 105, 106, 108, 109, 110, 111, 113n
Essential Science Fiction Television Reader (book) xxiii
Eyman, Scott 58
Erisman, John 130
Ermey, R. Lee 123

F
Fahn, Edward 166
Fandom xxvii, 85, 113n, 158, 177, 180, 186
Fantastic Journey (series) 60
Fantastic Voyage (film) 54, 56
Farscape (series) 80
Federal Communications Commission xv
Feuer, Jane 144
Fifth Element, The (film) 96n
Fillion, Nathan 128
film noir 28
Firefly (series) xvi, xxvii, 95n, 129, 127–40
Fischer, Dennis 36, 40
Fiske, John 144, 154
Flash Gordon (film) 7, 15; as adaptation 15–16
Flash Gordon (series) 12, 179
FlashForward (series) xvi
Fletcher, Anthony L. 17n
Fly, The (film) 39
Fontaine, Joan 39, 40
Forbidden Planet (film) 30, 33n, 34n, 130, 131
Ford, Carole Ann 147
Ford, Harrison 131, 186
Ford, John 130, 131
Foster, Alan Dean 103
Foucault, Michel xxii
Foundas, Scott 118
Frankenstein (film) 117
Friday Night Movie (series) 63
Friedberg, Anne xv-xvi
Friedman, Josh 96n
Fringe (series) xxviii n
Fryer, Richard 9
Fugitive, The (series) 60

G
Gangbusters (radio) 16
Garcia, Frank 45, 46, 47
Garner, Jennifer 88

Garson, Willie 74
Gatts, Strawberry 56
Gellar, Sarah Michelle 92
gender issues and science fiction xxvi, 6, 36, 82n, 84–89, 91–95; and stereotypes 123; and technology 153; and racial representation 180, 187
General Electric Theater (series) 21
Gentry, Ric 62
George, Susan 86, 87, 96n
Geraghty, Lincoln 73, 112n
Ghost in the Shell (film) 95
Giannetti, Louis 58
Gillan, Karen 156
Glass, Ron 136
Glassner, Jonathan 67
Glau, Summer 84, 85, 88, 89, 90, 94, 128, 131
Godzilla (film) 82n
Goff, Ivan 59
Gold, Murray 156
Goldstone, James 44
Goldwyn, Samuel 6
Gone with the Wind (novel) xiii
Goodgold, Ed 4, 17n
Goodman, John 154
Gore, Chris 179
Gould, Jack 18n
Graham, Jane 178
Grainge, Paul 143
Gray, Jonathan 178, 179, 187
Green Hornet, The (radio) 16
Greene, Eric 60
Gulf War 78
Gunning, Tom 17n, 69

H

Hamilton, Linda 88, 91, 92, 94, 96n
Haraway, Donna 89
Hark, Ina Rae 166, 173
Harrison, Gregory 62, 63
Hartley, John 188
Hartnell, William 148–49, 152, 153
Harwood, Bruce 121
Hawes, William 5
Hayes, Al 60
Headey, Lena 84, 85, 88, 91, 92
Hedison, David 41, 42
Helfer, Tricia 86
Henderson, C. J. 58
Henderson, Jay Allen 9
Hennesy, Dale 56
Heroes (series) xvi

Heroes Digital Experience (interactive media) 176
High and the Mighty, The (film) 27
Hill, Gladwyn 41
Hill, Jacqueline 148
Hills, Matt 112n, 161n
Hill, Rodney xxvi, 31
Hills, Matt 68
Hitchcock, Alfred 122
Hitchcock, Michael 133
Hoch, Winton 38
Hodge, Al 18n
Hoesterey, Ingeborg xxi–xxii
Holder, Nancy 130
Hontz, Jenny 118
Hooper, Toby 122
Hope Diamond Mystery, The (film) 4
Hugo Award 77, 82n
Huston, John 45
Hutcheon, Linda 178, 182, 186

I

I'm Gonna Spend My Christmas with a Dalek (song) 145
Incredible Hulk, The (series) 60
Independence Day (film) 82n
internet: and adaptation xxvii–xxviii; as convergence medium 20; and fan films 118, 143
Invasion of the Body Snatchers (film) 61
i-Pod 48
Iron Man (film) xvi
Iron Man 2 (film) xvi
I've Got a Secret (series) 42

J

Jameson, Fredric 78–79, 80
Jansen, David 60
Javna, John 18n
Jeffords, Susan 91, 94
Jenkins, Henry xv, xxi, xxviii n, 20, 33, 112n1, 144, 153, 156, 180, 181, 187
Johnson, Catherine xxv, xxvii, 20–21, 32
Johnson, Elmer A. 9
Johnson, George Clayton 54
Johnson-Smith, Jan 69
Jordan, Richard 55
Joseph-Witham, Heather R. 113n
Judge, Christopher 72
Jumper, John P. 81n
Jung, Carl 122, 123

K

Kanno, Yoko 173
Katic, Stana 88
Kelly, Kevin 94
Kennedy, John F. 120, 121
Kennedy, Robert F. 121
kinescope 3, 6
King, Martin Luther, Jr. 63, 121
King Features 16
King Kong (film) 55
Kinnard, Roy 4, 16, 17n
Klady, Leonard 67
Klein, Michael 159
Klemesrud, Judy 36
Klinger, Barbara 185
Knight, Peter 120, 121
Knockin' on Heaven's Door (film) 165
Koenig, Walter 103
Kraft Television Theatre (series) 21
Kraus, David 181
Krige, Alice 94
Krumholtz, David 135
Kubrick, Stanley xvi, 81n, 161n
Kuhn, Annette xvii, 22

L

Lahue, Kalton 17n
Lamb, John 38
Land of the Giants (series) 48
Landis, John 32
Lang, Fritz xxii, 39, 86
Lassie (series) 45
Laszlo, Ernest 56
Laura (film) 7
Leach, Jim 153
Lee, Wendell 166
Leekley, John 155
Leisen, Mitch 22
Leitch, Thomas xv, xix, xx, xxviii n, 177, 179
Leone, Sergio 171
Life (magazine) 14
Life on Mars (series) xvi, xxiii
Lights Out (series) 9, 16
Lilly, Evangeline 88
Lincoln, Abraham 150
Linden, Jennie 153
Lofficier, Jean-Marc 162n
Logan's Run (film) xiv, xxvi, xxviii n, 53–59; changes from novel 54–55; box office success 55, 58; special effects in 55–58; budget for 57
Logan's Run (series) xiv, xxvi, 53, 56, 58–64; creative team for 59–60; formulaic nature of 60–61, 62, 64; budget for 60, 62; special effects in 61–62, 64; ratings for 63; Episodes: "Capture" 60; "Carousel" 61–62; "The Collectors" 63; "Fear Factor" 61; "Man Out of Time" 61
Lone Ranger, The (radio) 16
Lost (series) xvi, 88
Lost City, The (film) 4
Lost Experience (interactive media) 176
Lost in Space (film) xiv, 138
Lost in Space (series) 37, 47, 54
Lostpedia (wiki) 177
Lowry, Brian 118
Lucas, George 63, 64, 176, 179, 181, 185; and ILM 64; and Lucasfilm 180, 184, 187
Lury, Karen 146
Lydecker, Howard and Theodore 9

M

MacRae, Henry 15
Magazine of Fantasy and Science Fiction 169
Maher, Sean 128
Maibaum, Richard 54
Maio, Kathi 160
Majors, Lee 62
Mannix (series) 59
Manson, Shirley 93, 96n
Marx, Karl 108
Mascot Pictures 17n
Master Mystery, The (film) 4
Matrix, The (films) xvi, 96n
McCarthy, Todd 117
McCoy, Sylvester 155, 156
McGann, Paul 155, 156, 161n
McGavin, Darren 115
McLeod, Norman Z. 22
McMahan, Alison 67
Meadows, D. H. 55
Melies Georges 35
Mellencamp, Patricia 53
Melville, Herman 45, 111
Melzer, Patricia 93, 94
Menzies, Heather 62
Meredith, Burgess 25
Metallious, Grace xv
Metropolis (film) xxii, 39, 86
MGM 17n, 32; back lot 22–23, 27–28
Mikita, Andy 76
Miles, Lawrence 161n
Miller, Cynthia xxv, 17n, 18n

Miller, Liz S. 143
Minton's Playhouse 164
Mitchell, Thomas 139n
Mittell, Jason 177
Moffat, Donald 62
Montalban, Ricardo 110–111
Moonlighting (series) 131, 156
Most Dangerous Game, The (film) 60
Movie Review Query Engine 118
Mulligan, Carey 158
Murch, Walter 182
My Favorite Martian (film) xiv, 138
My Favorite Martian (series) 45

N
Napier, Susan 169, 170, 172
Nautilus (ship) 37
NBC 5, 42, 45, 63, 101
NCIS (series) 88
New Adventures of Wonder Woman, The (series) 96n
Newman, Kim 153
New York Times 36, 92, 184
New York World's Fair (1939) 5, 26
Nichelle, Nichols 103
Nichols, Michael J. 181, 182
Nichols, Peter 58
Niebur, Louis 161n
Night Stalker, The 115
Nikita (series) 88
Nimoy, Leonard 102, 103, 105, 109, 110, 111, 112, 113n, 174
90 Bristol Court (series) 42
Noah, The (film) 55
Nolan, William F. 54, 55, 58, 59, 60
Nolte, John 187
Nouvelle vague 149

O
Oboler, Arch 16
O'Brien, Maureen 147, 148
O'Connor, Carroll 42
Of Mice and Men (novel) xiiii
Omega Man, The (film) 55
Oshii, Masamune 95
Osmond, Andrew 169
Oswald, Lee Harvey 121
Our Man Flint (film) 54

P
Pablo, Cote de 88
Pal, George 54, 56
Palmer, Lorrie xxvi
Paramount Pictures 17n, 101
Parish, James Robert 17n
Parker, Gillian 159
Parks, Lisa 144
pastiche xxi, xxii, 78–79, 128
pataphysical film 67–68
Patrick, Robert 93, 120
Patten, Fred 170
Perils of Pauline, The (film) 4
Perryman, Neil 153, 157
Peyton Place (film) xv
Peyton Place (series) xv
Phantom, The (film) 15
Phantom Edit, The (film) 181–182
Phantom Empire, The (film) 4, 5, 17n, 18n
Pharr, Mary xxv
Phillips, Mark 42, 45, 46, 47, 63
Pickens, James, Jr. 120
Pidgeon, Walter 39, 42
Pierson, Michele xviii, 22, 53
Pileggi, Mitch 120
Piper, Billie 156
Pirkle, Michelle xxvii
Planet of the Apes (film) xiii
Planet of the Apes (series) xiii, 60, 61
Playhouse 90 (series) 21
Poltergeist (film) 122
Poseidon Adventure, The (film) 48, 54
Post, Ted 24
postmodernism: and science fiction xvi–xvii, xxii–xxiii, 80; and pastiche xxi–xxii, 78–79, 128; and culture 22; and parody 78. *See* science fiction
Presnell, Don 23, 26, 33n
Primeval (series) xix
Psycho (film) 122, 125
Pugh, Casey 184, 135
pulp fiction 15, 16
Purves, Peter 160n

R
Radar Men from the Moon (film) 7
Rainey, Buck 17n
Rankopedia (web site) 84, 96n
Rating System (UK) 161n
Rawhide (series) 42
Raymond, Alex 15–16
Rebecca (film) 41
Remington Steele (series) 156
Republic Pictures 9, 17n
RKO 17n
Roberts, Ben 59
Robinson, Glen 56–57

Robinson, Murray 12
Robocop (film) xxiii
Rockford Files, The (series) 63
Rocky Horror Picture Show (film) 165
Rocky Jones, Space Ranger (series) 12, 14, 18n
Roddenberry, Gene xxvi, 56; and space exploration 37, 103, 113n, 138n, 180
Rogers, Jean 15, 16
Rogers, Roy 18n
Roley, Sutton 46
Rooney, Mickey 33n
Roseanne (series) 154
Rosemary's Baby (film) 122
Rosenfelt, Frank 54
Roswell (series) xxiii
Rothery, Teryl 77
Rubinek, Saul 76
Rubio, Kevin 181, 182, 183
Russell, Gary 155, 162n
Russell, M. E. 138n
Russell, William 148
Ryan, Jeri 87
Ryan, Michael E. 81n

S

Saddle the Wind (screenplay) 34n
Sarah Conner Chronicles, The (series) xxvi, 84–96; sexuality in 87; gender coding 88; Episodes: "Allison from Palmdale" 96n; "Automatic for the People" 92; "Born to Run" 93, 96n; "The Demon Hand" 96n; "Gnothi Seauton" 92; "Goodbye to All That" 93; "Heavy Metal" 90; "Pilot" 89; "The Turk" 95
See Terminator (films)
Saturn Award 82n
Sawtell, Paul 38
Scalzi, John 102
Scheib, Richard 35
Schwarzbaum, Lisa 169
Schwarzenegger, Arnold 84, 88, 89, 94; as Mr. Universe 87
science fiction: xiii–xvi; as self-conscious form xvii–xviii, 22, 33n, 72; and spectacle xvii–xviii, xxv, xxvii, 3, 8, 21, 22, 26, 35, 36, 38, 55, 58, 63, 68, 74, 78, 81, 95; and screens xix, 8, 35; and postmodernism xxii–xxiii, 78; criticism of xxii, xxiii, 82n; and fantasy xxv; and the internet xxviii; awards xxviii; and serials 4–5, 7–8, 9, 12–14, 16–17; and television aesthetics 20–21, 63; commercial appeal 35, 41–42; and the Western xxiii, 5, 18n, 41, 42, 56, 88, 113n, 128, 129, 130–31, 137, 171, 172, 179; and dystopia 55, 111; as cultural critique 63, 64, 80, 86; cyborgs in 83, 84, 86, 87, 89, 93–95, 96n, 167; and gender consciousness 84–89, 91–95, 153; and the double 89. *See* postmodernism
Science Fiction Film and Television (journal) xxiii
Sconce, Jeffrey 22, 30, 33n, 153
Scott, Fred 10
Scott, Ridley xxii
screen studies xv, xxiii, xxiv
Searchers, The (film) 131
Sea Around Us, The (film) 36, 37
Seatbelts, The (band) 164, 173
Segal, Philip 154, 155, 162n
Selznick, David O. 32
Serenity (film) xxiii, xxvii, 95n, 127–40, 131
seriality xiv, xxiv, xxvi, 7, 15, 16, 116, 127, 131, 147, 161n
serials xiv, 3–4, 91; conventions of xiv, 10, 17n; and the B-film xxv; popularity of 3; on broadcast television 3, 4; history of 4–5; on television 7–8, 14–15, 147, 153–54, 155–56, 160n, 161n; and product tie-ins 11–14; sources of 15–16; and the radio 16
Serling, Rod xxv, 20, 23, 30; as narrator 24, 27, 28, 29, 30, 32; writing background 31, 32. *See The Twilight Zone*
Shakespeare, William 130, 150
Shanks, Michael 72, 77
Shannon, Frank 15
Shatner, William 102–03, 105, 109, 110, 111–12, 112n, 174
Shefter, Bert 38
Sheldon, James 33n
Short, Sue 94
Showtime 68
Siegel, Don 22
Silent Running (film) 55
Simpsons, The (series) 131, 185

Index 209

Six Million Dollar Man, The (series) 62
Sliders (series) 155
Smallville (series) xxiii
Smight, Jack 33n
Smith, Dale 161n
Smith, David 91
Smith, Kevin 186
soap opera xv
Sobchack, Vivian 53
Sontag, Susan 21
Sound of Music, The (film) 62
Soylent Green (film) 55
Space: 1999 (series) 60
space opera xxv, 129, 129; and the serial 3–4, 17; adaptation of 3–4
Space Patrol (series) xxv, 7, 12; and product tie-ins 13–14
Spader, James 75, 76
special effects: and science fiction xv, 74, 75, 104; and television budgets 3–4, 8–9, 26, 61–62, 64, 67; on film 9, 38, 55–58, 104–05, 178, 181; and CGI 69, 70, 71, 81n, 156, 170
Spider Man (play) 57
Spielberg, Steven xvi, 32, 63
Spiner, Brent 86
Stableford, Brian 55
Stafford, Nikki 112n
Stagecoach (film) 130, 138n, 139n
Staiger, Janet 119
Stam, Robert 78, 81, 145, 159
Stanyard, Stewart T. 23, 24
Stargate (film) xiii, xxvi, 67, 69–73, 75, 78–79, 81
Stargate: The Ark of the Truth (film) 67
Stargate Atlantis (series) xiii, 67, 74
Stargate Continuum (film) 67
Stargate SG-1 (series) xiii, xxiii, xxvi, xxviiin, 67–82; and special effects 64, 69, 70–71, 74, 75; success of 67–68, 69, 78, 81n; as franchise 68; and scale 70–71; formulaic nature of 73, 75; as reflexive text 74–78, 79–80, 81n, 82n; as postmodern pastiche 78–79, 80–81; spin-off products 81n; Wiki for 81n. Episodes: "Arthur's Mantle" 79; "Avatar" 81n; "Children of the Gods" (pilot) 68–69, 70, 72, 82n; "Citizen Joe" 79, 81n; "Fragile Balance" 79; "Heroes" 76–78, 79, 80; "Inauguration" 79; "Lost City" 81n; "Moebius Part II" 82n; 131, 187; "The Other Guys" 79, 82n; "The Pegasus Project" 74; "Prodigy" 81n; "The Shroud" 79; "Smoke and Mirrors" 73; "200" 79–80, 82n; "Unending" 80–81; "Wormhole X-Treme" 74–77, 79
Stargate Universe (series) xiii, 67
Starlost (series) 60
Star Trek: (series) xiii–xiv, xviii, xix, xxvi, 37, 56, 60, 72, 74, 75, 80, 96n, 101–13, 174; spin-offs of xvi; utopianism xxvi; Borg in 86, 87, 94; as franchise 101–12, 173; novelizations 103; soundtrack 105. Episodes: "Amok Time" 109–10; "Prime Directive" 108; "Space Seed" 110–11; "This Side of Paradise" 109
Star Trek: The Animated Series 101, 103 *Star Trek: Deep Space Nine* (series) 79 *Star Trek: First Contact* (film) 86, 87, 94 *Star Trek: The Motion Picture* (film) xxiii, xxvi, 101, 102, 104, 105, 06, 107, 110, 111, 112, 166
Star Trek: The Next Generation (series) 35, 101, 104
Star Trek: Voyager (series) 87, 96n, 102, 105, 107
Star Trek II: The Wrath of Khan 101, 110–11, 112
Star Trek III: The Search for Spock 112
Star Trek VI: The Undiscovered Country 101
Star Wars (film) xxvii, 61, 67, 96n, 105, 182, 187; influence on television 58, 63, 101, 104; influence on other films, 131, 179, 186; influence on other media, 176, 181, 182, 183; on fan behavior, 180, 185, 186
Star Wars: A New Hope 176, 183–84
Star Wars Episode II: Attack of the Clones 182
Star Wars: The Phantom Menace 181
Star Wars Uncut (interactive media) 176–177, 184, 184–86
Stedman, Raymond William 17n
Stelter, Brian 184
Stephanie, Frederick 15
Stewart, Garrett 22, 128, 131
Sturgeon, Theodore 37, 39

Subotsky, Milton 161n
Summoned by Shadows (film) 159n
Superman (tv series) 74
Suvin, Darko xxii, 102, 106, 107
Swiss Family Robinson (novel) 37
SyFy Channel xxviiin, 68, 180

T
Takei, George 103
Tales from the Dark Side (series) 115
Tales of Tomorrow (series) 9
Tapping, Amanda 72
Tarzan and the Rocky Gorge (film) 180
Tasker, Yvonne 91, 94
Tate, Catherine 156
Taylor, Tamara 132
technology: and culture xvii, 94
Teed, Jill 75
telefantasy xxv, 20–21, 32
television: history 4–5, 20, 21, 23, 32; programming 5–6, 121, 143, 155, 176; audience of 6–7, 13, 53, 106, 121, 127, 154, 157, 158, 171, 174, 179, 180, 188; and domesticity 7, 12–17; budgets 8–9, 23; aesthetics of 20–21, 29, 31, 33n, 35, 48, 53–54, 68, 102–03, 104, 107, 127, 128, 144, 145, 149–50, 152, 157, 166, 170–71, 174, 178, 179, 183; dramatic structure 42–43, 118, 136, 166, 168, 173; and spectatorship 30, 69, 70, 74, 75n, 139n, 150, 177; and intertextuality 128, 153, 157, 164, 165, 172, 186. See seriality
Telotte, J. P. xxiii, 5, 15, 18n, 33n, 89, 94, 118
Tempest, The (play) 130
Terminator (films) xxvi, 84, 86, 87, 88, 89, 90, 91, 92, 93, 94, 95n, 96n; and fan culture 85
Theweleit, Klaus 96n
Thing, The (film) 115
Thing from another World, The (film) 115
Things to Come (film) xv–xvi, xviii
Thomas, Frankie 13, 14, 17n
Thompson, Howard 40
Thompson, Kristin 119
Thompson, Susanna 96n
300 (film) 91
Tibbetts, John 17n
Time Tunnel (series) 47
time travel xvi
Top of the Pops (Beatles) 151
To Tell the Truth (series) 42
Tom Corbett, Space Cadet (series) xxv, 7, 9, 13, 17n; and product tie-ins 12, 13–14, 17n; use of direct address 18n
Torchwood (series) xix, xxi
Tourneur, Jacques 22
Tovey, Roberta 153
Towering Inferno, The (film) 48
tradition of quality xix
Trapper John, MD (series) 62
Trevor, Claire 139n
Troops (film) 181, 182–183, 183
Troughton, Patrick 152
Trumbull, Douglas 113n
Tryon, Chuck xxvii
Tulloch, John 112n
20th Century-Fox 6, 17n, 36, 39, 42, 45, 154
20,000 Leagues Under the Sea (novel) 37
2001: A Space Odyssey 105, 107, 161n
2012 (film) 82n
TV Century 21 145
TV Comic 154
Twilight Zone, The (series) xvi, xxv, 20–33, 115; and live-action drama xxv, 21–22, 32; and genre 23; budgets 23; twist endings of 24, 29, 30, 31; and culture 27; as cultural critique 31–32. Episodes: "The Brain Center at Whipple's" 34n; "Eye of the Beholder" 30; "Five Characters in Search of an Exit" 25; "The Invaders" 34n; "It's a Good Life" 32; "The Monsters are Due on Maple Street" 23, 27–31, 29, 33n; "Nightmare at 20,000 Feet" 23, 25, 26–27, 31, 33n; "Nothing in the Dark" 25; "The Obsolete Man" 31; "The Odyssey of Flight 33" 25–26; "Showdown with Rance McGrew" 22, 31; "The Sixteen Millimeter Shrine" 22, 31; "Time Enough at Last" 23–24, 25, 30, 31; "Uncle Simon" 34n; "A World of Difference" 22, 24, 31
Twilight Zone: The Movie (film) xxiii, 32; literary character 21, 32–33

2001: A Space Odyssey (film) 63, 67, 72, 81n, 105, 107, 161n
TV III 68–69

U
United Federation of Planets (aka, Federation, *Star Trek*) 103, 106
United Nations 40
Universal Pictures 9, 15, 154
Uricchio, William 144
Ustinov, Peter 55
Utopianism 102, 103, 106, 107–08, 109, 110, 111, 112, 132–33, 136
Van Allen Radiation Belt 40, 43

V
Vanishing Shadow, The (film) 4
Variety (newspaper) 40, 54, 67, 117, 118, 139n
Verne, Jules 35, 38, 41; and *20,000 Leagues Under the Sea* (novel) 37
Vietnam War 60, 63
Village Voice 118
Vimeo (web site) 180
Vint, Sherryl xxvi
Virilio, Paul xxi, 20, 32, 132, 136, 139n
Von Ryan's Express (film) 54
Voyage dans la lune, Le (film) 35
Voyage to the Bottom of the Sea (film) 35–39, 38, 59; special effects in 38, 40–41; plot of 40–41; box office success 41, 42; camp elements in 47
Voyage to the Bottom of the Sea (series) xxiii, xxv, 35–48, 54, 59; guest stars 41–42; ratings for 42, 43, 45, 46–47; formulaic nature of 43; budget for 44; Episodes: "Eleven Days to Zero" 43; "The Ghost of Moby Dick" 44, 45; "Jonah and the Whale" 45–46; "The Lobster Man" 47; "The Phantom Strikes" 46; "The Price of Doom" 44; "The Sky's on Fire" 43; "The Wax Men" 47

W
Wagner, Geoffrey 159
Wagner, Lindsay 62
Wagon Train (series) 42, 56
Wallace, George 9
Warner Bros. 17n
Warren, Bill 17n, 40
Warren Report 121
Warwick, Edmund 148–149
Watanabe, Shinicohirô 166, 167, 168, 172
Wayne, John 139n
Weaver, Sigourney 92, 94, 96n
Weiss, Ken 4, 17n
Wells, H. G. xvi
Wells, Paul 168
Westerns xxiii, 5, 18n, 41, 56, 88, 113n, 128, 129, 130–31, 171, 172, 179
Whedon, Joss xxvii, 95n-96n, 127, 129, 130, 136–38, 139n
Whitaker, David 145
Wilcox, Roger M. 58, 60
Wilk, Max 5
Williams, Linda Ruth 92
Williams, Raymond 11, 15, 16, 18n, 143
Wise, Robert 57
Wizard of Oz (film) 154
Woman's Day (magazine) 12
Wonderful World of Color, The (series) 45, 46–47
Wonderful Wizard of Oz, The (novel) 95
Wood, Tat 161n
Wright, Brad 67
Wright, John C. 130
Wright, Leigh Adams 128
Wright, Peter 154, 161n

X
Xena: Warrior Princess (series) 96n
X-Files, The (films) xxiii, xxvi
X-Files, The (series) xxvi-xxvii, 96n, 115–26, 156; and religion 123–124; As creature features 115, 117, 119, 120; and mythology 122, 124–25. Episodes: "Biogenesis" 123–124; "En ami" 123; "Lone Gunman" 121, 126n; "Musings of a Cigarette-Smoking Man" 121; "Patience" 120; "Per Manum" 125; "Revelations" 123; "Shadows" 122; "The Sixth Extinction" 123, 124; "Sleepless" 123; "3" 123; "Three of a Kind" 121; "Tooms" 120; "Torbitt Document" 121

X-Files: Fight the Future (film) 116, 118, 119, 125
X-Files: I Want to Believe (film) 116, 117, 118, 127

Y
Yeoman, Owain 89

York, Michael 55, 57
Young, Clive 178, 180
Young, Paul xxiii–xxiv
YouTube 180, 186, 187

Z
Zanuck, Darryl F. 6

For Product Safety Concerns and Information please contact our EU representative GPSR@taylorandfrancis.com
Taylor & Francis Verlag GmbH, Kaufingerstraße 24, 80331 München, Germany

www.ingramcontent.com/pod-product-compliance
Lightning Source LLC
Chambersburg PA
CBHW070602300426
44113CB00010B/1363